Moral Psychology

For EJA (1983–2015)

"The charm of knowledge would be modest if not for the fact that, on the way to her, so much shame had to be overcome."

Friedrich Nietzsche, *Beyond Good and Evil*
(translated from the German by the author)

Moral Psychology
An Introduction

Mark Alfano

polity

First published in 2016 by Polity Press

Polity Press
65 Bridge Street
Cambridge CB2 1UR, UK

Polity Press
350 Main Street
Malden, MA 02148, USA

ISBN-13: 978-0-7456-7224-3
ISBN-13: 978-0-7456-7225-0(pb)

A catalogue record for this book is available from the British Library.

Library of Congress Cataloging-in-Publication Data

Alfano, Mark, 1983– author.
    Moral psychology : an introduction / Mark Alfano.
        pages cm
    Includes bibliographical references and index.
    ISBN 978-0-7456-7224-3 (hardback : alk. paper) – ISBN 978-0-7456-7225-0 (pbk. : alk. paper)   1. Ethics–Psychological aspects.   2. Moral development.   I. Title.
    BJ45.A44 2016
    170.1'9–dc23
                                                                    2015026465

Typeset in 10.5 on 12 pt Palatino
by Toppan Best-set Premedia Limited
Printed and bound in the UK by Clays Ltd, St Ives PLC

For further information on Polity, visit our website:
politybooks.com

Contents

Acknowledgments

This book is the product of years of preparation (some of it intentional, much not), research, and writing. In May 2012, Sarah Lambert contacted me on behalf of Polity Press to ask for advice: she wanted to know who might be in a position to write a monograph on moral psychology for advanced undergraduate students. Flattered that anyone would consider my opinion worthwhile, I assembled some suggested contents and a list of four names (none of them "Mark Alfano"), and wished her well. A couple of months later, Sarah emailed me again to ask whether I would consider writing the book myself. I'd just finished a final draft of my first book, *Character as Moral Fiction*, and was thinking about what to do next. At the time, I had three monograph-length projects in mind: (1) *Desire, Preference, and Value*, which would grapple with the normative implications of prospect theory, implicit biases, and what Paul Slovic calls the "collapse function" (the more people who need help, the less we help); (2) *Nietzsche's Socio-Moral Psychology*, which would offer a naturalistic interpretation of Nietzsche and argue that he anticipated a number of important insights of twentieth-century empirical psychology; and (3) *To See As We Are Seen*, which would expand the discussion of the ethics of (in)visibility I began in chapter 8 of *Character as Moral Fiction* to include Plato, Epicurus, Bentham, Buber, Levinas, and Foucault, as well as contemporary psychological and philosophical work on faces, recognition, and privacy. In other words, an undergraduate textbook was not foremost in my mind. With a little cajoling, though, Sarah managed to get me to see that all three of my other projects would benefit from a comprehensive survey of contemporary moral psychology. (The Nietzsche book is next. After that – who knows?)

In preparing this manuscript, I've benefited from presenting research on moral psychology at a number of university colloquia and conferences. If extended memory serves, I discussed work related to this book as early as 2011 (Yale, Washington University in Saint Louis, New York University, Northwestern, Cardiff, University at Buffalo (SUNY), London School of Economics, the Eastern and Pacific APAs, and the North Carolina Philosophical Society Conference), then pretty steadily in subsequent years: 2012 (Princeton, University of Victoria, University of Illinois Urbana-Champaign, the London Conference on Experiments on Ethical Dilemmas, the Sorbonne Conference on Ethics and the Architecture of Personal Dispositions, the Buffalo Experimental Philosophy Conference, the New Jersey Regional Philosophical Association); 2013 (Edinburgh's Eidyn Center, Universidad Nacional Autónoma de México Instituto de Investigaciones Filosóficas, the Northwest Philosophy Conference again); and 2014 (Pacific APA, Zurich Center for Ethics, and the Bled Conference on Ethical Issues).

I've also learned a great deal from attending and presenting to the University of Oregon Institute for Cognitive and Decision Sciences research groups in Decision-Making, Social and Personality Psychology, and Scientific Study of Values. In the fall of 2013, I taught a graduate seminar titled "Naturalizing Virtue." I hope my students (Jacob Levernier, Kathryn Iurino, Phil Mayo, Jesse Chambers, and Rain Baker) learned as much from me as I did from them. In the winter of 2014, I taught an undergraduate honors seminar on moral psychology; the students (Alex Harris, Aurora Laybourn-Candlish, Kendall Mack) in this course weren't mere guinea pigs; but they did provide me an excellent opportunity to pilot some material.

I've also learned a great deal from informal conversations with many, many people. I list them here in alphabetical order, since trying to weight how much I owe to each would be impossible: Abrol Fairweather, Adam Carter, Adam Morton, Aderemi Artis, Adriana Renero, Alex Voerhoeve, Alexander Todorov, Alexandra Plakias, Andrew Bailey, Andrew Conway, Andrew Higgins, Anthony Appiah, Azim Shariff, Brian Kim, Brian Robinson, Bryce Huebner, Chandra Sripada, Christian Miller, Colin Klein, Colin Koopman, Cristina Bicchieri, Dan Haybron, Dan Korman, Dan Shargel, Dana Rognlie, Daniel Kelly, Daniel Lapsley, Daniel Star,

Danielle Wylie, David Morrow, David Rosenthal, David Wong, Derek Powell, Dhananjay Jagannathan, Don Loeb, Duncan Pritchard, Elliot Berkman, Emma Gordon, Eric Schwitzgebel, Fiery Cushman, Gabe Abend, Gerard Saucier, Gideon Rosen, Gilbert Harman, Gunnar Bjornsson, Hannes Schwandt, Hanno Sauer, Heather Battaly, Holly Arrow, Jacob Berger, James Beebe, Jason Baehr, Jason Stanley, Jennifer Cole Wright, Jennifer Corns, Jennifer Nagel, Jennifer White, Jesse Prinz, Jesse Summers, John Basl, John Doris, John Mikhail, Jonathan Webber, Jorah Dannenberg, Josh May, Joshua Alexander, Joshua Knobe, Julia Driver, Kate Manne, Kate Norlock, Kristina Gehrman, Lauren Olin, Liezl Van Zyl, Lorraine Besser-Jones, Lynn Kahle, Marc Fleurbaey, Mark Johnson, Markus Christen, Mike Otsuka, Myisha Cherry, Myrto Mylopoulos, Ned Block, Neera Badhwar, Neil Sinhababu, Nina Strohminger, Owen Flanagan, Paul Katsafanas, Paul Slovic, Paul Stey, Peggy Desautels, Peter Singer, Petter Johansson, Philip Pettit, Philipp Koralus, Rachel Cristy, Rachel Fedock, Robert Roberts, Roxanne Desforges, Sanjay Srivastava, Sara Hodges, Shannon Spaulding, Shaun Nichols, Shyam Nair, Stephen Brence, Stephen Stich, Sven Nyholm, Tad Zawidzki, Victoria McGeer, Wesley Buckwalter, Christopher Murtagh, and Zachary Horne. I'm sure there are others, and I can only hope they will forgive my oversight.

Valerie Tiberius deserves special thanks. She and I are, in a sense, competitors, as she also recently wrote a moral psychology textbook (the first to be published in English, as far as I know). Despite this, she generously shared a draft of her manuscript with me. Let a thousand flowers bloom!

I'm also extremely grateful to the Princeton University Center for Human Values and Center for Health and Wellbeing, where I spent the 2012–13 academic year as a research post-doc. Without the time and vibrant intellectual culture this made available, this book would have been completed sooner, and would have been the worse for it.

I am also grateful to the three anonymous referees of this manuscript, especially to reviewer 2, who taught me to appreciate more fully the basic charity accorded by referees 1 and 3.

Finally, two people deserve special thanks: my publishers, Emma Hutchinson and Pascal Porcheron. Emma and Pascal displayed remarkable patience, as I missed multiple deadlines to turn in the manuscript. Without their forbearance, this book would not exist.

Introduction

1 Setting the stage

Moral psychology is the systematic inquiry into how morality works, when it does work, and breaks down when it doesn't work. The field therefore incorporates questions, insights, concepts, models, and methods from various parts of psychology (personality psychology, social psychology, cognitive psychology, developmental psychology, evolutionary psychology), neuroscience, sociology, anthropology, criminology, and of course philosophy (applied ethics, normative ethics, metaethics). These fields are – or at least can be – mutually informative. Indeed, one guiding theme of this book is that moral philosophy without psychological content is empty, whereas psychological investigation without philosophical insight is blind. Given their characteristically synoptic perspective, philosophers are ideally situated to organize and moderate a productive conversation among these sciences. Nevertheless, there is always the risk that investigators with different training and expertise may misinterpret, misconstrue, or misunderstand one another. In this book, I attempt to put the relevant disciplines in dialogue. They sometimes speak with different accents, jargons, vocabularies, even grammars. My aim is to make their conversation intelligible to the reader, even if they cannot all be brought to speak exactly the same language in exactly the same way.

Systematic inquiry depends on systematic questions. Science is not just a collection of facts about the same thing or class of things.

Imagine how stupid it would be to conduct moral psychology by assembling all and only the motives that every person has ever had while responding to a moral problem (assuming this to be possible in the first place). This would be an utterly disorganized, uninformative, overwhelming mess. In the annals of the illustrious British Royal Society, you find descriptions of "experiments" like this: "A circle was made with powder of unicorne's horn, and a spider set in the middle of it, but it immediately ran out severall times repeated. The spider once made some stay upon the powder" (Weld 1848, p. 113). This would be a caricature of bad science if it hadn't actually happened. We might call this *empiricism run amok*. Science doesn't just ask what happens, as if this were a question that, when completely answered, would satisfy human inquirers. Science asks questions systematically. It asks, for instance, what the effect of X on Y is. It asks whether that effect is mediated by M. It asks whether the effect is moderated by Z.[1] It attempts to determine which variables, organized in which configuration, accounts for the variability observed and experimentally induced in the field of inquiry.

In this endeavor, science is guided by insightful identification of relevant variables, careful distinction between similar phenomena, creative elaboration of alternative models, and skeptically imaginative construction of potential counterexamples. As the economist Paul Krugman put it recently on his blog, you can't just let "the data speak for itself – because it never does. You use data to inform your analysis, you let it tell you that your pet hypothesis is wrong, but data are never a substitute for hard thinking. If you think the data are speaking for themselves, what you're really doing is implicit theorizing, which is a really bad idea (because you can't test your assumptions if you don't even know what you're assuming)."[2] One way to help make theorizing explicit rather than implicit is to ask systematic questions.

Unfortunately, in universities and in the contemporary education system more broadly, we typically spend far too much time answering (and learning to answer) questions and far too little asking (and learning to ask) questions. So, in this introduction, I'll try to show how questions are asked, how they become more nuanced and complicated, and how conditions of adequacy for answers are (tentatively) established.

Here's a moral question I've asked myself:

What should I do to him for her?

Picture this: I'm headed to work on a downtown subway car at 8:30 AM. Two seats to my right, a 20-something woman is intently reading a magazine, obviously somewhat tense because a man is standing over her, leaning in a bit too close, leering slightly, and alternating between asking her name and telling her to smile. She's presumably on her way to work and obviously uninterested in his conversation. She rolls her eyes and sighs. He seems obnoxious but mostly harmless. She casts about from time to time. Is she looking for help? for someone to share a moment of derisive eye contact with? for reassurance that, if her unwelcome interlocutor escalates to insulting or assaulting her, fellow passengers will not remain apathetic bystanders?

2 Patiency

What should I do to him for her?

This question presupposes an immense amount.

First, it presupposes **patiency**[3] – that is, the fact that things happen to people. My fellow commuter can be made uncomfortable. She can feel threatened. She can be threatened. She can be assaulted. Things – some of them good and some of them quite bad – can happen to her. Some of them might be done by that jerk who keeps insinuating himself on her attention. The fact that good and bad things can happen to her – that she is, in technical terms, a patient – is presupposed by my question.

Things can also happen to him. He can be ignored and accommodated. He can be egged on. He can, alternatively, be confronted and challenged. He can be distracted or redirected. The fact that good, bad, and neutral things can happen to him – that he too is a patient – is also presupposed by my question.

Finally, things can happen to me. One reason I might do nothing is that I'm afraid of what might happen to me if I confront or even just accost him. Probably nothing – but I'm useless in a fight, and strangers can be unpredictable. She might express gratitude to me for intervening. Alternatively, she might be annoyed that a second stranger has made her business his business. I aim to be helpful, which among other things includes stymieing creeps, but I also aim to avoid trampling through strangers' lives uninvited. As I decide what to do, her patiency, his patiency, and my patiency are all quite salient.

Things happen to people. When they do, we have an example of patiency. In other words, when something happens to someone, she is the patient of (is passive with respect to) that event or action. Moral psychology asks what it is about us that makes us patients, and how our patiency figures in our own and other people's moral perception, behavior, decision-making, emotions, characters, and institutions. Several chapters of this book are directly related to patiency. For instance, in chapter 1 on preferences, we will see that some philosophers argue that your life goes well to the extent that your preferences are satisfied. In other words, your life is better when you get what you want than when you don't get it. If you, like most people, want to be healthy, but you end up contracting influenza, your life goes worse. Something happens to you that contravenes your preferences. On the flipside, if you, like most people, prefer temperate weather to frigid cold, and the weather where you are is temperate, then your life goes better. Something happens to you that satisfies your preferences. In chapter 4 on character, we will see that benevolence is typically considered a virtue. What makes someone benevolent? Wishing others well, and at least sometimes acting successfully on those wishes. If a benevolent person helps you in some way, you are the patient of her action.

Thus, patiency is a crucial concept in moral psychology. When I ask what I should do to him for her, I'm asking what follows from her patiency, his patiency, and my own patiency. This is an example of how questions are asked systematically: we start with something seemingly simple and comprehensible ("What should I do to him for her?") and parse out some of the deeper questions and concepts it presupposes.

3 Agency

What should I do to him for her?

This question presupposes **agency**. Things don't just happen to people: sometimes people do things.

Return to the example of the woman on the train. She might do something. She might stand up and walk to the next train car. She might lean back and hold her magazine up in front of her face, blocking the stranger's attempt to make eye contact and muffling his voice. She might tell him off. She might kick him in the shin.

Likewise, he might do something. He might continue to bug her until she escapes the train car. He might sit down next to her. He might call her a bitch. He might throw his hands in the air and walk away. He might switch to bothering someone else. He might grow bored and start playing with his smartphone.

I, too, might do something. (There'd be little point in asking myself *what I should do* if I couldn't.) If my usual wariness of strangers holds up, I might cautiously eye the situation and hope impotently that nothing too bad happens. I might instead stride over and command him to stop bothering her. More helpfully, I might stroll over and ask her quietly whether she's OK.

People do things. When they do, we have an example of agency. In other words, some person is the agent of (is active with respect to) some event or action. Moral psychology asks what it is about us that makes us agents, and how our agency figures in our own and other people's moral perception, behavior, decision-making, emotions, character, and institutions.

Several chapters of this book are directly related to agency. Chapter 1 discusses how our preferences affect our choices, and hence our actions. It's tempting to assume that our preferences are stable, at least once we reach adulthood. Empirical research suggests otherwise. It's even more tempting to assume that our preferences are transitive: if I prefer chocolate ice cream to vanilla and prefer vanilla to strawberry, then I'd better prefer chocolate to strawberry. Again, empirical research suggests that, at least in some cases, transitivity breaks down. To what extent can we be the authors of our own actions if our preferences are unstable and inconsistent? Chapter 2 is about the relation between deliberative agency, on the one hand, and implicit biases, on the other. The vast majority of people in the developed world would, if asked, reject racist and sexist beliefs. But social psychologists have demonstrated that most of us nevertheless implicitly harbor and even act on racist and sexist associations. When we do, are we fully responsible for our actions? If we aren't, why not? Chapter 3 asks whether we are more or less agentic when we are motivated by emotions. Particularly intense emotions seem to come over us like a hurricane, swamping our planning, deliberation, and policies. But deficits in emotion have been shown to correlate with demonstrably bad decision-making. Chapter 4 connects agency with virtue, which for many theorists is a matter of acting in accordance with practical reason.

If people were incapable of agency, if they were entirely passive beings, the contours of whose lives were completely determined by outside forces, there wouldn't be much for moral psychologists to think about. We could construct theories about what it meant for one person to have a better life than another, what it meant for one person to have as good a life as possible for such an impoverished creature, what it meant for such a life to improve or deteriorate. But that would be about it. The introduction of agency greatly complicates moral psychology. Now, things don't just happen to us; we *do* things. Some of those things turn out as we want or intend them to. Others don't. This imposes some constraints on what it means to act well, to be a successful agent. Sometimes we do what we want, but then we are disappointed by the result. This suggests that we need a better understanding of our own preferences. Sometimes we accomplish one goal but in so doing thwart our striving for a second goal. This suggests that we need to understand agency holistically, so that it involves progress toward a complete set of goals without too much self-undermining. Such constraints are discussed in chapter 1.

Thus, agency, like patiency, is a crucial concept in moral psychology, and it's a concept that complicates the inquiry. When I ask what I should do to him for her, I'm asking what follows from her agency, his agency, and my own agency. This is a further example of how questions are asked: we start with something seemingly simple and comprehensible ("What should I do to him for her?") and parse out some of the deeper questions and concepts it presupposes.

4 Sociality

What should I do to him for her?

This question presupposes **sociality**. Things happen to people: they get sick, they enjoy pleasant weather, they endure the many small indignities of youth and the even more numerous small indignities of aging. People do things: they stand up and walk away, they shrink into their seats, they write books. In many interesting cases, though, one person does something to someone else. Indeed, some of the examples I gave above had this flavor. The only reason I asked myself what I should do to him for her was that he was doing something to her in the first place: he was harassing her. As I deliberated about what to do, I considered the fact that there were things she might do to him, such as pointedly ignoring him, additional things he might do to her, such as insulting her, and various things

Table I.1 Agency x patiency examples

	Y is a patient	**Y is not a patient**
X is an agent	X harasses Y X kicks Y in the shin X confronts Y	X stands up X shrinks into his seat X writes a book
X is not an agent	Y gets sick Y enjoys pleasant weather Y grows old	

I might do to him on her behalf, such as confronting him for harassing her. Moral psychology asks what it is about us that makes us social, and how our sociality figures in our own and other people's moral perception, behavior, decision-making, emotions, character, and institutions.

As table I.1 illustrates, people can be simple patients, to whom things just happen; they can be simple agents, who just do things; but they can also be complex agents and patients: they can do things to each other. In such cases, agency and patiency are inextricably intertwined. One person's agency is the cause or even a constitutive part of another person's patiency. One person's patiency is the effect of another person's agency. When asked, "What happened to you?" my fellow commuter would be giving an incomplete answer if she responded, "I was harassed." Being harassed is not like enjoying pleasant weather; it's not something that can happen to someone all on their own. A more complete answer would be, "I was harassed by a stranger." Likewise, if someone later asked the creep, "What did you do on the train?" he would be giving an incomplete response if he answered, "I harassed." Harassing isn't like standing up; it's not something someone can do all on their own.

We can represent these relations with the schematic diagram illustrated in figure I.1.[4] In this diagram (and others of its sort that I'll use below), a dot represents a person. An arrow proceeding away from a dot represents that person exercising agency. An arrow pointing at a dot or other array represents that entity enduring patiency (good, bad, or neutral). I'll put a box around each such relation.

Figure I.1 represents the simplest sort of sociality: one agent does something to another agent. Gray et al. (2012) suggest that the fundamental template for moral judgment is an agent (potentially)

Figure I.1 Agent–patient relation

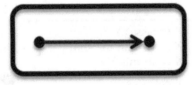

Figure I.2 Agent–patient relation

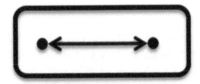

harming a patient. I agree in large part, but as the following sections show, I think things are more complicated. A more complex form of sociality emerges when two people are agents and patients with respect to each other at the same time: you do something to me while I do something to you. For instance, we dance together, each making suggestions to the other through subtle bodily movement, gestures, glances, and words. Call this **interactivity**. Figure I.2 represents interactive sociality of this sort.

Things happen to people; people do things; sometimes, these are the same event. But sociality is often more complicated than that. Interactivity is one source of complexity, but a minor one. Another source of complexity is the possibility – indeed, the prevalence – of recursively embedded agent–patient relations. This might sound frighteningly technical, but don't worry. **Recursion** is all over the place, and I'm certain that you're already familiar with it, if only informally. Recursion is a process in which objects of a given type are generated by or defined in terms of other objects of the same type. For instance, think of your *ancestors*. What makes someone an ancestor of yours? The answer to this question relies on recursion: the parents of X are ancestors of X (that's the non-recursive step) and ancestors of ancestors of X are ancestors of X (that's the recursive step). Your grandparents are your ancestors because they're the parents of your parents. Your great-grandparents are your ancestors because they're the parents of the parents of your parents. Your great-great-grandparents are your ancestors because they're the parents of the parents of the parents of your parents. The great-great-grandparents of your great-great-grandparents are your ancestors because they're the ancestors of your ancestors. And so on.

Social agent–patient relations can also be recursively embedded. The majority – probably the vast majority – of the complexity of moral psychology derives from such embedding. In fact, the example I started off with has a recursive structure. When I asked myself what I should do to him for her, I was thinking of myself as an agent who acts on a preexisting agent–patient relationship. After all, I would have had no reason to intervene if he hadn't been harassing her in the first place.

Figure I.3 illustrates the situation in which one person acts on a second person acting on a third person. Since this relation is recursive, it can be expanded yet another step (and another, and another…), as illustrated in figure I.4. Although figure I.4 might seem complicated, I think we can pretty easily conjure up a situation that it characterizes. For instance, imagine that I decide to stride over to the creep and aggressively command him to cut it out. As I confront the harasser, my friend intervenes between us, saying, "Look, everybody just knock it off." My friend acts on me acting on him acting on her. This sort of thing happens all the time. And, as

Figure I.3 Recursively embedded agent–patient relations

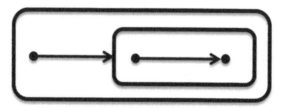

Figure I.4 Doubly recursively embedded agent–patient relations

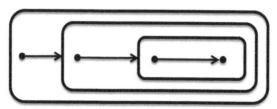

you can see, the more recursion there is, the most complicated the situation becomes.

Moral judgments, likewise, can be embedded in other moral judgments to produce novel moral judgments (Harman 2008, p. 346). Indeed, there seem to be productive moral principles based on recursion: if it's wrong to x, then generally it will also be wrong to coerce someone to x. Similarly, if it's wrong to x, then generally it will also be wrong to command someone to x. From this it follows that if it's wrong to x, then it's wrong to command someone to coerce someone to x. Such moral embedding has been experimentally investigated by John Mikhail (2011, pp. 43–8), who argues on the basis of experiments using variants on the "trolley problem" (Foot 1978) that moral judgments are generated by imposing a deontic structure on one's representation of the causal and evaluative features of the action under consideration. One might also think that this feature of morality helps to explain the troubling "banality of evil" (Arendt 1963), which crops up when multiple layers of bureaucracy and other institutional structures lead to cases where an individual, like Adolf Eichmann, orders someone to order someone to order someone to murder someone. At a great many recursive removes, this might feel like dull paper-pushing, but from a moral point of view it might be at least as bad as committing the murder oneself.

Moral psychology asks what it is about us that makes us social, and how our sociality figures in our own and other people's moral perception, behavior, decision-making, emotions, characters, and institutions. Sociality is what makes moral psychology so complicated but also so interesting. In a way, it's the underlying theme of every chapter of this book, but it features most prominently in chapters 3, 4, and 5. In chapter 3 on emotion, we will see that emotions often function as signaling devices. When I display anger, I signal to you that I am prepared and committed to react aggressively to offenses. When you display disgust, you signal to me that the object of your disgust is contaminated and to be avoided. Emotional signaling fits well into the recursive embedding structure discussed here. When I display anger toward you, I also often signal to other people that they should be indignant over the offense you've caused me (a relationship like the one in figure I.3). When you display contempt toward my behavior, you also often signal to other people that they should feel superior to me. Chapter 4 on character discusses the interlocking virtues of generosity and gratitude. Chapter 5 on moral disagreement investigates the ways in which sociality influences agreement on moral values, norms, heuristics, and decisions.

Arguably, sociality is the key concept required to provisionally carve off the moral domain from related evaluative domains, such as the epistemic, the conventional, and the prudential. One common way of marking this distinction, due in part to Hare (1952), is to hold that the concept of morally wrong action involves four main components: seriousness, generality, authority-independence, and objectivity. This conception has been challenged by, among others, Sinnott-Armstrong & Wheatley (2014) and Haidt & Joseph (2007). At this early stage, I will settle for gesturing at a very broad moral domain including anything susceptible to judgments of being good, bad, better, worse, best, worst, obligatory, permissible, impermissible, virtuous, and vicious. As we proceed, these concepts will be fleshed out and made more precise, and conceptual and empirical connections among them will emerge. Already, we can see that this broad construal of morality encompasses the assessment of states of affairs (as good, bad, and so on), actions (as obligatory, forbidden, permissible), and states of character (as in various ways virtuous or vicious). Not all such assessments are properly *moral*; I will contend (especially in chapter 3 on emotion) that the properly moral involves the presuppositions of social emotions. If you express moral resentment toward me, your emotion involves an implicit call for me to respond with guilt (or to explain why your resentment is inappropriate) and for others to respond with indignation toward me (or likewise to explain to you why your resentment is inappropriate). This point will be familiar to some readers from Peter Strawson's "Freedom and resentment" (1960). This helps to explain why moral norms are sometimes conceived as those that demand not just retaliation by victims of their violation, but also third-party punishment (Fehr & Fischbacher 2004). Failure to respond appropriately is then itself considered a moral violation (Sripada 2005): if I respond to your justified anger not with guilt but with derision, I have committed another moral offense; if others respond to your justified anger not with indignation but with callousness, they have committed a moral offense just as much as I have.

Thus, sociality, like patiency and agency, is a crucial concept in moral psychology, and it's a concept that greatly complicates the inquiry. When I ask what I should do to him for her, I'm asking what follows from our sociality, that is, from the fact that I can act on him acting on her. This is another example of how questions are asked: we start with something seemingly simple and comprehensible ("What should I do to him for her?") and parse out some of the deeper questions and concepts it presupposes.

5 Reflexivity and temporality

What should I do to him for her?

This question presupposes **reflexivity**. People do things; things happen to people; people do things to people. In some cases, the agent and the patient are the same person. In other words, people can do things to themselves. This is easiest to see if we also introduce the last main conceptual presupposition of my question: **temporality**. As I decide what to do to him for her, here are some considerations that might cross my mind:

> *If I don't intercede somehow, I'll feel guilty all day.*
> *If I manage to distract him without starting a fight, I'll be proud.*
> *If I act like a coward now, I'll be cultivating bad habits.*

All these considerations involve thinking of my future self as the patient of my current self. Another way of putting the same point is that I'm taking a social perspective on myself: on the one hand, me-now is the agent who does something to a patient; on the other hand, me-in-the-future is the patient to whom something is done by that agent. These concepts also interact with sociality and the recursive embedding of agent–patient relations. For instance, suppose I make a bad decision on Monday (agent) that leads me to make an even worse decision on Tuesday (patient-to-Monday-me) that leads me to suffer immensely on Wednesday (patient-to-Tuesday-me). This is the sort of structure represented in I.3, except that all three nodes represent me – just at different stages of my life.

Whenever we engage in long-term projects – especially long-term projects that are meant to have some effects on our future selves – patiency, agency, sociality, reflexivity, and temporality are all involved. Were you to think of your future self as a stranger or even a friend, rather than as your*self*, your planning would look very different. Likewise, if you were to think of your past actions as those of a stranger or even of a friend, rather than of your*self*, your trajectory would change radically. It doesn't make sense to feel regret, remorse, guilt, or shame for the actions of a stranger, even a stranger who resembles you in some way. Moral psychology asks what it is about us that makes us reflexive and temporal, and how our reflexivity and temporality figure in our own and other people's moral perception, behavior, decision-making, emotions, characters, and institutions.

Several chapters of this book are directly related to reflexivity and temporality. The instability of preferences discussed in chapter 1 is a temporal instability, and it threatens agency because human agency as we normally conceive of it is meant to be temporally extended. I don't just do things now. I do things now so that I can do and experience things later. If my preferences change in the meantime, then setting myself up to do or experience something later may be pointless. The interaction between deliberative agency and implicit biases discussed in chapter 2 concerns, among other things, whether I'm able to reflectively endorse my own choices. Emotions, discussed in chapter 3, can function as social signals; they can also function as commitment devices. If I have a particular emotion, I'm committing myself (if only unconsciously and tentatively) to a plan of action in the future. If I act wrongly, one of the things that may happen to my future self is the suffering of remorse. Virtue, discussed in chapter 4, is acquired (according to Aristotle and many who follow in his footsteps) through long-term, goal-directed cultivation; I have a plan for my own life over time, which I proceed to carry out, making me my own patient over the course of months, years, and even decades.

Reflexivity and temporality complicate moral psychology in various ways. This is easiest to see if we imagine creatures that are otherwise just like humans but who have no long-term memory, no sense of self, and no capability to plan, to feel proud of their accomplishments, or to experience remorse. Although such creatures would be patients (things would happen to them) and agents (they would do things) who were in some ways social (they would do things to each other), they would be very unlike us insofar as they could not intentionally do things to and for themselves, could not be grateful to or disappointed with their past selves, could not engage in long-term projects, and could not enjoy long-term friendships. Clearly, these are crucial aspects of human moral psychology.

Thus far, we have explored five crucial concepts in moral psychology: patiency, agency, sociality, reflexivity, and temporality. I don't mean to suggest that these are the only concepts moral psychologists find worth studying, but I do think they are among the most central. Other important concepts will crop up throughout this book. Some, such as emotion and intuition, will be treated at greater length. Others, such as imagination and mindfulness, will receive less attention. I encourage you to follow up on any and all of the concepts that capture your interest, and will provide lists of secondary sources at the end of each chapter to help direct and slake your curiosity. In the remainder of this introduction, I will characterize some of the major normative theories that you might already be aware of in terms of their emphases on patiency, agency, sociality, reflexivity, and temporality. After that, I'll conclude by considering an objection to moral psychology that might be raised because of the ever-fraught relationships among contingency, necessity, and normativity. In particular, I'll focus on the truism that one can never deduce a normative claim from a descriptive claim, an *ought* from an *is*.

6 Comparing emphases of major normative theories

In the history of Western philosophy, four major normative theories have emerged: **utilitarianism**, **Kantian ethics**, **virtue ethics**, and **care ethics**. Since it's likely that you've encountered at least some of these views before reading this book, in this section, I compare how they relate to the five core concepts of moral psychology.

6.1 *Utilitarianism*

Utilitarianism is the best-known variety of a family of views called **consequentialism**. According to consequentialism, the goodness of an act is determined solely by the goodness of the consequent state of affairs. This view is typically combined with a theory of what makes a state of affairs good and a theory of right action. For instance, hedonist act utilitarianism says that the only thing that contributes to the goodness of a state of affairs is pleasure, that the only thing that detracts from the goodness of a state of affairs is pain, and that an action is right if (and only if) it maximizes the amount of goodness in the consequent state of affairs.

Pleasure and pain are mental states that humans and other animals enjoy and suffer. Thus, utilitarians and other consequentialists place their primary emphasis on patiency. Jeremy Bentham, one of the foremost utilitarian thinkers in philosophical history, exemplified this attitude, while asking what determines whether a creature has moral worth and bears moral consideration:

> Is it the faculty of reason, or, perhaps, the faculty of discourse? But a full-grown horse or dog is beyond comparison a more rational, as well as a more conversable animal, than an infant of a day, or a week, or even a month, old. But suppose the case were otherwise, what would it avail? the question is not, Can they *reason?* nor, Can they *talk?* but, Can they *suffer?* (1789/1961, ch. 17, fn.)

For someone like Bentham, it doesn't matter whether you can engage in reasoning (including the practical reasoning required for agency and the reflexivity required for long-term planning). It doesn't matter whether you can talk. The main moral question for him is whether you can suffer, whether things can happen to you – in particular, bad and painful things.

Utilitarianism thus gives pride of place to patiency and de-emphasizes agency and reflexivity. Bentham's lack of concern for talking might lead one to think that he and other utilitarians have no regard for sociality. In one sense, that's correct. However, utilitarians and other consequentialists also tend to think that every being capable of suffering matters equally. And they recognize that people are capable of both inflicting suffering on one another and alleviating one another's suffering. For this reason, utilitarians put a great deal of emphasis on sociality, though deriving that emphasis from its relation to patiency and suffering.

Naturally, there are more sophisticated versions of consequentialism that shift the emphasis to some extent away from patiency. For example Amartya Sen (1985) has developed a consequentialist framework in which the primary bearers of value are not occurrent states of pleasure, but human capabilities (e.g., literacy, being ambulatory, having enough food to eat even if one chooses to fast, a full emotional repertoire, political control), along with the freedom to exercise agency in choosing the set of capabilities one eventually acquires.

Lastly, utilitarians tend to put great emphasis on temporality. What I have in mind here is the fact that the consequences of an action are typically construed not just as what happens immediately afterwards, but as everything that flows from the action. Everything, for all time? At the very least, everything that could be foreseen by a very intelligent and dedicated investigator. Utilitarians care so much about such long-term consequences that they have debates about *population ethics*, asking questions such as "How many people should there be?" (Blackorby et al. 1995)

6.2 *Kantian ethics*

Kantian ethics, the best-known exemplar of **deontological ethics**, puts most emphasis on the two concepts that utilitarianism de-emphasizes (agency and reflexivity), while according less weight to the concepts utilitarianism emphasizes (patiency, sociality, and temporality). Kant thought that an account of moral obligation could be derived from the structure of agency itself. In his *Groundwork of the Metaphysics of Morals*, he called this the *categorical imperative*, because it applies to every agent in every action they undertake regardless of their desires, preferences, and values. The best-known formulation of the categorical imperative states that you must "act only in accordance with that maxim through which you can at the same time will that it become a universal law" (*Groundwork* 4:421). My book is not an introduction to major moral theories, let alone the history of philosophy, so I will not go into much detail interpreting the categorical imperative. Kant's idea, though, is that simply in virtue of being an agent you are constrained to act from some motives rather than others. Clearly, then, agency figures importantly in Kantian ethics.

The other core concept that receives primary emphasis in Kantian ethics is reflexivity. This is already somewhat evident from the first formulation of the categorical imperative, which requires you to reflect on and extrapolate from your own motives, but it comes into focus if we consider the third formulation: act as if you were, through your maxim, always a legislating member in the universal kingdom of ends (*Groundwork* 4:439). On this view, a moral act is one that can be *self*-legislated – i.e., an act that is in accordance with a law one could give not only to others but also to oneself.

Agency and reflexivity have pride of place in Kantian ethics, but the other three core moral psychological concepts receive some attention. Patiency and sociality get their due in the second formulation of the categorical imperative: treat humanity – whether your own or someone else's – never merely as the means to some end, but always as an end in its own right. In this formulation, we can see that Kant cares not only about agency, but also about what's done to people. He thinks it's always wrong to treat someone as a mere means to your own end. However, patiency matters for Kant only derivatively because he thinks that what's wrong with treating someone as a mere means is that, in so doing, you don't respect their agency. Thus, the importance of what happens to us and what we do to each other depends on the antecedent importance of agency.

Finally, Kantian ethics doesn't totally discount temporality (Kant argues that we have an imperfect duty to develop our own talents, for instance), but it also doesn't place primary emphasis on it.

6.3 *Virtue ethics*

Virtue ethics is a family of views that focuses less on what it's right to do and more on what sort of person it's good to be. A good person is someone with many virtues (compassion, courage, honesty, trustworthiness) and few vices (selfishness, laziness, unfairness, rashness). Ancient Greek philosophers were basically all virtue ethicists of one kind or another. Plato emphasized the virtues of courage, temperance, wisdom, and justice. Aristotle famously thought that every virtue was a middle state between a pair of vices. For instance, courage is the disposition to fear neither too many things nor too few things, to fear them neither too intensely nor not intensely enough, to fear them neither for too long nor for too short a period, and so on.

Utilitarian ethics focuses primarily on patiency, sociality, and temporality; Kantian ethics focuses primarily on agency and reflexivity. Virtue ethics has a more balanced approach (this isn't necessarily a good or a bad thing – it's just a matter of emphasis), putting moderate to high emphasis on all five central concepts. A virtuous person is characteristically active, doing things for reasons. A virtuous person is also quite social. Aristotle, for instance, devotes two whole books (out of ten) of the *Nicomachean Ethics* to friendship and another to justice. Additionally, because virtue ethicists are concerned with the shape of a person's whole life and the slow acquisition of virtuous traits, they pay more attention to temporality and moral development than utilitarians and Kantians do. They place slightly less emphasis on patiency and reflexivity, though these too figure in their account.

6.4 Care ethics

The other three views surveyed in this section are venerable, traditional approaches to morality. The ethics of care is much more
recent. The dawn of care ethics can be dated with some precision
to the publication, in 1982, of Carol Gilligan's *In a Different Voice:
Psychological Theory and Women's Development*. Gilligan explored the
ways in which women (at least the women she researched) tend to
talk in terms of care, emphasizing personal relationships and attachments (motherhood, siblinghood, friendship, etc.) and the special
responsibilities that flow from these. She accused existing moral
theories, such as Lawrence Kohlberg's (1971) Kantian approach to
moral psychology, of ignoring and even sometimes denigrating
such caring relationships in favor of a completely impartial, legal-
istic notion of rights and justice. Although this criticism is somewhat overbroad (as I mentioned above, Aristotle devotes twice as
much attention to friendship as he does to justice), popular versions
of both utilitarian and Kantian ethics clearly deserve Gilligan's
rebuke. Since 1971, various philosophers, including Kittay (1999),
Noddings (1984), and Slote (2007), have formulated care-based
approaches to ethics in the wake of Gilligan's critique.

Like the other theories canvassed here, care ethics is actually a
family of views. What unites them is their emphasis on personal,
face-to-face relationships and attachments, as well as their recognition that we all come into this world as helpless, dependent, scream-
ing, fragile lumps of flesh (and we don't tend to leave it in better
shape). Care ethicists therefore focus primarily on human sociality
and patiency, with derivative interest in agency and temporality.
Reflexivity receives little attention in the care tradition, though there
is some fascinating work on self-care and self-forgiveness in this
literature (e.g., Norlock 2008).

7 Is and ought

To some people, the idea of combining scientific psychology with
philosophical ethics to investigate moral psychology will seem only
natural. Philosophy helps to set the terms of the investigation (in
this case, patiency, agency, sociality, reflexivity, and temporality),
proposes questions and models, and dreams up potential counterexamples; psychology empirically determines whether the terms

refer to anything in the world, answers the questions, tests the models, and checks whether the potential counterexamples can be realized. Psychology as an academic discipline split off from philosophy less than two centuries ago; it's unsurprising that the two fields would sometimes collaborate. To other people, though, this project might seem to be doomed from the start. Science studies how things *are*, whereas philosophy studies how things *ought* to be and how they *must* be. According to these critics, science can never, even in principle, help to answer philosophical questions.

As you've probably guessed, I disagree, and for several reasons. First, science can investigate modal reality (how things not only are but *can* and *can't* be). To the extent that we accept the truism that people can't be morally required to do things or be in ways that are impossible, scientific investigation of moral psychology constrains moral theory. Second, scientific psychology can also investigate not just *whether* various kinds of behavior, character, and attachments are possible, but also how demanding it would be for people to act, be, and relate in those ways. Beyond a certain threshold, the harder it is to live up to a moral theory's requirements, the more suspicious we should be of that theory. This is not to say that morality can't make legitimate, even extreme, demands on us, but just that the more extravagant those demands grow, the more dubious we should be of the theory that generated them. This problem is familiar to normative ethicists as the *demandingness problem*, and it has been taken to challenge various normative views, including not just utilitarianism (Donner 2011) but any ethical theory whatsoever (Audi 2015). Third, even if we decide to hold onto very demanding norms, psychological science can help us to see how to live up to those norms. In the same way, even if we hold onto extremely idealized norms of physical health, biological science can help us to see how to approximate those norms in our own lives. Fourth, moral arguments and theories often contain implicit or explicit empirical premises. These need to be validated using our best scientific psychology.[5]

Finally, morality is an important part of human behavior and cognition; as such, it's something psychologists want to study, even if their investigations never end up suggesting revisions to moral norms. The idea that this aspect of psychology is simply off-limits, as if philosophers could somehow call "dibs" on it, is preposterous. As Levitin put it, those who think that science cannot study values typically commit a fallacy: "they seem to have confused *making* value judgments, which is incompatible with scientific objectivity,

with studying objectively *how other people make them* – a phenomenon as amenable to psychological study, in principle, as other forms
of human learning and choice" (1973, p. 491). Moral psychology
doesn't aim to replace consequentialism, deontology, virtue ethics,
or the ethics of care. In the case of care, this should be especially
obvious: the entire edifice of care ethics was inspired by empirical
research on moral psychology. Instead of taking their ball and going
home, philosophers need to learn to share their insights, theories,
and models with their scientist neighbors.

It's not all good news for traditional normative ethics, though.
As I mentioned above, moral theories have empirical presuppositions. Moral psychology can investigate those presuppositions.
Sometimes, to the moral theorist's delight, they turn out to be well-
supported. Sometimes, the foundations look pretty shaky. The relation between philosophy and psychology doesn't need to involve
confrontation or scorn, though. A better attitude for both sides to
take, I contend, is one of curiosity and intellectual humility. A
curious investigator is committed to her views, but she's also
delighted to find out that she's wrong because that spurs her to
construct a better model, a stronger theory, a more nuanced hypothesis. There's no part of reality that's specially marked off for philosophers and only philosophers to investigate. By the same token,
there's no part of reality that's specially marked off for psychologists and only psychologists to investigate.

By the same token, there's no part of reality that's specially
marked off for psychologists and only psychologists to investigate.
There is an unfortunate tendency among some – though by no
means even a majority – of scientists to dismiss philosophy as out-
dated, old-fashioned, irrelevant, or nonsensical. This tendency has
recently been manifested by such luminaries as physicist Stephen
Hawking, who declared at a conference in 2011 that philosophy is
dead, and astronomer Neil DeGrasse Tyson, who insisted during a
televised interview that philosophy is "distracting" because it
involved "too much question asking." Needless to say, I reject such
philistinism, whether it comes from people involved in the hard
sciences or people in the human scientists. A prominent example of
the latter is Daniel Gilbert, who blithely claims that "For two thousand years philosophers" have committed obvious logical fallacies
related to happiness and virtue because "[h]appiness is a word that
we generally use to indicate an experience and not the actions that
give rise to it" (2007, pp. 34–5).

Such remarks are not uncommon in the movement that marches under the banner of "positive psychology," where arguments of the form "philosophy used to say BLAH, but now science has discovered that..." often frame the debate. It should be clear that a single study does not a refutation make, especially since there are so many ways for philosophical theories to dodge empirical bullets.

In my own research, I favor a more irenic approach that seeks to put empirical flesh on the conceptual bones furnished by various philosophical models. I often find that I don't really understand such a model until I've adequately operationalized its terminology in a way that can be tested. And as any responsible scientist would tell you, the data obtained in experimentation are typically more complicated than any reductive tagline would suggest. Furthermore, the data never speak for themselves: they always need to be interpreted in light of a theory, which will be supplied either as an explicit philosophical or conceptual model or as the implicit assumptions of the scientist

If you don't believe me now, perhaps you will when you finish this book.

Further readings

Annas, J. (2009). *Intelligent Virtue*. Oxford University Press.

Doris, J. (2012). *The Moral Psychology Handbook*. Oxford University Press.

Flanagan, O. (1993). *Varieties of Moral Personality: Ethics and Psychological Realism*. Harvard University Press.

Gilligan, C. (1982). *In a Different Voice: Psychological Theory and Women's Development*. Harvard University Press.

Korsgaard, C. (2009). *Self-Constitution: Agency, Identity, and Integrity*. Oxford University Press.

Morton, A. (2013). *Emotion and Imagination*. Polity.

Nussbaum, M. (2000). *Women and Human Development: The Capabilities Approach*. Cambridge University Press.

Sinnott-Armstrong, W. (2008–14). *Moral Psychology*, vols 1–4. MIT Press.

Study questions

1 Give an example of patiency that does *not* involve agency.
2 Give an example of agency that does *not* involve patiency.
3 Give an example of reflexivity that does *not* involve temporality.

4 Which of the four major normative theories discussed in section 6 do you find most attractive? Do you think it doesn't pay sufficient attention to one of the core concepts (patiency, agency, sociality, reflexivity, temporality) discussed in this chapter? Why or why not?

5 How would your life be different if you felt no attachment to your future self? How would it be different if you felt no attachment to your past self? How would it be different if you felt no attachment to any of your friends?

6 Imagine someone who was never the patient of others' actions. Is that a good kind of life? Why or why not?

7 If I hadn't noticed that he was harassing her, it never would have occurred to me to deliberate about how to intervene. Does this suggest that moral psychology presupposes a particular kind of perceptual awareness? How would you characterize such awareness?

8 Are you still worried that moral psychology isn't "real" philosophy? Why or why not?

9 Are agency-in-patiency and patiency-in-agency possible? For instance, does it make sense to think about someone allowing something to happen to herself, or for someone to allow herself to do something? Give examples.

1

Preferences

1 The function of preferences: prediction, explanation, planning, and evaluation

Among our diverse mental states, some are best understood as representing how the world is. If I *know* that wine is made from grapes, I correctly represent the world as being a certain way. If I *think* that Toronto is the capital of Canada, I incorrectly represent the world as being a certain way (it's Ottawa). Other mental states are best understood as moving us to act, react, or forbear in various ways. I *want* to see the Grand Canyon before I die. I *desire* to know how to speak Spanish. I *prefer* to use chopsticks rather than a fork to eat sushi. I *intend* to keep my promises. I *aim* to be fair. I *love* to hear New Orleans-style brass band music. Depending on their longevity, their intensity, their specificity, their malleability, and their idiosyncrasy, we use different words to describe these mental states: values, drives, choices, appraisals, volitions, cravings, goals, reasons, purposes, passions, sentiments, longings, appetites, aspirations, attractions, motives, urges, needs, acts of will. Such mental states are sometimes referred to as **pro-attitudes**, and related states that move someone to avoid, escape, or prevent a particular state of affairs are correspondingly called **con-attitudes**.

If you put together an agent's representations of how the world is and the mental states that move her to act, you have some hope of predicting and explaining her actions. Suppose, for instance, that you know that I want a snack, and that I have some crackers in my kitchen. What am I going to do? It's not unreasonable to predict that I will go to the kitchen, open the cupboard where I keep the crackers, take them out and eat them. Now suppose that you know that my memory of where I store my own comestibles is pretty weak. I still want a snack, but I mistakenly think that my crackers are in the pantry, not the cupboard. What do you think I'll do now? It's reasonable to predict that I'll still walk into the kitchen, but that instead of opening the cupboard I'll look in the pantry. Someone's representations and purposes combine to lead them to act. If you know what someone's representations and purposes are, you can to some extent predict what they'll do.

In the same vein, knowing what someone's representations and purposes are puts you in a position to explain their actions. Suppose you see me stand up, walk across the room, open a door, and walk through the doorway. On the door, you notice the following icon:

Figure 1.1

Why did I do what I did? A plausible explanation isn't too hard to assemble. If you saw the sign indicating that the door led to the men's bathroom, then presumably I did too; so I probably had a relevant representation of what was on the other side of the door. What desire (preference, goal, intention, need) might I have that would rationalize my behavior? The most obvious suggestion is that I wanted to relieve myself. Of course, it's possible that I went to the men's bathroom to participate in a drug deal, to conceal myself while I had a good long cry, or for some other reason. But if you're right in thinking that I wanted to urinate, then you've successfully explained my action. If you know what someone's representations and purposes are, you can to some extent explain what they've done.

To predict and explain other people's actions, we need some idea of what they prefer (want, desire, value, need). But that's not all that preferences are for. Preferences also figure in planning and evaluation, and when they're structured appropriately, they contribute to the agent's autonomy. Think about your best friend. Imagine that her birthday is in a week. You love your friend, and want to do something special for her birthday. You don't need to predict your own action here, nor do you need to explain it. Your task now is to plan: in the next week, what can you do for your friend that will simultaneously please and surprise her without emptying your bank account? To give your friend a special birthday present, you need to know what she enjoys (or would enjoy, if she hasn't experienced it yet). To be motivated to give your friend a special birthday present in the first place, you need to want to do something that she wants. In philosophical jargon, you must have a **higher-order desire** – a desire about another desire (hers). You want to give her something that she wants.

It's remarkable how adept people can be at solving this sort of problem, which involves the sort of recursively embedded agent–patient relations discussed in the introduction. Think about it. To plan a good gift, you need to know *now* not just what your friend currently wants, but what she *will* want in the future. You can't just give her what you yourself want or what you will want in a week. You can't give her what she wants now but won't want in a week. To successfully give your friend a good present, you have to figure out in advance what she'll want in a week.

The same constraints apply when you plan for yourself. Think about choosing your university major. What do you want to specialize in? Musicology is interesting, but will you still be interested in it three years from now? Will it set you up to earn a decent living (something you'll presumably want in five, ten, and twenty years)? Marketing might earn you a decent living, but will you find it boring (not want to do it, or even want not to do it) after a few years? Are you going to want to have children? In that case, you may need more income than you would if you didn't want (and didn't have) children. Living a sensible life requires planning. You need to make plans that affect your friends, your family, your colleagues, your rivals, and your enemies. You also need to make plans for yourself. Doing this successfully requires intimate knowledge of (or at least some pretty good guesses about) your own and others' future desires, needs, and preferences.

Thus, preferences figure in the prediction, explanation, and planning of action. They're also important when we morally evaluate action. Imagine that I reach out violently and knock you over, causing you some pain and surprising you more than a little. What should you think of my action? It depends in part on what moved me to do it. If I've shoved you because I want to hurt you, if I'm engaged in an assault, you're going to think I'm doing something wrong. If I'm not depraved, I'll also feel guilty. If I'm just clumsily gesturing at a pretty tree over there, I should probably know better, but you'll temper your anger. I may not feel guilty, but I'll probably be embarrassed or even ashamed. If I'm knocking you out of the way of a biker who's zooming down the sidewalk toward you, perhaps you'll feel grateful, while I'll feel relieved or even proud.

What marks the difference between your reactions to my action? What marks the difference between my own assessments of it after the fact? It's not that my shoving you and your falling hurts more or less in one case or the other. Instead, what leads you to evaluate my action as wrong, misguided, or benevolent is the pro- (or con-) attitude that moves me to act. Likewise, what leads me to feel guilt, embarrassment, or relief is the pro- (or con-)attitude that moved me to act. If I want to hurt you, if I want to do something to you that you prefer not to happen, you'll say that I've acted wrongly. If my aim is to do something relatively harmless (something you neither prefer nor disprefer) like pointing out a feature of the environment, you'll perhaps think I'm a klutz, but you won't think I've done something morally wrong. If I'm trying to prevent you from being run down by an out-of-control cyclist, if I want to do something to you that (once you understand it) you prefer that I do, you'll presumably think I've done something morally good.

Preferences are important and versatile. They help us predict and explain actions. They help us exercise agency on our own behalf and for those we care about. They help us evaluate the actions of others and ourselves. They also play a role in autonomy. According to some philosophers, such as Harry Frankfurt (1971, 1992; see also Katsafanas 2013 and, if he is on the right track, Nietzsche 1886/1966), a person is autonomous or free to the extent that she wants what she wants to want, or at least does not want what she would prefer not to want. An autonomous agent is someone whose will has a characteristic structure. This idea is discussed in more depth in chapter 2.

As I mentioned above, we have dozens of terms to refer to pro- and con-attitudes. But the title of this chapter is "Preferences." Why? Preferences are sufficiently fine-grained to help in the prediction, explanation, and evaluation of action in the face of *tradeoffs*. Other motivating attitudes lack this specificity. Consider, for instance, values.[1] At a high enough level of abstraction, just about everyone values the same ten things: power, achievement, pleasure, stimulation, self-direction, universalism, benevolence, tradition, conformity, and security (Schwartz 2012). If you want to know what someone will do, why someone did something, or whether someone deserves praise or blame for acting as they did, knowing that they accept these values gives you no purchase. Qualitatively weighting values doesn't improve things much. Consider someone who values pleasure "somewhat," stimulation "a lot," and security "quite a bit." What will she do? It's hard to say. Why'd she go to the punk rock show? It's hard to say. Does she merit some praise for engaging in a pleasant conversation with a stranger at the coffee shop? It's hard to say.

Preferences set up a rank ordering of states of affairs. This is easiest to see in the case of tradeoffs. Suppose two desires are moving you to act. You're exhausted after a long day, so you want to take a nap. But your friend just texted to suggest meeting up for a drink at a local bar, and you want to join her. This tradeoff is represented in table 1.1.

In this simplified choice matrix, there are four ways things could turn out. You could take a nap and join your friend (A); you could join your friend without taking a nap (B); you could take a nap without joining your friend (C); and you could neither nap nor join your friend (D). If you have a complete set of preferences over these options, one of them is optimal for you, another is in second place, another is in third place, and the final one is in last place. Presumably A is your top outcome and D is your bottom outcome. Unfortunately, although you most prefer A (i.e., you prefer it to B, C, and D), it's impossible. So you're in a position where you need to weigh a tradeoff. This is where preferences become important. If you

Table 1.1 Choice matrix

	Nap	Don't nap
Join friend	A	B
Don't join friend	C	D

Preferences

simply value the nap and value socializing with your friend, there's no saying whether you'll go with B or C. But if you *prefer* socializing to napping, we can predict that you'll opt for B over C. By the same token, if you prefer napping to socializing, we can predict that you'll opt for C over B.

So preferences are especially helpful in predicting behavior. They're also great for explaining and evaluating behavior. A useful rule of thumb for explaining behavior is that people act in such a way as to bring about the highest-ranked outcome they think they can achieve. Imagine someone who prefers A to B, B to C, C to D, D to E, E to F, F to G, and G to H. She acts in such a way as to produce C. How can we explain this? If we posit that she believes that A and B are out of the question (perhaps she takes them to be impossible or at least extremely difficult to achieve), then we can explain her behavior by saying that she went with the best outcome available to her.

2 The role of preferences in moral psychology

We're now in a position to see how preferences relate to the five core concepts of moral psychology (patiency, agency, sociality, reflexivity, and temporality).

2.1 The role of preferences in patiency

Even if no one else is involved, even if you're not exercising agency, your preferences matter for your patiency. According to one attractive theory of personal **wellbeing**, what it means for your life to go well is that your preferences are satisfied (Brandt 1972, 1983; Heathwood 2006). Your preferences might be satisfied through your own agency. You might prefer, among other things, to exercise agency in pursuit of some goal or other. Your preferences might be satisfied because you are involved in social relations with other people. Even so, there will be cases in which what you prefer happens or fails to happen simply by luck, accident, unanticipated causal necessity, or the agency of other people. Fundamentally, then, wellbeing is associated with patiency, with what happens to you.

The preference-satisfaction theory of wellbeing is attractive for several reasons. It explains why one aspect of morality is intrinsically motivating. If my wellbeing is a matter of whether my preferences are satisfied, then I can't help caring about my wellbeing. Preferences are a way of caring about things. Of course I care about what I care about. The preference-satisfaction theory of wellbeing also accounts for cases in which hedonic (pleasure-based) theories of wellbeing fail. Sometimes, it seems like my life goes no better, and may even go worse, when I experience some pleasures. I struggle with alcohol dependency and end up drinking to excess. While I *enjoy* the drinks, I *prefer* to stop. Arguably, I'm worse rather than better off because, even though I experience pleasure, my preferences are frustrated. Similarly, sometimes it seems like your life goes no worse, and may even go better, when you experience some pains. You exercise vigorously at the gym. You force yourself to study extra hard for an exam. You watch a frightening or depressing or horrifying movie. You eat a meal spiced with more than a little wasabi. These are painful experiences, but in each case you *prefer* to suffer through the pain. Arguably, you're better rather than worse off because, even though you experience pain, your preferences are satisfied.

The preference-satisfaction theory of wellbeing also provides a way to understand wellbeing comparatively. People don't just have *good* or *bad* lives. They have *better* or *worse* lives. Someone whose life is going poorly could be even worse off. Someone whose life is going well could be even better off. This distinction maps nicely onto the idea of a preference ranking. Since preferences can in principle put *all* the ways the world could be in order from best to worst, it's possible to identify someone's wellbeing with how far up their ranking things actually are. If you prefer A to B, B to C, C to D, D to E, E to F, F to G, and G to H, and the actual state of affairs is C, then your level of wellbeing is better than many ways it could be, but not maximal. If things change to B, your wellbeing improves one notch; if things change to D, your wellbeing goes down a notch.

The most plausible version of the preference-satisfaction theory of wellbeing claims that what really contributes to your wellbeing is not the extent to which your actual preferences are satisfied, but the extent to which your *better-informed* preferences are satisfied. Why? And what does it mean for preferences to be informed? Imagine that you're about to take a bite of a delicious chile relleno. It's your favorite dish. The cheese is perfectly melted. The poblanos are fresh. The tomatoes are local. Everything is perfect except for one little thing: unbeknownst to you, the cook accidentally used rat poison rather than salt. If you eat these chiles, you're going to end up in the hospital or the ground. But you don't know this; in fact, you have no clue. It won't improve your life to eat those chiles. It'll make your life (much!) worse.

Philosophers recognize this, and that's why they say that your wellbeing is a function not of what you want but of what you would want if you were better informed. If you knew that the chiles relleno were poisoned, you would prefer quite strongly not to eat them, so even though you currently prefer to eat them, doing so would detract from rather than contribute to your wellbeing.

Knowledge of potential poisons is clearly not the only thing you need in order to construct better-informed preferences, so philosophers of wellbeing argue that your *better*-informed preferences are your *fully* informed preferences. According to this approach, the preferences that determine someone's wellbeing are not the preferences that person *actually has*, but the ones they *would have if they were fully informed*. Specifying what full information means in a way that doesn't collapse into omniscience is tricky, but one attractive suggestion is to take into account "all those knowable facts which, if [you] thought about them, would make a difference to [your] tendency to act" (Brandt 1972, p. 682) or "everything that might make [you] change [your] desires" (Brandt 1983, p. 40) – a process Richard Brandt dubbed **cognitive psychotherapy**.[2]

2.2 The role of preferences in agency, reflexivity, and temporality

I briefly described the role of preferences in agency, reflexivity, and temporality above. Several points are relevant. First, to act at all, you must have pro-attitudes like preferences. Without states that move you to act, you'd never act in the first place, never exercise agency at all. Second, to act in the face of tradeoffs, you must have some way of ranking potential outcomes. That's what preferences do: they put potential outcomes in a rank order. Third, to be the sort of agent that the vast majority of adult humans are, you need to engage in long-term plans and projects. This involves having some idea in advance what your future self's preferences will or might be. It involves having temporally extended preferences, so that you want *now* for your *future* preferences, whatever they end up being, to be satisfied. It involves thinking of that future person as *yourself* and therefore having a special regard for him or her. If your future self mattered to you no more or less than some random stranger, long-term projects would be pointless.

To be a recognizably human agent, your preferences must not violate certain constraints. Put less dramatically, your agency is undermined to the extent that your preferences violate certain constraints. You'll fail to act successfully to the extent that you suffer from preference reversals (preferring A to B one moment and B to A the next moment). You'll fail to act successfully if you have cyclical preferences (preferring A to B, B to C, but C to A). You'll fail to act successfully over time if you cannot rely on your current representation of your future preferences to be largely accurate (thinking that you'll prefer A to B when in fact you'll prefer B to A).

2.3 The role of preferences in sociality

We tend to think that people deserve praise and blame only, or at least primarily, for their motivated actions. As I pointed out above, if someone inadvertently brings about a consequence, we tend to withhold or at least temper praise (even if the consequence was good) and blame (even if it was bad). Moral good luck is nice, but not particularly praiseworthy. Negligence is blameworthy, but less so than malignance.

The role of preferences in sociality is most directly comprehensible from a utilitarian or other consequentialist framework, but does not depend essentially on the truth of such a view. Utilitarians such as Brandt analyze right action in terms of preference-satisfaction. According to Brandt (1983, p. 37), an action is permissible if (and only if) "it would be as beneficial to have a moral code permitting that act as to have any moral code that is similar but prohibits the act." Obligatory and forbidden actions can then be defined in terms of permissibility using well-known equivalences in deontic logic: an obligatory action is one that it's not permissible not to do, and a forbidden action is one that it's not permissible to do. The connection with preferences is that benefit (and harm) are understood on this account in terms of wellbeing. In other words, according to Brandt, an action is permissible if and only if it would satisfy as many fully informed preferences, across all people, to have a moral code permitting that act as to have any moral code that is similar but prohibits the act.

Brandt's theory is a *rule* utilitarian approach to right action. One could instead adopt an *act* utilitarian theory, according to which an action is permissible if and only if performing it in the circumstances would be as beneficial as performing any alternative action

(Smart 1956). Or one could adopt a *motive* utilitarian theory, according to which an action is permissible if and only if it's what a person with an ideal motivational set (i.e., a psychologically possible motivational set that, over the course of a lifetime, is as beneficial as any alternative psychologically possible motivational set) would perform in the circumstances (Adams 1976). Regardless of the precise flavor of utilitarianism one adopts, then, it's clear that, for utilitarians, preferences are immensely important on the dimension of sociality. To act in such a way as to satisfy the most preferences, you must take into account the effects of your action not just on yourself but on everyone else. In other words, you need to take into account how your agency affects others as patients. Recursively embedded agent–patient relations also play a role here. What you do (or fail to do) to one person will often have some effect on what they do (or fail to do) to another person, which will have an effect on what the second person does (or fails to do) to a third person, and so on.

As I mentioned above, the relevance of preferences to sociality is easiest to see from a utilitarian perspective, but it doesn't rely on such a perspective. Virtue ethicists and care ethicists (though perhaps not Kantians) all accept the centrality of preferences in their approaches to sociality. For instance, one nearly universally recognized virtue is benevolence, the disposition both to want to benefit other people and to succeed, typically, in doing so. Even if a virtue ethicist thinks that there are benefits other than preference-satisfaction, they admit that preference-satisfaction is *one* kind of benefit. In the same vein, Aristotle and other ancient virtue ethicists gave pride of place to friendship. Friends aim, among other things, to benefit each other (and typically succeed), which again involves (perhaps among other things) preference-satisfaction. Similarly, in the care tradition, the one-caring aims among other things to benefit the cared-for. This typically involves not only satisfying the cared-for's informed preferences but actively *helping* the cared-for to get their actual preferences to approximate their idealized preferences.

3 Preference reversals and choice blindness

Thus, preferences matter in multiple ways to the core concepts of moral psychology. What does the scientific literature on preferences tell us about these important mental states? Two convergent lines of evidence suggest that preferences are neither determinate nor stable: the heuristics and biases research on **preference reversals**, and the psychological research on **choice blindness**.

Preferences are dispositions to choose one option over another. You strictly prefer *a* to *b* only if, if you were offered a choice between them, then *ceteris paribus* you would choose *a*. If your preferences are stable, then what you would choose now is identical to what you would choose in the future. If your preferences are determinate, then there is some fact of the matter about how you would choose. That is to say, exactly one of the following subjunctive conditionals is true: if you were offered a choice, then *ceteris paribus* you would choose *a*; if you were offered a choice, then *ceteris paribus* you would choose *b*; if you were offered a choice, then *ceteris paribus* you would be willing to flip a coin and accept *a* if heads and *b* if tails (or you would be willing to let someone else – even your worst enemy – choose for you). The kind of indeterminacy and instability I argue for in this section is modest rather than radical. I want to claim that preferences are unstable in the sense of *sometimes* changing in the face of seemingly trivial and normatively irrelevant situational influences, not in the sense of *constantly* changing. Similarly, I want to claim that preferences are indeterminate in the sense of there *sometimes* being no fact of the matter how someone would choose, not in the sense of there *always* being no fact of the matter how someone would choose.

3.1 *Preference reversals*

Two distinctions are worth making regarding the types of possible preference reversals. In a *chain-type* reversal, you prefer *a* to *b*, prefer *b* to *c*, and prefer *c* to *a*; such reversals are sometimes labeled failures of *acyclicity*. In a *waffle-type* reversal, you prefer *a* to *b*, but also prefer *b* to *a*. The other distinction has to do with temporal scale. Preference reversals can be synchronic, in which case you would have the inconsistent preferences all at the same time. More commonly, they are diachronic, in which case you might now prefer *a* to *b* and *b* to *c*, and then later come to prefer *c* to *a* (and perhaps give up your preference for *a* over *b*). Or you might now prefer *a* to *b*, but later prefer *b* to *a* (and perhaps give up your preference for *a* over *b*). In my (2012b) paper, I call diachronic waffle-type reversals the result of Rum Tum Tugger preferences, after the character in T. S. Eliot's *Book of Practical Cats* who is "always on the wrong side of every door."

Preference reversals were first systematically studied by Daniel Kahneman, Sarah Lichtenstein, Paul Slovic, and Amos Tversky as part of the heuristics and biases research program.[3] In study after study, they and others showed that people's **cardinal preferences** could be reversed by strategically framing the choice situation. When faced with a high-risk/high-reward gamble and a low-risk/low-reward gamble, most people choose the former but assign a higher monetary value to the latter. These investigations focused on choices between lotteries or gambles rather than choices between outcomes, because the researchers were attempting to engage with theories of rational choice and strategic interaction, which – in order to generate representation theorems – employ preferences over probability-weighted outcomes. While this research is fascinating, its complexity makes it hard to interpret confidently. In particular, whenever the interpreter encounters a phenomenon like this, it's always possible to say that the problem lies not in people's preferences but in their credences or subjective probabilities. Since evaluating a gamble always involves weighting an outcome by its probability, one can never be sure whether anomalies are attributable to the value attached to the outcome or the process of weighting. And since we have independent reason to think that people's ability to think clearly about probability is limited and unreliable (Alfano 2013), it's tempting to hope that preferences can be insulated from this line of critique.

For this reason, I will focus on more recent research on preference reversals in the context of choices between outcomes rather than choices between lotteries. A choice of outcome *a* over outcome *b* can only reveal someone's **ordinal preferences**; it can only tell us *that* she prefers *a* to *b*, not *by how much* she prefers *a* to *b*. This limitation is worth the price, however, because looking at choices between outcomes lets us rule out the possibility that any preference reversal might be attributable to the agent's credences rather than her preferences.

Some of the most striking investigations of preference reversals in this paradigm have been conducted by Dan Ariely and his colleagues. For instance, Ariely et al. (2006) used an arbitrary anchoring paradigm to show that preferences ranging over baskets of goods and money are susceptible to diachronic waffle-type reversals.[4] In this paradigm, a participant first writes down the final two digits of her social security number (a national identification number, henceforth SSN-truncation[5]), then puts a "$" in front of it. Next, the experimenters showcase some consumer goods, such as chocolate, books, wine, and computer peripherals. The participant is instructed to record whether, hypothetically speaking, she would pay her SSN-truncation for the goods. Finally, the goods are auctioned off for real money. The surprising result is that participants with high SSN-truncations bid 57–107 percent more than those with low SSN-truncations.

To better understand this phenomenon, consider a fictional participant whose SSN-truncation was 89. She ended up bidding $50 for the goods, so, at the moment of bidding, she preferred the goods to the money; otherwise, she would have entered a lower bid. However, one natural interpretation of the experiment is that, prior to the anchoring intervention, she would – or at least might – have chosen that amount of money over the goods (i.e., she would have bid lower); in other words, prior to the anchoring intervention, she preferred the money to the goods. Anchoring on her high SSN-truncation induced a diachronic waffle-type reversal in her preferences. Prior to the intervention, she preferred the money to the goods, but after, she preferred the goods to the money. This way of explaining the experiment entails that her preferences were unstable: they changed in response to the seemingly trivial and normatively irrelevant framing of the choice.

Another way to explain the same result is to say that, prior to the anchoring intervention, there was no fact of the matter whether she preferred the goods to the money or the money to the goods. In other words, it was false that, given a choice, she would have chosen the goods, but it was equally false that, given a choice, she would have chosen the money or been willing to accept a coin flip. Only in the face of the choice in all its messy situational details did she construct a preference ordering, and the process of construction was modulated by her anchoring on her SSN-truncation. This alternative explanation entails that her preferences were indeterminate.

Furthermore, these potential explanations are mutually compatible. It could be, for instance, that her preferences were partially indeterminate, and that they became determinate in the face of the choice situation. Perhaps she definitely did not prefer the money to the goods prior to the anchoring intervention, but there was no fact of the matter regarding whether she was indifferent or preferred the goods to the money. Then, in the face of the hypothetical choice, this local indeterminacy was resolved in favor of preference rather than indifference. Finally, her newly crystallized preference was expressed when she entered her bid.

Such a robust effect calls for explanation. My own suspicion is that a hybrid of indeterminacy and instability is the right theory of what happens in these cases, but it's difficult to find evidence that points one way or the other. In any event, for present purposes, I'm satisfied with the inclusive disjunction of indeterminacy and instability.

3.2 Choice blindness

There are many other – often amusing and sometimes depressing – studies of preference reversals, but the gist of them should be clear, so I'd like to turn now to the phenomenon of choice blindness, a field of research pioneered in the last decade by Petter Johansson and his colleagues. As I mentioned above, preferences are dispositions to choose. You prefer *a* to *b* only if, were you given the choice between them, then *ceteris paribus* you would choose *a*. Preferences are also dispositions to make characteristic assertions and offer characteristic reasons. While it's certainly possible for someone to prefer *a* to *b* but not to say so when asked, the linguistic disposition is closely connected to the preference. Someone might be embarrassed by her preferences. She might worry that her interlocutor could use them against her in a bargaining context. She could be self-deceived about her own preferences. In such cases, we wouldn't necessarily expect her to say what she wants, or to give reasons that support her actual preferences. But in the case of garden-variety preferences, it's natural to assume that when someone says she prefers *a* to *b*, she really does, and it's natural to assume that when someone gives reasons that support choosing *a* over *b*, she herself prefers *a* to *b*. Research on choice blindness challenges these assumptions.

Imagine that someone shows you two pictures, each a snapshot of a woman's face. He asks you to say which you prefer. You point to the face on the left. He then asks you to explain why, displaying the chosen photograph a second time. Would you notice that the faces had been surreptitiously switched, so that the face you hadn't pointed at is now the one you're being asked about? Or would you give a reason for choosing the face that you'd initially dispreferred? Johansson et al. (2005) found that participants detected the ruse in fewer than 20 percent of trials. Moreover, when asked for reasons, many of the participants who had not detected the manipulation gave reasons that were inconsistent with their original choice. For instance, some said that they preferred blondes even though they had originally chosen a brunette.

This original study of choice blindness has been supplemented with experiments in other domains. For instance, Hall et al. (2010) found that people exhibited choice blindness in more than two-thirds of all trials when the choice was between two kinds of jam or two kinds of tea. After tasting both, participants indicated which of the two they preferred, then were asked to explain their choice while sampling their preferred option "again." Even when the contrast between the items was especially large (cinnamon apple versus grapefruit for jam, pernod versus mango for tea), fewer than half the participants detected the switch.

Choice blindness in the domain of aesthetic evaluations of faces and comestibles might not seem weighty enough to support the argument that preferences are often indeterminate and unstable. But perhaps choice blindness in the domain of political preferences and moral judgments is. Johansson et al. (2011) used the choice blindness paradigm to flip Swedish participants' political preferences across the conservative–socialist gap.[6] Participants filled in a series of scales on their political preferences for policies such as taxes on fuel. Some of these scales were then surreptitiously reversed, so that, for example, a very conservative answer was now a very socialist answer. Participants were then asked to indicate whether they wanted to change any of their choices, and to give reasons for their positions. Fewer than 20 percent of the reversals were detected, and only one in every ten of the participants detected enough reversals to keep their aggregate position from switching from conservative to socialist (or vice versa). In a similar study, Hall et al. (2012) used a self-transforming survey to flip participants' moral judgments on both socially contentious issues, such as the permissibility of prostitution, and broad normative principles, such as the permissibility of large-scale government surveillance and illegal immigration. For instance, an answer indicating that prostitution was morally permissible would be flipped to say that prostitution was never morally permissible, and an answer indicating that illegal immigration was morally permissible would be flipped to say that illegal immigration was morally impermissible. Detection rates for individual questions ranged between 33 percent and 50 percent. Almost seven out of every ten of the participants failed to detect at least one reversal. Do preference-reversing or choice-blinding conditions obtain at the polling station? We don't know, especially because the results just canvassed were all obtained by a single lab. But even if these results exaggerate the extent to which preferences are unstable and indeterminate, there is reason for concern about the determinacy and stability of preferences.

As with the behavioral evidence for preference reversals, the evidence for choice blindness suggests that people's preferences are unstable, indeterminate, or both. The choices people make can fairly easily be made to diverge from the reasons they give. If preferring *a* to *b* is a disposition both to choose *a* over *b* and to offer reasons that support the choice of *a* over *b* (or at least not to offer reasons that support the choice of *b* over *a*), then it would appear that many people lack preferences, or that their preferences do exist but are extremely labile. Not only is there sometimes no fact of the matter about what we prefer, but also our preferences are often seemingly constructed on the fly in choice situations, and their ordering is shaped by seemingly trivial and normatively irrelevant factors.

3.3 *An attractive way to accommodate the data*

While it is of course possible to dispute the validity of these experiments or my interpretation of them, I want to proceed by considering some of the philosophical implications of that interpretation, assuming for the sake of argument that it is sound. I've already explored some of the implications of this perspective in Alfano (2012b; see also Kim forthcoming), where I argue that the indeterminacy and instability of preferences infirm our ability to explain and predict behavior. Predictions of behavior often refer to the preferences of the target agent. If you know that Karen prefers vanilla ice cream to chocolate, then you can predict that, *ceteris paribus*, when offered a choice between them she will go with vanilla. Likewise for explanations: you can base an explanation of Karen's choice of vanilla on the fact that she prefers vanilla. But if there's no fact of the matter about what Karen prefers, you cannot so easily predict what she will do, nor can you so easily explain why she did what she did. A related problem arises when considering instability. If Karen prefers vanilla to chocolate now, but her preference is unstable, then the prediction that she will choose vanilla in the future – even the near future – is on shaky ground. For all you know, by the time the choice is presented, her preferences will have reversed. Similarly for explanation: if Karen's preferences are unstable, you might be able to say that she chose vanilla because she preferred it at that very moment, but you gain little purchase in explaining her patterns of choices over time.

I've responded to these problems by proposing a model in which preferences are interval-valued rather than point-valued. A traditional valuation function v maps from outcomes to points. The binary preference relation is then defined in terms of these points: a is strictly preferred to b just in case $v(a) > v(b)$, b is strictly preferred to a just in case $v(a) < v(b)$, and the agent is indifferent as between a and b just in case $v(a) = v(b)$. In the looser model I propose, by contrast, the valuation function maps from outcomes to closed intervals, such that a is strictly preferred to b just in case $\min(v(a)) > \max(v(b))$ and the agent is indifferent as between a and b just in case there is some overlap in the intervals assigned to a and b. The basic idea behind this model is that, while preferences may be modestly indeterminate and unstable, they are not in general wildly indeterminate or unstable. Various interventions like the ones explored in this chapter may reverse or blind preferences between things that are fairly similarly ranked to begin with, such as flavors of ice cream, but they are less likely to reverse or blind preferences between things that are extremely different. An intervention might get you to prefer eating cake to eating pie, or eating pie to eating cake, but it will not get you to prefer suicide to eating cake. If this is on the right track, then there are some genuinely preferred and some genuinely dispreferred outcomes or prospects for almost everyone, even if there is a penumbra of indeterminacy and instability around this zone. Though this model preserves the transitivity of strict preference, it does not preserve the transitivity of indifference. This, however, may be a feature rather than a bug, since ordinary preferences as exhibited in choice behavior themselves seem not to preserve the transitivity of indifference.

4 Philosophical implications of the indeterminacy and instability of preferences

In this section, I consider some possible philosophical implications of the indeterminacy and instability of preferences, drawing on the descriptive model outlined in the previous section. Moving from the descriptive to the normative domain is always fraught, but, as I argued in the introduction, the two need to be explored in tandem, with mutual theoretical adjustments made on each side. Moral psychology without normative structure is a baggy monster. Normative theory without empirical support is a castle in the sky.

4.1 Implications for patiency, reflexivity, and temporality

The primary worry raised for the theory of personal wellbeing by the indeterminacy and instability of preferences is that, if the extent to which your life is going well depends on or is a function of the extent to which you're getting what you want, then wellbeing inherits the indeterminacy and instability of preferences. In other words, there might be no fact of the matter concerning how good a life you're living at this very moment, and if there is such a fact, it might fluctuate from moment to moment in response to seemingly trivial and normatively irrelevant situational factors.

By way of example, imagine someone who is eating toast with apple cinnamon jam. Is his life as good as it would be if he were eating toast with grapefruit jam? If he is like the people in the choice blindness studies mentioned above, there might be no answer to this question. If he's told that he prefers apple cinnamon, he will prefer the present state of affairs, but if he is told that he prefers grapefruit, he'll be less pleased with the present state of affairs than he would be with the world in which he is eating grapefruit jam. Whether his life is better in the apple cinnamon jam-world or the grapefruit jam-world is indeterminate until his preferences crystallize in one ordering or the other.

Or consider someone who has a brand new hardbound copy of *Moby Dick*, for which she just paid $50 when it was marked down from $70. Is her life going better now that she has the book, or was it going better before, when she had the money? If she is like the participants in Ariely's preference reversal study, the answer may be "yes" to both disjuncts. Before she bought the book, she preferred the money to the book. But then she anchored on the manufacturer's suggested retail price of $70, raised her valuation of the book, and ended up preferring it to $50. Her unstable preferences mean that she was better off with the money than the book, *and* that she is better off with the book than the money. It's not a contradiction, but it makes her wellbeing a pain in the neck to evaluate.

Fortunately, though, there is a ready response to this worry, which begins by pointing out that the indeterminacy and instability of preferences is not radical but modest, a feature captured by the descriptive model sketched above. Although there may be no fact of the matter whether the life of the consumer of cinnamon apple jam is better than the life of the consumer of grapefruit jam, there is a fact of the matter whether either of these lives is better than that of someone who, instead of eating jam, is enduring irritable bowel syndrome. Although preference orderings may fluctuate between owning a book and having $50, they do not fluctuate between owning the same book and having $50,000. These observations are consistent with the interval-valued preferences of the descriptive model outlined in the previous section. In the first example, the intervals for cinnamon apple jam and for grapefruit jam overlap with each other, but neither overlaps with the interval for irritable bowel syndrome. Thus, we can still make a whole host of judgments about the quality of various possible lives, even if, when we "zoom in," such judgments cannot always be made.[7] In the second example, the intervals for having $50 and having the book overlap with each other, but neither overlaps with the interval for having $50,000.

Thus, for the price of this local indeterminacy and instability, the theoretician of wellbeing can purchase an answer to an objection to the preference-satisfaction theory of wellbeing. The objection goes like this: when assessing whether it would be better to have the life of a successful lawyer or a successful artist, it seems trivial or even perverse to ask whether the artist's life would involve slightly more ice cream, even if the agent considering what to do with her life likes ice cream. Such preferences shouldn't bear normative weight in this context.

However, if we assume, as seems reasonable in light of the evidence, that her preference for a little more ice cream is weak enough that it could be shifted by preference reversal or choice blindness, then its normative irrelevance is unmasked. The life of the ice cream-deprived artist and the life of the ice cream-enjoying artist are assigned nearly identical intervals on the scale of preference – intervals that differ less from each other than from that assigned to the life of the lawyer. Hence, if we learn to cope with a little indeterminacy and instability, we can avoid more serious objections to the preference-satisfaction theory of personal wellbeing.

4.2 Implications for sociality and agency

The main worry raised by the indeterminacy and instability of preferences in the context of sociality is that, if right action depends on preference-satisfaction (perhaps among other things), then it inherits the indeterminacy and instability of preferences. It might turn out that there's just no fact of the matter what it would be right to do, or that that fact is in constant flux. This worry is perhaps most pressing for preference-utilitarians, such as Brandt (1983) and Singer (1993), but it casts a long shadow. Even if you don't think that right action is a function of preferences and only preferences, it's hard to deny that preferences matter *at all*. For instance, as I pointed out above, virtue ethicists typically countenance benevolence as an important virtue. If, as I argued in the previous section, wellbeing is affected by the indeterminacy and instability of preferences, then benevolence is too. In particular, even an ideally benevolent person will have trouble exercising her trait if the *target* of benevolence has indeterminate preferences. The ideally benevolent person might have cultivated a coherent, determinate set of other-regarding preferences, but if the target of benevolence – like many or perhaps most people – has incoherent or indeterminate preferences, there will be no fact of the matter about how to benefit that person. And even if one thinks that benevolence is not a virtue, virtually any tolerable theory of right action is going to say that maleficence is a vice and that there is a duty – whether perfect or imperfect – of non-maleficence.

In the remainder of this section, I will concentrate on the normative implications of indeterminacy and instability for preference-utilitarianism, but it should be clear that these are just some of the more straightforward implications.

Before considering some responses I find attractive, I should point out that the problem we face here is not the one that is solved by distinguishing between a decision procedure and a standard of value. An objection to utilitarianism that was lodged early and often is that it's either impossible or at least extremely computationally complex to *know* what would satisfy the most preferences. This knowledge could only be acquired by eliciting the preference orderings of every living person – or perhaps even every past, present, and future person. The correct response to this objection is that utilitarianism is meant to be a standard of value, not a decision procedure.[8] It identifies what it would be right to do, but that doesn't mean that you can use it to *find out* what it would be right to do every time you make a moral decision. The distinction is meant to parallel other general theories: Newtonian mechanics would have identified, if it had been the correct physical theory, what a projectile will do in any circumstances whatsoever, even if people were unable to apply the theory in a given instance.

This response is unavailable in the present context. There are two ways in which it might be impossible to know what would satisfy someone's preferences: one epistemic, the other metaphysical. You would be unable to know what someone wants if there was a fact of the matter about what that person wants, but you couldn't find out what that fact is. This would be a merely epistemic problem, and the distinction between a decision procedure and a standard of value handles it nicely. But you would also be unable to know what someone wants if there simply was no fact of the matter concerning what that person wants. If I am right that preferences are indeterminate, then this is the problem we now face, and it does no good to have recourse to the distinction between a decision procedure and a standard of value.

Preference-utilitarianism is not without resources, however. As in the case of wellbeing, one attractive response is to point out that preferences are only modestly indeterminate and unstable. Although there may be no uniquely most-preferred outcome for a given individual (or indeed for any individual), there will be many genuinely dispreferred outcomes, and hopefully a manageably constrained subset of preferred outcomes. These would all be outcomes than which nothing is determinately and stably better, but there is no unique best outcome among them. In a similar vein, Webber (forthcoming) argues that only strongly held attitudes and preferences – ones that are not susceptible to reversal or blindness – should be accorded normative weight.

Furthermore, from among this subset of alternatives it might be possible to winnow out those that satisfy preferences which we have independent normative grounds to reject – preferences that are silly, ignorant, perverse, or malevolent. As I pointed out above, it's commonly argued in the context of right action that brute preferences carry less weight than fully informed preferences. According to those who argue in this way, whether it's right to do something depends less on whether it would satisfy people's *actual* preferences than on whether it would satisfy their fully informed preferences. It might be hoped that idealizing preferences would cut down or even eliminate their indeterminacy and instability.

Here's what that might look like. Suppose that someone's actual preferences are captured by my interval-valued model. As such, they present two problems: they fail to uniquely determine how it would be right to treat that person, and they may even rule out the genuinely right way to treat her because her actual preferences are normatively objectionable. It might be possible to kill these two birds with the single stone of idealization if idealization leads to unique, point-valued preferences that are no longer normatively objectionable. Perhaps there is only one way that her preferences could turn out after she undergoes cognitive psychotherapy. This is a big "perhaps," but it is worth considering. What evidence we have, however, suggests that idealizing in this way would not lead to determinate, stable preferences. When Kahneman, Lichtenstein, Slovic, and Tversky began to investigate preference reversals, many economists saw the phenomenon as a threat, since it challenged some of the most fundamental assumptions of their field. Accordingly, they tried to show that preference reversals could be removed root and branch if participants were given sufficient information about the choices they were making. Years of attempts to eliminate the effect proved fruitless.[9]

The burden is therefore on the idealizer to say what information participants lack in the relevant experiments. What does someone who bids high on a bottle of wine after considering her SSN-truncation not know, or not know fully enough? Perhaps she should be allowed first to drink some of the wine. While Ariely et al. (2006) did not investigate whether this would eliminate the anchoring on SSN-truncation, they did conduct other experiments in which participants sampled their options and thus had the relevant information. In one, participants first listened to an annoying sound over headphones, then bid for the right not to listen to the sound again. As in the consumer goods experiment, before bidding, participants first considered whether they would pay their SSN-truncation in cents to avoid listening to the sound again. And as expected, those with higher SSN-truncations entered higher bids, while those with lower SSN-truncations entered lower bids. It's unclear what further information they could have acquired to inform their preferences. It seems more plausible that they had *too much* information, not too little. If they hadn't first considered whether to bid their SSN-truncation, they would not have anchored on it and would therefore have had "uncontaminated" preferences. But cognitive psychotherapy says to take into account "everything that might make [one] change [one's] desires" (Brandt 1983, p. 40). Anchoring changed their desires, so it counts as part of cognitive psychotherapy. Perhaps the process can be revised by saying that one should take into account everything that might *correctly* or *relevantly* change one's desires, but then the problem is to come up with an account of what makes an influence on one's desires correct or relevant that doesn't involve either a vicious regress or a vicious circle. No one has managed to do this.

Another response, which I find more attractive, is to embrace rather than reject the indeterminacy and instability of preferences. There are several ways to do this. One is to figure out which preferences are wildly indeterminate or unstable and disqualify their normative standing. Just as it makes sense to ignore the Rum Tum Tugger's begging to be let inside because you know he'll just beg to get back out again, perhaps it makes sense to hive off Jake's indeterminate and unstable preferences, leaving a kernel of normatively respectable ones behind. Only these would matter when considering what it would be right to do by Jake, or what would promote his wellbeing.

A second way to embrace indeterminacy and instability is to make a less heroic assumption about the effect of cognitive psychotherapy. Instead of taking it for granted that this process is bound to converge on unique, point-valued preferences, perhaps it will merely shrink the width of Jake's interval-valued preferences. In that case, even after idealization, there would be no unique characterization of what it would be right to do by Jake or what would most promote his wellbeing. As I've argued in the context of prediction and explanation (Alfano 2012b), however, this might be a feature rather than a bug. Suppose that idealization yields a preference ordering that rules out most actions as wrong and condemns many outcomes as detrimental to Jake's wellbeing, but does not adjudicate among many others. The remaining actions would then all be considered morally right in the weak sense of being permissible but not obligatory, and the remaining outcomes would all be vindicated as conducive to wellbeing. This strategy might help to solve the so-called demandingness problem by expanding what James Fishkin calls "the zone of indifference or permissibly free personal choice" (1982, p. 23; see also 1986). Thus, while it is possible to try to resist the evidence for indeterminacy and instability, or to acknowledge the evidence while denying its normative import, it may be better instead to embrace these features of preferences and use them to respond to existing problems.

5 Future directions in the moral psychology of preferences

Because preferences are involved in multiple ways in patiency, agency, sociality, temporality, and reflexivity, there are many avenues for further research. In this closing section, I list just a few of them.

First, further conceptual work by philosophers and theoretically minded psychologists and behavioral economists may reveal or clarify relevant distinctions, such as a contemporary version of Mill's distinction between higher and lower pleasures. Perhaps a useful distinction can be made between satisfaction of higher and lower preferences. According to Mill, one pleasure is higher than another if an expert who was acquainted with both would choose any amount of the former over any amount of the latter. This maps fairly directly onto the idea of **lexicographic preferences**: one good or value is lexicographically preferred to another if (and only if) any amount of the former would be chosen over any amount of the latter. Such values would be in principle immune to preference reversals. Jeremy Ginges and Scott Atran (2013) have found that when a value becomes "sacred," it becomes lexicographically preferred in this way. Moral, political, and religious values seem to be the only values that are capable of becoming sacred. However, tradeoffs have only been studied in one direction (giving up a sacred value to gain a secular value, not giving up a secular value to gain a sacred value).

Second, further empirical research would help to determine whether the hiving off strategy succeeds. Is there some identifiable class of preferences that are especially susceptible to reversals and choice blindness? We currently lack sufficient evidence to say. It seems that effects may be stronger in business and gambling domains, weaker in social and health domains (Kuhberger 1998), but these distinctions are neither mutually exclusive nor exhaustive. This is yet another area in which collaboration between philosophers, who are specially trained in making this sort of distinction, and psychologists, who know how to design relevant experiments, would be useful.

Third, to what extent do preference reversals and choice blindness disappear when people are informed about them? Are psychologists who know all about these effects less susceptible to them? More susceptible? The same as other people?

Fourth, are there some people who are congenitally more susceptible to preference reversals and choice blindness than others? There is very little research on this, though one study suggests that roughly a quarter of the population is highly susceptible and another quarter is immune (Bostic, Herrnstein, & Duncan 1990). Perhaps the preferences of people who are clear on what they want deserve more normative weight than the preferences of people who don't know what they want. Perhaps the second group would benefit not so much from getting what they (think they) want (for the moment) but from having their preferences shaped in more or less subtle ways.

Finally, on a related note, perhaps public policy should sometimes aim not so much to satisfy existing preferences, but to shape people's preferences in such a way that they are (more easily) satisfiable. The idea here is to take advantage of the instability of preferences, cultivating them in such a way that the people who have them will be most able to satisfy their own wants. If you're not getting what you want, either change what you're getting, or change what you want. Of course, this proposal may seem objectionably paternalistic, but I tend to agree with Richard Thaler and Cass Sunstein (2008) in thinking that in some cases such policies may be permissible. In fact, it's a striking asymmetry that almost no one objects to the shaping of beliefs, provided they are made to accord with (what we take to be) the truth, whereas it's hard to find someone who doesn't object to the shaping of desires and preferences. However, I would argue that the choice we often face is not *whether* to mold preferences but *how*. Given how easily preferences are influenced, it's highly likely that they are constantly being socially shaped without our realizing it. If this is right, existing policies already shape preferences; we just don't know how. The choice is therefore between negligently influencing preferences and doing so strategically. I tend to think that society has not just a right but an obligation to help people develop appropriate preferences – a point with which feminists such as Serene Khader (2011) concur. The worry that such interventions might be objectionably paternalistic can be assuaged somewhat by insisting, as Khader does, that the very people whose preferences are the targets of policy intervention participate in designing the interventions.

Further readings

Bicchieri, C. (2005). *The Grammar of Society: The Nature and Dynamics of Social Norms*. Cambridge University Press.

Haybron, D. (2008). *Pursuit of Unhappiness*. Oxford University Press.

Kahneman, D. (2013). *Thinking, Fast and Slow*. New York: Farrar, Straus, & Giroux.

Lewis, D. (1972). Psychophysical and theoretical identifications. *The Journal of Philosophy*, 67(13): 427–46.

Pettit, P. (1990). In defense of folk psychology. *Philosophical Studies*, 59(1): 31–54.

Singer, P. (1993). *Preference Utilitarianism*. Cambridge University Press.

Study questions

1 This chapter argued that preferences and other motivating mental states are crucial for the prediction, explanation, planning, and evaluation of action. What else might they be important for?

2 Some philosophers have argued that it's impossible to complete what Brandt called cognitive psychotherapy. In light of the discussion of preference reversals in this chapter, what do you think of this criticism?

3 Psychologists claim to have demonstrated that your preferences are irrational. Do you agree? Why or why not?

4 Psychologists claim to have demonstrated that you don't even know what you want, let alone what you will want or what other people do or will want. Do you agree? Why or why not?

5 What are some potential implications of preference indeterminacy and instability for virtue ethics?

6 What are some potential implications of preference indeterminacy and instability for care ethics?

7 Would it bother you if social policies aimed to shape your preferences? What if you contributed to the formulation and/or implementation of those policies?

2

Responsibility

1 Some incidents

At 12:40 AM, February 4, 1999, Amadou Diallo, a student, entrepreneur, and African immigrant, was standing outside his apartment building in the southeast Bronx. In the gloom, four passing police officers in street clothes mistook him for Isaac Jones, a serial rapist who had been terrorizing the neighborhood. Shouting commands, they approached Diallo. He headed toward the front door of his building, then stopped on the dimly lit stoop and took his wallet out of his jacket. Perhaps he thought they were cops and was trying to show them his ID; maybe he thought they were violent thieves and was trying to hand over his cash and credit cards. We will never know. One of them, Sean Carroll, mistook the wallet for a gun. Alerting his fellow officers, Richard Murphy, Edward McMellon, and Kenneth Boss, to the perceived threat, he triggered a firestorm: together, they fired 41 shots at Diallo, nineteen of which found their mark. He died on the spot. He was unarmed. All four officers were ruled by the New York Police Department to have acted as a "reasonable" police officer would have acted in the circumstances. Subsequently indicted for second-degree murder and reckless endangerment, they were acquitted on all charges.

Sean Bell, a black resident of Queens, had some drinks with his friends the night before his wedding, which was scheduled for November 25, 2006. As they were leaving the club, though, something less typical happened: five members of the New York City

Police Department shot about fifty bullets at them, killing Bell and permanently wounding his friends, Trent Benefield and Joseph Guzman. The first officer to shoot, Gescard Isnora, claimed afterward that he'd seen Guzman reach for a gun. Detective Paul Headley fired one shot; officer Michael Carey fired three bullets; officer Marc Cooper shot four times; officer Isnora fired eleven shots. Officer Michael Oliver emptied an entire magazine of his 9mm handgun into Bell's car, paused to reload, then emptied another magazine. Bell, Benefield, and Guzman were unarmed. In part because Benefield's and Guzman's testimony was confused (understandably, given that they'd had a few drinks and then been shot), all the police officers were acquitted. New York City agreed to pay Benefield, Guzman, and Bell's fiancée just over seven million dollars (roughly £4,000,000) in damages, which prompted Michael Paladino, the head of the New York City Detectives Endowment Association, to complain, "I think the settlement is a joke. The detectives were exonerated... and now the taxpayer is on the hook for $7 million."[1]

The gun lobby and related special interest groups have made it more or less impossible to find out how many people (let alone people subdivided by race, gender, and class) are killed by the police in America in a given year. The lowest plausible estimate is just over 400; more reasonable estimates indicate the number is more than 1,000.[2]

In 1979, Lilly Ledbetter was hired as a supervisor by Goodyear Tire & Rubber Company. Initially, her salary roughly matched those of her peers, the vast majority of whom were men. Over the next two decades, her and her peers' raises, which when awarded were a percentage of current salary, were contingent on periodic performance evaluations. In some cases, Ledbetter received raises. In many, she was denied. By the time she retired in 1997, her monthly salary was $3,727. The other supervisors – all men – were then being paid between $4,286 and $5,236. Over the years, her compensation had lagged further and further behind those of men performing substantially similar work; by the time she retired, she was making between 71 percent and 87 percent what her male counterparts earned. Just after retiring, Ledbetter launched charges of discrimination, alleging that Goodyear had violated Title VII of the Civil Rights Act, which prohibits, among other things, discrimination with respect to compensation because of the target's sex. Although a jury of her peers found in her favor, Ledbetter's case was appealed all the way to the American Supreme Court, which ruled 5–4 against her. Writing for the majority, Justice Samuel Alito argued that

Ledbetter's case was unsound because the acts of discrimination occurred more than 180 days before she filed suit, putting them beyond the pale of the statute of limitations and effectively immunizing Goodyear. In 2009, Congress passed the Lilly Ledbetter Fair Pay Act, loosening such temporal restrictions to make suits like hers easier to prosecute.

Though appalling, Ledbetter's example is actually unremarkable. On average in the United States, women earn 77 percent of what their male counterparts earn for comparable work. A longitudinal study of the careers of men and women in business indicates that Ledbetter's case fits a general pattern. Although no gender differences were found early-career, by mid-career, women reported lower salaries, less career satisfaction, and fewer feelings of being appreciated by their bosses (Schneer & Reitman 1994). Over the long term, many small, subtle, but systematic biases often snowball into an unfair and dissatisfying career experience.

Why consider these cases together? What – other than their repugnance – unites them? The exact motives of the people involved are opaque to us, but we can speculate and consider what we should think about the responsibility of those involved, given plausible interpretations of their behavior and motives. This allows us to evaluate related cases and think systematically about responsibility, regardless of how we judge the historical examples used as models. In particular, in this chapter I'll consider the question whether and to what extent someone who acts out of bias is responsible for their behavior. The police seem to have been in some way biased against Diallo and Bell; Ledbetter's supervisors seem to have been in some way biased against her. To explore the extent to which they were morally responsible for acting from these biases, I'll first discuss philosophical approaches to the question of responsibility. Next, I'll explain some of the relevant psychological research on bias. I'll then consider how this research should inform our understanding of the moral psychology of responsibility. Finally, I'll point to opportunities for further philosophical and psychological research.

2 The moral psychology of responsibility

Let's start with some intuitive distinctions. When we talk about responsibility, at least four parameters need to be fixed: (1) the thing or person that *bears* responsibility, (2) the *kind* of responsibility, (3) the *conduct* it or she is responsible *for*, and (4) the *authority to whom* it or she is accountable, if any. In 2012, Hurricane Sandy was responsible for more than $68 billion worth of damage in North America. This is a case of an inanimate object (1) being causally responsible (2) for property damage (3) and being accountable to no one in particular (4). In the Netherlands, if a car collides with a cyclist, the driver of the car (1) is considered legally responsible (2) for property damage and injury (3) to the cyclist (4). While causal and legal responsibility are interesting, they are not our concern here. After all, it's obvious that the police were causally responsible for the deaths of Diallo and Bell, and it's obvious that her supervisors were causally responsible for Ledbetter's salary. Moreover, legal responsibility has already been assigned in these cases. One might worry that it was assigned incorrectly, but what we are interested in now is *moral responsibility*.

In cases of characteristically moral responsibility (2), a human agent (1) is or at least could be held accountable by some moral authority (4) for an action, omission, mental state, or state of character (3). Adult humans are generally assumed to be at least partially morally responsible for their behavior, their mental states, and their character provided that at least two conditions are met: a *knowledge condition* and a *control condition*.[3] According to the knowledge condition, if you lacked certain kinds of relevant knowledge, then you are not responsible for what you did (or failed to do). According to the control condition, if you lacked certain kinds of relevant control, then you are not responsible for what you did (or failed to do). As you might expect, what exactly counts as "relevant" knowledge and control is highly contested.

Responsibility thus has the same kind of recursively embedded structure explored in the introduction to this book (see figure 2.1). In a typical case of holding someone responsible for doing something, there are three people involved. There's the agent whose

Figure 2.1 Recursively embedded agent–patient relations

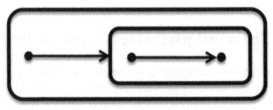

responsibility is being assessed. There's the patient of her activity. And there's the person who holds her to account. The patient of the initial action may be identical to the person who holds the accountable. For instance, if I lie to you, you can call me to account. This identity needn't hold in all cases, however. Your friend could hold me to account for lying to you.

2.1 The knowledge condition on responsibility

The knowledge condition has two main components. First, arguably, you can't be held responsible for doing something when you didn't even know that you were doing it. For example, suppose I'm backing my car out of my driveway when, unbeknownst to me, a suicidal neighbor sneaks up behind my car and lies down in such a way that I run him over. It's true that I did run him over. It's also true that I knew in some sense what I was doing: I knew I was backing out of my driveway. But it's false that I knew what I was doing in the relevant sense: I didn't know I was running him over. As Elizabeth Anscombe (1957; see also Davidson 2001a) pointed out, action is always under some description. The same event, described in one way, is an intentional action, yet described in another way, is not.

This knowledge constraint also applies to actions that result in good consequences. If, while backing my car out of my driveway, it ends up blocking a sniper's bullet aimed at my neighbor, I'm not morally responsible for saving his life. I am causally responsible, since I was the one who interposed the vehicle between the bullet and its target, but since I didn't know that that was what I was doing, it makes no sense to praise me as a life-saver. I and my neighbor are, instead, lucky.

Contrast this with a case in which I know that my poor neighbor has suicidal tendencies. I've seen him trying to get himself run over by other neighbors who were, thankfully, more observant than me. Arguably, I now acquire a duty to investigate whether he's behind my car. This suggests an important revision to the first component of the knowledge condition: you can't be held responsible for doing something when you didn't even know you were doing it *unless you shirked your duty to know*. Life is short, and there are far too many knowable things for any of us to get even close to knowing them all. The duty to know, then, applies only in some cases. I'll leave up for grabs precisely what those cases are.[4]

The second component of the knowledge condition is that you can't be held responsible for doing something when you didn't know why you were doing it. To understand this condition, we need to distinguish between motivating and normative reasons. A motivating reason is a psychological state that moves the agent to perform (or omit) some action; in the terminology introduced in the previous chapter, a motivating reason is either a pro-attitude or a con-attitude. By contrast, a normative reason is a consideration that counts in favor of performing (or omitting) some action. In at least some cases, we don't hold people responsible for their behavior unless their motivating reasons match the normative reasons that apply to the case at hand *even if* their behavior corresponds to what someone with matched motivating and normative reasons would have done. For instance, imagine that a brown recluse spider is crawling its deadly way toward a sleeping child, and I reach out and squash it with a rolled up newspaper. I knew exactly *what* I was doing: I was killing the spider. But why was I doing it? The normative reason to kill the brown recluse is that it has such deadly venom that it could kill the child. If that's what was motivating me, then I deserve to be held responsible for (potentially) saving the child's life. If instead I was doing it because I find bugs disgusting and kill them whenever I have the chance, I don't deserve to be held responsible in this way. We can even suppose that I knew that it was a brown recluse, that it might kill the child, and hence that I was (potentially) saving the child's life, but that I didn't care at all about the child's life. I just callously wanted to smash the disgusting bug. Lack of knowledge of the relevant normative reasons, ignorance of *why* I should act, relieves me of responsibility both for my good and for my bad behavior.

As with the other component of the knowledge condition, though, I can sometimes be held responsible despite my lack of knowledge if my ignorance is culpable. I can't be held responsible for doing something when I didn't even know why I was doing it *unless I shirked my duty to know*.

2.2 *The control condition on responsibility*

Knowledge is one constraint on responsibility; the other main constraint is control. Most philosophers would agree that you can't straightforwardly be held responsible for what you do (or omit) when you lack appropriate control over your behavior. One way in which control can be undermined is constraint or coercion. For example, suppose I promised to meet you today at noon in the library, but on my way there I was kidnapped. It hardly makes sense to hold me responsible for my failure to live up to my commitment: I was physically constrained.

There are other kinds of constraints. For instance, it often makes less sense to hold someone responsible for their behavior when it is biologically, economically, or psychologically constrained. Someone who steals a loaf of bread because she's so hungry she might starve is, in a sense, less responsible for her behavior than someone who steals just because she is too stingy to pay.[5] Someone who fails to rescue a child from the edge of a cliff because he has a paralyzing fear of heights is less responsible for his behavior than someone who fails to help just because he doesn't care. Similar arguments apply to coercion. And as with the knowledge condition, I can sometimes be held responsible for my behavior when I face constraint or coercion if the constraint or coercion is culpable. For instance, if I'm economically constrained in such a way that I can't support my family because I gambled my savings away, it would seem that I'm less easily absolved of responsibility.[6]

Like the knowledge condition, the control condition has two components. Someone who faces a constraint or operates in the face of a coercive incentive structure may nevertheless exercise control over her behavior. Given that I've been kidnapped, there are still various things I can do. Given that you're terrified of heights, there are still certain things you can do. Given that I've gambled away my savings, there are still a number of things I can do. The second component of the control condition is more fundamental: even supposing lack of constraint or coercion, was the agent sufficiently and in the right way in control of her behavior?

What does it mean to be sufficiently in control of your behavior? What does it mean to be in control of your behavior in the right way? As you might expect, philosophers have proposed a bewildering variety of answers to these questions. Among the kinds of control they've suggested might be essential are mental control (Wegner 1994), ultimate control (Kane 1989), regulative control (Fischer & Ravizza 1999), guidance control (Fischer & Ravizza 1999), intervention control (Snow 2009), evaluative control (Hieronymi 2006), indirect control (Arpaly 2003), long-range control (Feldman 2008), fluent control (Railton 2008), habitual control (Romdenh-Romluc 2011), skilled control (Annas 2011), real-self control (Frankfurt 1971, 1992), and ecological control (Clark 2007).[7] And that's not even close to a comprehensive catalogue.

We can impose some structure on this profusion of notions of control by classifying them on three dimensions: proximal vs. distal, first-order vs. higher-order, and degrees of freedom. A concept of control is proximal to the extent that it requires the agent to be in control of her behavior *in or just prior to the moment of acting*; a concept of control is distal to the extent that it allows her control over her behavior to be temporally distant from the moment of action. A view counts as distal, then, if it requires the agent to have selected or designed her environment to facilitate one choice rather than another; it also counts as distal if it requires her to have habituated herself to act in one way rather than another (either by rote or through a more skilled, reasons-responsive mechanism), even if she then cannot act otherwise than she's habituated herself to act. For instance, the Kantian concept of control as autonomy (Korsgaard 2009) requires that, for every action, at the moment of acting, the agent be able to exercise conscious, reflective control over her behavior – acting contrary to her strongest inclinations and desires to bring about an alternative outcome if she wills it.[8] The Kantian notion of autonomy is thus highly proximal. By contrast, Clark's (2007) notion of ecological control merely requires that the agent be so positioned in a social and material environment, partially through her own temporally distant choice and design, that in the moment of choice she does what her prior or better self would have wanted.

A concept of control is higher-order to the extent that it requires the presence or absence of particular higher-order (typically second-order) mental states, such as thoughts and desires; a concept of control is first-order to the extent that it does not require such mental states. For instance, Frankfurt's (1971, 1992) notion of *identification* requires either that the agent have the desires that she wants to have, or at least that she not have desires she wants not to have. Higher-order desires are easiest to understand in a two-person example. Suppose that you don't want to go to a movie with me, but I want to go to a movie with you. In the ordinary case, though, I don't just want you to come to the movie with me no matter what. I want you to come to the movie because you yourself want to be there with me. Otherwise, I'd just be dragging you along or kidnapping you. Thus, I have a higher-order desire: a desire that you desire to go to the movie with me. People often have higher-order desires about others' desires, but they can also have higher-order desires about their own desires.

Such phenomena are familiar from fiction. For example, in season 3, episode 11 of the television series *Friday Night Lights*, Tyra Collette is a high school senior who's recently turned her academic life around. Despite earning mediocre grades in her first two years of high school, she puts her nose to the grindstone and achieves significant improvements, yet her chances of acceptance at a reputable university are in doubt. When she sees her unambitious older sister whisked off her feet by an unemployed but good-natured man, the following conversation ensues with her mother, Angela:

TYRA: I don't know what's wrong with me.
ANGELA: Nothing's wrong with you. What are you talking about?
TYRA: Why can't I want that? They look so happy together. I mean, I spend all this time trying to go to college, and it's seeming more and more impossible.

Tyra wants to attend a good university, but she realizes that doing so will be extremely difficult, even impossible. She concludes that it might be better for her if her first-order desires were different, and even expresses a higher-order desire not to want to go to college.

Though Frankfurt's identification view is perhaps the best-known higher-order theory, there are others. Paul Katsafanas (2013), for example, argues that someone exercises responsible agency when and only when two conditions are met: first, she approves of her action, and second, her approval would not be undermined by further knowledge of the origins of her own motivations. Indeed, any concept of control that requires the agent to be conscious of her motivating reasons for action counts as higher-order, since a mental state such as a motivating reason is conscious if (and only if) one is somehow aware of oneself as being in it (Rosenthal 2005; Prinz 2012).

Finally, a concept of control may require any non-negative number of degrees of freedom. In other words, *holding constant her desires, preferences, and emotions*, it may require that the agent be able to do at least one thing other than what she actually does or many things other than she actually does; alternatively, it may not impose any requirement that alternative possibilities be open to her. Libertarian accounts of free will infamously require that the agent have some positive degrees of freedom. By contrast, Fischer & Ravizza's (1999) notion of guidance control merely requires the agent's decisions and deliberation be part of the causal chain that leads her to act. Likewise, Frankfurt's notion of identification does not require

Table 2.1 Illustrative concepts of control on three dimensions

Proximal vs. distal	First-order vs. higher-order	Degrees of freedom	Exemplar
Proximal	First-order	0	Fischer & Ravizza
		>0	
	Higher-order	0	Frankfurt
		>0	Kant
Distal	First-order	0	Clark
		>0	
	Higher-order	0	Annas
		>0	

positive degrees of freedom. These distinctions are displayed in table 2.1.

Although table 2.1 presents the distinctions as categorical, it should be clear that different concepts of control can be more or less proximal. For instance, Annas's (2011) notion of skilled control has certain proximal elements (a skilled individual can exercise some proximal control *because* she's developed a skill over time), and Clark's notion of ecological control has certain conscious elements (one can consciously choose, at least sometimes, to strategically select and design one's environment). Similarly, a notion of control might be framed almost entirely in terms of higher-order mental states, as Frankfurt's is, or it might give them only a minor role. Although these concepts of control are often pitted against one another as competitors, it might be more useful to think of them as a moral psychological palette. Perhaps sometimes we care about (and have) Frankfurt-style identification. Perhaps sometimes we care about (and have) Fischer and Ravizza-style guidance control. Perhaps sometimes we care about (and have) Clark-style ecological control. It may be that no single account of control suits all our purposes in predicting, explaining, evaluating, and controlling people's behavior (our own behavior included).

2.3 Interactions between knowledge and control

Like the other conditions, the second component of the control condition is not exceptionless. In particular, although we generally do not hold someone responsible for their behavior if they were not sufficiently and in the right way in control, sometimes we do none-theless because their lack of control was culpable. Just as someone can be culpably ignorant of the fact that he is doing something or why he is doing something, just as someone can be culpably con-strained, so someone can be culpably lacking in the appropriate form of control.

One important way in which such culpability arises is through the interaction of the knowledge and control conditions. Quite gen-erally, there is an important bidirectional link between knowledge and successful action. Knowledge is an epistemic achievement. Suc-cessful action is a practical achievement. Knowledge results from reliable cognitive processes. Successful action results from reliable practical processes.[9] It should be unsurprising, then, that there might be a kind of ping-ponging back and forth between knowl-edge and action, between cognitive and practical success. For instance, the more you know, the more possibilities you're able to entertain. The more possibilities you're able to entertain, the more fine-grained your preferences can be. The more fine-grained your preferences can be, the more fine-grained your controlled actions can be. Thus, more knowledge enables more finely controlled action. In the other direction, more controlled action sometimes puts one in a position to acquire more knowledge. The more reliably and precisely you're able to plan and control your behavior, the more successful you'll be as an inquirer, and hence the more high-grade knowledge you'll tend to acquire. Or consider another possibility: if you acquire knowledge of *how to gain and exercise control*, then you are one step away from having and exercising such control. By the same token, if you have sufficient control to gain certain kinds of knowledge, you're just one step away from acquiring that knowledge.

This sort of bidirectional feedback between the cognitive and the practical is appealing in many ways, but it also engenders addi-tional responsibility through a kind of bootstrapping we might call, in the language of rock climbers, *chimneying*. Chimneying is a method for climbing a narrow vertical tunnel by pushing with one's right arm and leg on one side of the tunnel, while pushing with one's left arm and leg on the other side of the tunnel; to chimney is to exploit one constraint to put oneself in a position to exploit another constraint, which then allows one to exploit the first con-straint again, and so on. In this case, the constraints aren't rock faces but the conceptual limitations imposed by the knowledge and control conditions. Suppose I learn that I'm susceptible to a rare visual bias: when driving, I tend to overestimate the distance between my car and the car directly in front of me. Up until I learn this, I've been systematically tailgating, but I had no idea that's what I was doing. Arguably, until I learn about my visual impairment, I'm not responsible for tailgating because I don't know that that's what I have a tendency to do, and I have no reason to suspect it either. Once I learn, though, I acquire a responsibility to exercise additional control over my driving. It would be irresponsible of me to drive at what felt to me like a safe distance, since I now know that my feeling safe is consistent with systematic risk. So I start to follow at a greater distance. In so doing, I come to realize that this same feeling is also present when I'm playing soccer and when I'm having a conversation. Now I should also ask myself which of my other activities may be more dangerous because of my visual impairment. Perhaps I'm a dangerous soccer player who's far too likely to accidentally foul my opponent because I underestimate my distance from him. Perhaps I'm an obnoxious conversation partner because I tend to stand too close to my interlocutor. Arguably, I acquire a responsibility to investigate – to acquire better knowledge of – my own potential biases. And if I do, I'll then acquire a responsibility to control my behavior better, which may lead me to discover yet further biases, and so on. In the remainder of this chapter, I argue that exactly this sort of chimneying process characterizes how we should respond to recent empirical work on implicit bias.

3 Implicit bias

Someone embodies a bias for Xs to the extent that she favors Xs in virtue of their being Xs; someone embodies a bias against Ys to the extent that she disfavors Ys in virtue of their being Ys. An **explicit bias** is one that the biased individual has some introspective awareness of, whereas an **implicit bias** is inaccessible to the biased individual's consciousness.[10] Someone who endorses the claim that women are less competent than men exhibits an explicit bias against women; someone who rejects this claim but nevertheless unknowingly associates competence more closely with men than with women embodies an implicit bias. The distinction between these two types of bias is cross-cutting, and biases come in degrees. For instance, someone could have a strong implicit bias in favor of one group despite a weak explicit bias against it, and someone could have a weak implicit bias in favor of one group while also harboring a strong explicit bias for it. In this section, I'll primarily consider issues arising because of implicit bias. This is not because explicit biases are irrelevant. Nor do I mean to suggest that – in our supposedly enlightened day – explicit biases have been eradicated. Far from it. Racism, sexism, ableism, homophobia, and plenty of other pernicious explicit biases are unfortunately alive and well. But they are also easier to explain and evaluate than implicit biases. This chapter therefore focuses on the trickiest cases, in which a moral agent explicitly rejects an objectionable bias but implicitly retains it.

3.1 Two recipes for disaster

There are two main ways in which implicit biases that their bearers consciously reject can lead to systematically unfair outcomes. Both depend on the potential targets of bias facing many instances in which prejudicial decisions can be made. In the first instance, each biased decision has an extremely harmful effect. In the second, no particular biased decision has an extremely harmful effect, but the cumulative, longitudinal effect of multiple biased decisions is extremely harmful:

1 A large number of interactions (e.g., police interactions with civilians), each with a very low probability of an extremely bad outcome (mistaken brutalization of the civilian).
2 A large number of interactions (e.g., career-relevant interactions between boss and employee), each with a moderate probability of a slightly bad outcome (e.g., giving a raise that's slightly lower than deserved), but the badness of later outcomes compounding exponentially the badness of earlier bad outcomes (e.g., because raises are a percentage of current salary).[11]

Consider the second recipe first: imagine five people starting their first jobs in the year 2000. Each of them has an initial yearly salary of $50,000 and yearly performance reviews that determine a percentage increase to their salary for the next year. For the sake of simplicity, let's suppose that all five are equally meritorious, deserving 3 percent raises every year. However, the implicit biases of their boss against some of them lead two to receive only 1 percent and 2 percent raises per year, and the implicit biases of their boss for some of them lead two others to receive 4 percent and 5 percent raises

Table 2.2 Yearly salaries for victims and beneficiaries of implicit bias

Annual raise[13]	Y0	Y1	Y2	Y5	Y10	Y20	Y30	Y40
1%	$50,000	$50,500	$51,005	$52,551	$55,231	$61,010	$67,342	$74,443
2%	$50,000	$51,000	$52,020	$55,204	$60,950	$74,297	$90,568	$110,402
3%	$50,000	$51,500	$53,045	$57,964	$67,196	$90,306	$121,363	$163,102
4%	$50,000	$52,000	$54,080	$60,833	$74,012	$109,556	$162,170	$240,051
5%	$50,000	$52,500	$55,125	$63,814	$81,447	$132,665	$216,097	$352,000

every year. The employees all receive raises, though, and out of decorum they don't brag about how much they're earning, so they all feel (at least for a while) that they've been fairly treated. After the first annual raise, the lowest-paid employee is now earning $50,500, whereas the highest-paid employee receives $52,000. The difference is just fifteen hundred bucks over the course of the year. After taxes, that's just a couple of lattes per day. No big deal, right? But watch what happens over the course of a 40-year career – see table 2.2. By the end of year five, the highest earner is pulling down 21 percent more than the lowest earner. By year twenty, the highest earner receives more than double the lowest earner. By the ends of their careers, the differences are stark. The lowest earner is vastly outpaced even by the other victim, receives less than half what the fairly treated employee makes, and is out-earned by almost 400 percent by the most favored employee. And that's just the difference in their incomes. Assuming that they each invested 10 percent of their income each year and made market returns on their investments, the differences in their wealth will be vast indeed.[12]

The other recipe is a little harder to envisage, but we can get a feel for it by modeling it as the number of times an individual can expect to be mistakenly brutalized by the police over the course of their lifetime. Suppose (falsely) that law enforcement officers never mistakenly brutalize children below the age of 12 or adults above the age of 62. That means each of us has fifty years of potential victimization. In a given year, someone may be available for interaction with the police (walking past them while they're on patrol, being seen by them on security footage, driving past or near them on a highway, etc.) 200 times. That means people have on average 10,000 chances, over the course of a lifetime, to have an unfortunate interaction with the cops.[14]

Imagine three otherwise comparable people, Q, R, and S, and suppose that the police are very slightly biased against Q because of his race, and very slightly biased for S because of his race and socioeconomic status. This means two things. First, while their probability of initiating an interaction with R in any given situation is 0.1 percent, their probability of initiating an interaction with Q in any given situation is 1 percent, and their probability of initiating an interaction with S is .01 percent. They rarely bother any of these men, but they're ever so slightly more disposed to bother R than S, and ever so slightly more disposed to bother Q than R. They don't think of themselves as unfairly bothering anyone; indeed, they'd reject the charge of bias. Anscombe would say that they are not acting under the description of racism. Nevertheless, they pay slightly more attention to Q and his behavior, and they pay slightly less attention to S and his behavior. They're slightly more inclined to construe Q's movements as "furtive." They're slightly more inclined to construe his possessions as weapons rather than wallets. And so on.

In addition, *given* that they're already interacting with Q, R, or S, the police are again implicitly biased. They're slightly more inclined to construe Q's intentions as aggressive, slightly more inclined to construe his utterances as threats, etc. And they're slightly less inclined to construe S's intentions as aggressive, slightly less inclined to construe his utterances as threats, etc. Thus, they have a 0.01 percent chance of unfairly brutalizing S given that they're already interacting with him, a 0.1 percent chance of unfairly brutalizing R given that they're already interacting with him, and a 1 percent chance of unfairly brutalizing Q given that they're already interacting with him.

What does this mean? Take a look at Table 2.3. On any given occasion, Q, R, and S all have minuscule chances of having an interaction with the police. Moreover, even given that they are interacting with the police, they have miniscule chances of being unfairly brutalized. Despite this, S can basically assume that he'll never be unfairly brutalized by the cops: his expected number of brutalizations is 0.0001. In other words, if there were ten thousand people like S, we should expect only one of them to be brutalized in the course of their lifetimes. R is also in pretty good shape: his expected number of lifetime brutalizations is only 0.01. In other words, if there were one hundred people like R, we'd expect only one of them to be unfairly brutalized. Q is in worse shape. Given the implicit biases against him, he can expect with some certainty to be unfairly

Table 2.3 Lifetime expectations of unfair brutalization for victims of and beneficiaries of implicit bias

	# of possible interactions over lifetime	Probability of an interaction	Expected # of interactions	Probability of unfair brutality given an interaction	Expected # of unfair lifetime brutalizations
S	10,000	.01%	1	.01%	.0001
R	10,000	.1%	10	.1%	.01
Q	10,000	1%	100	1%	1

brutalized once in his lifetime. Maybe the event will "only" involve getting roughed up. Maybe, like Benefield and Guzman, he'll be shot but not killed. Maybe, like Diallo and Bell, he'll be killed.

3.2 A few points about methodology

Thus far, I've only discussed the potential for harm resulting from implicit bias through simplified, speculative models. What does empirical psychology have to say about this? I'll explore this question through some illustrative experiments as well as the most recent meta-analyses that have been published. Before proceeding, it's worthwhile to explain what the differences between these two sorts of analysis are.

Psychologists conduct studies and experiments. An experiment draws a (more or less) representative sample from a population, then randomizes the participants to condition (at least two – control and experimental – but sometimes there are multiple experimental conditions). A study, by contrast, doesn't randomize. Experiments allow more confident prediction and explanation, since studies are prone to more uncontrolled confounding variables. But there are various reasons why a scientist might conduct a study rather than an experiment. First, sometimes it's impossible to randomize participants to condition. For instance, if you want to compare Americans to Japanese, you can't just take a bunch of people and randomly assign them a nationality. Second, sometimes it's unethical to randomize participants to condition. For instance, if you want to compare victims of violent assault to non-victims, you could collect a representative sample of people and choose half of them at random to assault. This would obviously be unethical, so researchers don't do it. Most psychology and other social science papers you will come across report between one and five studies or experiments conducted by the authors. The authors explain who their participants were (the "participants" section), what they had participants do (the "method" section), and how things turned out (the "results" section). They then interpret their results in a "discussion" section.

In the results section, you'll encounter a number of statistical tests that the researchers ran on their data to determine whether the effects they observed were significant. One of the most common statistics you'll see is a p-value, which is the conditional probability of observing results at least as extreme as those seen in the experiment *given* that nothing interesting is going on (the **null hypothesis**; the test itself is called a **null hypothesis significance test**). When the p-value is sufficiently low (below .05, or .01, or .001, depending on who you ask), the researchers conclude that, since it's so unlikely that their results would have been observed given the null hypothesis, something interesting in fact was going on. As a deductive inference, this is obviously invalid: X doesn't follow from the fact that it would be improbable that X. Scientists aren't making deductive inferences, though; they're making inductive and abductive inferences. When you're dealing with empirical inquiry, that's the best you can do. The problem this introduces, though, is that any given supposedly significant result a researcher reports might be a false positive, and any given non-significant result a researcher reports might be a false negative.

This is not to impugn psychological science; it's just a note of caution. When you read an interpretation of a psychological experiment, you should always ask yourself, "Is the effect they're reporting real, or is it instead a false positive? Is the failure to find an effect really evidence that there is no effect, or is it instead a false negative?" One way to convince yourself that the (lack of) effect is "real" is to look at the **effect size**. One common measure of effect size is Cohen's d, which is the ratio of the difference in means between conditions to the standard deviation of the relevant variable. So, for example, a d of 1.0 would indicate that a manipulation moved the mean of the experimental condition an entire standard deviation away from the mean of the control condition – a huge effect.[15] Another, perhaps even more common, measure of effect size is r, the correlation between an independent variable and a dependent variable. In social psychology, the average r is .21 (Richard et al. 2003).[16]

Even a well-designed, conscientiously analyzed experiment with a large effect size can result in a false positive, though. To help filter out false positives and false negatives, scientists use **meta-analysis**. In a typical meta-analysis, the unit of analysis is not a given participant's responses, but the results of a given study. Different studies are treated, as it were, as different "people" submitting data. This is why meta-analysis deserves its name: it's an analysis of analyses. The main point of this kind of approach to the empirical evidence is that it gives us a more comprehensive picture of all the relevant research, rather than focusing on a few dramatic (and sometimes atypical) results.

In recent years, some famous and provocative results have failed to replicate. One researcher or team of researchers reports a finding, but then when they or other researchers do the same thing with a new group of participants, a different result obtains. If you just know that some studies report significant results and some don't, it's very hard to decide how to interpret the literature. Meta-analysis goes beyond "some studies say X, but some studies say not-X." It combines the results of all relevant published (and sometimes unpublished) investigations of the same phenomenon (by comparing their p-values, their effect-sizes, and various other statistics) to arrive at a more accurate and precise estimate of the direction and magnitude of the effect, if any. Below, I report some relevant results from recent meta-analyses of studies of implicit and explicit bias.

3.3 Explicit attitudes, implicit attitudes, and behavior

Thought guides action. We can use three main kinds of test to figure out what people think: explicit, implicit, and behavioral. An explicit test just asks people what they think. For instance, mention a person, group of people, topic, or whatever, and ask them to report their attitudes. Their responses are a kind of action – one that's directly related to what they think. Scientists use this method, and laypeople do it all the time. Open as it is to whatever the respondent has to say, this is an information-rich explicit test of someone's attitudes. But it's hard to aggregate responses to open-ended questions. The researcher needs to code responses in some way so they are comparable across participants. This is resource-intensive in terms of both time and cost. Moreover, coding responses introduces its own biases and reduces the richness of the information drastically.

A different way to measure attitudes explicitly is to ask participants not to provide content directly but to agree or disagree with pre-crafted statements designed by the researcher to elicit participants' attitudes. As you can imagine, some measures of explicit attitudes will be more reliable than others. For instance, some people are jerks. If you ask a non-jerk whether she's a jerk, she'll probably say no. If you ask a jerk whether he's a jerk, he'll probably say no too. By contrast, some people are left-handed. At least in contemporary Western societies, there's no serious prejudice against the left-handed, so if you ask someone whether they're left-handed you can probably treat their response as accurate.

When explicit measures of attitudes are likely to fail (and even when they aren't), it's useful to approach things from a different angle. One of the potential sources of bias in explicit measures of attitudes is mediated by the time that participants have to deliberate about and revise their answers. If I'm prejudiced and you ask me whether I'm prejudiced, I can pause to ask myself whether I want to admit what I really think, how you might react, how someone who overhears me might react, whether I'll feel ashamed of myself if I'm honest, and so on. Of course, letting people deliberate about what they really think can also make their answers more accurate. If I ask you a question you've never considered before, it's natural to think that I'll get a better response by giving you some time to mull it over. But when the mulling is likely to introduce uncontrollable biases, it can be useful to supplement the investigation by forcing people to respond quickly – within limits, the quicker the better. The idea here is that, under sufficient time pressure, you won't have the chance to revise your answer in a self-serving or socially acceptable direction – or at least that you'll do it less uniformly and successfully. This technique dates back at least to Freud's notion of free association, but contemporary psychologists have made it more rigorous and quantified.

In 1998, Greenwald et al. published the first paper to use an **implicit association test** (IAT) to investigate attitudes in this way. An IAT measures the strength of associations between contrasted concepts by observing participants' reaction times (also known as latencies) in a computerized categorization task. The basic idea is this: if you associate X more closely with A than with B, you'll be quicker to categorize something as an example of X-or-A than an example of X-or-B. The details of the test are a bit more complicated. Here's how Greenwald et al. summarize them in their recent meta-analysis:

In an initial block of trials, exemplars of two contrasted concepts (e.g., face images for the races Black and White) appear on a screen and subjects rapidly classify them by pressing one of two keys (for example, an *e* key for Black and *I* for White). Next, exemplars of another pair of contrasted concepts (for example, words representing positive and negative valence) are also classified using the same two keys. In a *first combined task*, exemplars of all four categories are classified, with each assigned to the same key as in the initial two blocks (e.g., *e* for *Black* or *positive* and *I* for *White* or *negative*). In a *second combined task*, a complementary pairing is used (i.e., *e* for *White* or *positive* and *I* for *Black* or *negative*)....The difference in average latency between the two combined tasks provides the basis for the IAT measure. For example, faster responses for the {Black+positive/White+negative} task than for the {White+positive/Black+negative} task indicate a stronger association of Black than of White with positive valence. (2009, p. 18)

There are other implicit measures of attitudes, but the IAT has been studied and documented most extensively. Here are a few of the more important and well-validated results, based on two recent meta-analyses:

1 Explicit measures of attitudes and implicit measures of attitudes positively correlate. The strength of the correlation ranges from roughly .011 (very low) to .471 (very high). The correlation tends to be higher for attitudes about consumer goods (e.g., brand preference) and group attitudes (e.g., preference over racial and ethnic groups), lower for gender stereotypes and self-concept (Hofmann et al. 2005, p. 1377).
2 IATs are better at measuring affective or emotional attitudes than cognitive attitudes (Hofmann et al. 2005, p. 1377).
3 IATs predict relevant behavior better than explicit measures in the domains of race/ethnicity and socioeconomic status, but worse in the domains of gender, consumer preferences, political preferences, and personality traits (Greenwald et al. 2009, p. 24).
4 IATs are better predictors of behavior especially when self-report measures "might be impaired in socially sensitive domains" (Greenwald et al. 2009, p. 25).

Together, these results suggest several conclusions. First, explicit and implicit measures of attitudes correlate. This is both a blessing and a curse. If the measures correlated too highly (say, above .80), there'd be no reason to prefer one to the other, nor even to treat them as measures of distinct constructs. If they didn't correlate at all or correlated negatively, it would be unclear whether they were actually measures of attitudes rather than some other construct or (even worse) nothing.[17] Second, since both explicit and implicit measures of attitudes predict behavior, it seems that implicit measures of attitudes contribute information over and above what one learns from an explicit measure, especially on socially sensitive topics. Third, implicit measures are especially suited to domains in which emotions are salient and influential.

With this in mind, it's plausible to conclude that we can learn from implicit measures things about people's dispositional beliefs, desires, and emotions that they themselves would not and perhaps could not report explicitly. What things? In the context of race, it seems that even people who explicitly disavow racist attitudes, even people who are themselves victims of negative racial stereotypes, may nevertheless harbor negative implicit attitudes toward blacks, among others. For instance, American undergraduate students are more likely and quicker to "shoot" unarmed black men in a computer simulation (Correll et al. 2002; Greenwald et al. 2003). This may partially explain cases like those of Diallo and Bell, which I described at the start of this chapter.[18] It may also partially explain the fact that, in recent decades in the United States, the rate at which blacks were killed by police has been between 300 and 700 percent higher than the rate at which whites were killed by police (Brown & Langan 2001).[19] In the context of gender, it may also help to partially explain the systematic differences in compensation between men and women cited above.

4 Philosophical implications of implicit bias

What does any of this mean for the philosophical understanding of responsibility? Before you read further, I suggest taking a few of the IATs available at www.implicit.harvard.edu. This will help you to contextualize the discussion. When I took these tests, I found that I had a strong implicit preference for whites over blacks, a strong implicit preference for able-bodied people over disabled people, a strong implicit preference for straight people over gay people, and a weak implicit association of men with careers and women with home life. As you might have guessed, I explicitly reject all of these attitudes. I'd like to be the sort of person who doesn't have race-based preferences, who doesn't think that the able-bodied are preferable to the disabled, who likes and treats homosexuals (and other gender minorities) the same as heterosexuals, and who treats women who have careers and men who devote themselves to home life with the same degree of respect as men who have careers and women who devote themselves to home life. The meta-analyses discussed above suggest that, at least sometimes, I don't live up to these standards. Perhaps you were disappointed by your own IAT results, too.

4.1 Implications for agency and reflexivity

Effective agency involves pursing your goals successfully. Agency is thus undermined to the extent that your own behavior and dispositions make it harder for you to achieve those goals. For instance, suppose you want to be healthy, so you decide to go on daily jogs. Unfortunately, you live in an area with immense amounts of pollen or other allergens in the air. Every time you exercise, you end up wheezing and sneezing, and you spend the next day in bed suffering from flu-like symptoms. When you're bedridden, you get no exercise and often find yourself snacking on ice cream and nachos. Your own attempts to improve your health undermine your health. It would be foolish to ignore this and just keep going on jogs when you recover. If you're serious about your goal of becoming healthy, effective agency means investigating a different way to exercise and implementing it. In other words, when you realize that what comes naturally to you takes you away from your goal rather than toward it, the smart response is to *acquire knowledge* and *use* it.

If this sounds familiar, that's because it maps directly onto the knowledge and control conditions for responsibility discussed above. A moral agent who explicitly rejects racist, sexist, and homophobic attitudes but who learns that he might harbor implicit biases against these groups faces a choice, whether he likes it or not. If he's serious about his rejection of these biases, he can exercise effective agency by investigating how to combat his biases and putting the knowledge he acquires into practice. Otherwise, he's not serious about rejecting bias. He might pay lip service to it. He might engage in a variety of self-deceptive psychological acrobatics. But the only responsible way to handle the unwelcome news about his own biases is to find out how severe they are, figure out some strategies for obviating or overcoming them, and implement those strategies. As he proceeds with this strategy, he may end up chimneying between the knowledge and the control conditions on responsibility: every time he learns something new (about himself, about how to manage his biases, about the consequences of his biases when he doesn't manage them), he acquires a responsibility to take further control, and every time he takes control over a new aspect of himself or his situation, he's put in a position where he can learn even more.

In the meantime, how should he feel about himself, his attitudes, and his behavior? How should others feel about him, his attitudes, and his behavior? Some of the more prominent and early philosophical discussions of implicit attitudes argued on pragmatic grounds against the idea that "acknowledging that one is biased means declaring oneself to be one of those bad racist or sexist people" (Saul 2013).[20] Why? Why give oneself the benefit of the doubt? There are several answers, based on pragmatic, epistemic, and control considerations.

Pragmatically, it may do one no good in reforming one's ways to think of oneself as racist, sexist, and so on. As I argue in the chapter on virtue below, self-concept is often self-confirming: if I think of myself as an X, I'm more likely to act like an X than I would be otherwise. For this reason, it's dangerous to think of oneself as racist, sexist, ableist, and so on. Likewise, it may not help others to convince him to reform his ways if they accuse him of being racist, sexist, and so on. As I also argue in my discussion of virtue in chapter 4, such attributions also tend to be self-confirming. One might worry, though, that these considerations cut no ice. Sure, it might not be *useful* for him to think of himself or for others to think of him as a biased person, but that doesn't indicate one way or the other whether he *is* a biased person. Maybe he needs to lie to himself to escape his bias. Maybe other people need to lie to him to avoid putting him on the defensive. But that doesn't make his or their lies any more true.

Perhaps, instead of thinking of himself as a racist or sexist person, he should think of himself as someone who strives to be fair to targets of negative stereotypes but who suffers in his human, all-too-human, way from various biases. Perhaps, instead of thinking of him as a racist or sexist person, other people should think of him as someone who strives to be fair but who suffers in human, all-too-human, ways from various biases. These attitudes have the

benefit of ascribing good will (or at least lack of ill will) while recognizing serious defects. It's unclear whether they're pragmatically
worse than pretending there's nothing wrong; they might even be
better. They do, though, put salutary emphasis on the responsibility
he must take to acquire both knowledge of and control over his
biases.

Epistemically, there's a little more wiggle room. As I explained
above, there are different kinds of bias. Someone who embodies an
explicit bias knows, at least to some extent, where she stands and
what she's inclined to think, feel, and do. Someone who embodies
an implicit bias might not – at least not directly. Suppose a boss has,
but is completely unaware of, a subtle implicit bias against his
women employees. Like me when I don't know that I'm systematically tailgating, he has no reason to think he might be biased. He
might even explicitly reject misogynistic stereotypes. But when the
time comes to make a hiring or promotion decision, he acts like the
boss described above in table 2.2. Along the same lines, suppose
that a law enforcement officer has, but is completely unaware of, a
subtle implicit bias against black people. Like me when I don't
know that I'm systematically tailgating, she has no reason to think
she might be biased. She might even be a racial minority herself.
She might reject racial stereotypes. But when the time comes to
make a flash decision about a passing civilian or a potentially dangerous encounter, she acts like the police described in table 2.3.

Arguably, these people fail to meet the knowledge conditions on
responsibility, and so should not be held responsible for their bias.[21]
As noted above, action is always under a description. The boss
wouldn't describe his action as discrimination; the police officer
wouldn't describe her action as discrimination. Indeed, they'd both
reject that description were it suggested to them. Is their ignorance
culpable, though? It's hard to say precisely when ignorance becomes
culpable, but arguably the ignorance displayed here is innocent.

Things get interesting if we vary the cases slightly. Suppose that
the boss does a survey of his employees and notices that the women
consistently make less than the men. Suppose that the police officer's supervisor tabulates her likelihood of initiating interactions
with people of different races and her likelihood of escalating to
violence given that she's already interacting with them. Now they
have some evidence that they might be biased. Of course, it's not
decisive (empirical evidence never is), but it is suggestive. Arguably, they now acquire a duty to investigate their own dispositions:
the sort of chimneying back and forth between epistemic and

practical that I described above kicks in. If they end up concluding that they are indeed biased, they then acquire a responsibility to systematically correct that bias. Even if their self-examination is inconclusive, they arguably acquire a responsibility to obviate their own potential biases. As Kelly & Roedder (2008) point out, in general we have a duty to give people the benefit of the doubt; to the extent that someone's implicit bias prevents her from doing so, she is at least negligent and perhaps reckless in allowing that bias to guide her behavior. Even more to the point, when someone acquires evidence of her own potential bias, she manifests the vices of callousness and perhaps even hatred if she does not bother to understand and correct her bias. This is a point Kelly & Roedder (2008) draw from Garcia's (2004, p. 43) analysis of the vice of racism, which he diagnoses not simply as a mistaken belief or cluster of mistaken beliefs, but rather as "disregard for, or even hostility to, those assigned to the targeted race," which makes racism a deformation not primarily of the intellect but of the will.

Things get more interesting if we vary the cases further. Suppose that the boss reads a newspaper headline about implicit bias against women in the workplace, or that a friend sends him a link to an academic article on the topic. Suppose that the police officer reads a newspaper headline about implicit bias against racial minorities in law enforcement, or that her supervisor mentions some relevant research. Simply knowing that people in general have these tendencies doesn't guarantee that *they* have these tendencies, but it certainly suggests that they might. Now they have even stronger evidence that they might be biased. It seems even more likely, then, that they acquire a duty to investigate their own dispositions, which could lead through chimneying to a responsibility to control their actions. In addition, they probably also acquire a responsibility to systematically correct their own potential biases even if they can't confirm that they have them.

Things get even more interesting if we vary the cases one more time. Suppose that the boss and the police officer go to www .implicit.harvard.edu, take the relevant IATs, and discover that they do harbor implicit biases. Chagrinned, they try again, with the same result. Now they have very strong evidence indeed. Arguably, they now *know* that they are biased in ways that they explicitly reject, so appeal to the knowledge condition does them no good. They're like me when I realize for sure that I'm disposed to tailgate while driving down the highway. At this point, if they do nothing about their own biases, they're like someone who drives around knowing that he's tailgating people.[22] Unless something else absolves them, they're culpably responsible for their future biased behavior.

Thinking of control, there's again some wiggle room. Consider the hardest cases first: suppose that I know that I harbor implicit biases and want to correct for them. One might worry that, even though the knowledge condition is met, I nevertheless lack control. As Saul (2013) says, "Even once [people] become aware that they are likely to have implicit biases, they do not instantly become able to control their biases, and so they should not be blamed for them." As I pointed out above, there are many different conceptions of control. Saul may be right that people don't "instantly" gain control over their biases, which indicates that proximal notions of control may not be particularly helpful in this context.[23] That doesn't mean, though, that more distal notions of control are inapplicable. For instance, Annas's (2011) notion of skilled control may be relevant. Skills take time and deliberate practice to acquire, and constant renewal to maintain. Imagine that I agree to do the cooking for my family. Presumably, I need to acquire enough skill in preparing food that I don't poison my wife (at the very least!). This doesn't mean that I automatically acquire the skills of the Iron Chef. It means that I now need to devote myself to learning how to store and prepare food safely. In the same way, if I want to go on thinking of myself as a non-racist, non-sexist, non-ableist person after I take the relevant IATs and discover that I harbor implicit biases, I don't automatically acquire the skills of a fair person, but do need to devote myself to learning how to act in an unbiased way to the extent possible. It's beyond the scope of this book to delve into the vast literature on skills and skill-acquisition, but there do seem to be systematic ways to acquire the relevant skills. Getting a friend to confront me when I might be acting in a biased way seems to help (Czopp et al. 2006), as does my confronting others when they seem to be biased (Rasinski et al. 2013). As McGeer (2015) argues, being a member of the moral community seems to involve both being a valid target for such acts of holding responsible and being situated to hold others responsible oneself. Going to the trouble to confront bias – whether explicit or implicit – is a way of demonstrating one's own commitment to norms of fairness, and therefore a way of putting oneself on the hook to be held responsible by others and oneself.

Another, perhaps even more tractable, notion of control in the context of overcoming implicit bias is Clark's (2007) notion of ecological control.[24] Instead of changing myself (narrowly conceived), I can take control by selecting or designing my environment.

Research into the controllability of implicit biases is still at an early stage, but there are already some useful suggestions available. For instance, I could commit myself to not trusting my gut when making important decisions. Of course, just deciding not to trust my gut doesn't guarantee that I will blunt my bias, so instead of trying to combat my biases directly, I could make efforts to ensure that they're not triggered. For instance, when making decisions about hiring a new employee, I could ensure that their applications were anonymized in such a way that I couldn't determine a particular applicant's gender, race, or disability status. Other interventions that have shown some promise of mitigating implicit bias in a longitudinal study (Devine et al. 2012) include stereotype replacement (a proximal, higher-order strategy of recognizing, labeling, and replacing an initially negative stereotype activation), counter-stereotypic imaging (a distal, higher-order strategy of dwelling on real or imaginary counter-stereotypic exemplars), individuation (a wide-ranging strategy that involves seeking and obtaining specific information about members of stereotyped groups, in order to recognize differences among them), perspective taking (another wide-ranging strategy that involves imagining oneself into the shoes of a member of a stereotyped group, thereby reducing psychological distance), and increasing opportunities for contact (a distal strategy that puts one in a position to individuate members of the stereotyped group and have positive interactions with them).

At this point it's helpful to distinguish again between the two recipes for disaster identified above. When it comes to slow decisions that have the potential to compound biases, I can use technologies like anonymizing. I can also force myself to use rubrics rather than forming holistic judgments. I can implement decision procedures that require me always to consider reasons for and reasons against a given course of action (e.g., hiring or promoting someone).

If these techniques don't suffice, I could build in a counter-bias to my own decision-making, giving a bonus at the end of any evaluation to people who belong to groups I know myself to be biased against. As Aristotle puts it in the *Nicomachean Ethics*, if you're trying to straighten a bent stick, it's often best to bend it too far in the other direction. One might worry that this technique would lend an unfair advantage. It's important to emphasize how wrongheaded this worry is. Compare it to the tailgating example. If I know that I have a tendency to underestimate my distance from vehicles in front of me, I should increase my following distance. Will I sometimes introduce even more distance than I need? Probably. Nothing's perfect. We're talking here about a policy that aims to hit the mark as often and closely as possible. By the same token, then, if I know that I'm disposed to express implicit biases against a particular group, I need to adjust my generic way of interacting with members of that group so that, overall, my behavior hits the mark as often and closely as possible. Will I sometimes treat members of that group better than they might deserve? Sure.[25] If I'm treating members of a group fairly in general, then it's pretty much guaranteed that I'll sometimes treat some of them better than they deserve and sometimes treat some of them worse than they deserve. Since implicit biases are, by definition, hard to detect while they are influencing my behavior, perhaps the best I can do is to introduce a systematic counter-bias.

What about low-probability, high-stakes decisions – the other recipe for disaster? Deciding not to trust one's gut doesn't work here, since these decisions are often made quickly (e.g., police reacting to an ambiguously threatening situation). Cops can't always avoid situations in which they have to make decisions about whether someone poses a threat, though they can reduce the over-patrolling of minority neighborhoods that currently (in the United States) increases the odds of having a confrontation in the first place, and thence of having a violent confrontation. Anonymizing doesn't work in such a context. Nor do rubrics. Implementing a counter-bias after making a decision is out of the question.

It might seem that, in this second kind of situation, it's impossible to counteract bias. I think not. One way of seizing distal control is to ensure that it's harder to make snap decisions with potentially disastrous consequences. For instance, don't arm most police. Don't allow public safety officers on college campuses to carry guns. Put double- or triple-safeties on pistols. Don't allow anyone to possess – let alone carry – high-capacity weapons. From the point of view of some Americans, this might seem like an extreme, perhaps unworkable, solution. From the point of view of Western Europeans, on the other hand, it will seem obvious. Any specific solution needs to be tailored to the political and policy landscape of the community in which it is proposed.

4.2 Implications for sociality and temporality

Taking even more distal control of this sort of situation may require solutions that cannot be implemented in the short term by a single agent. For instance, it's likely that the prevalence of some implicit biases is explained by the ways different groups are treated in the media. If members of a group typically only make the news when they do something strange, bad, or evil, people are likely to acquire implicit biases against members of that group. If members of a group typically make the news for their accomplishments and positive qualities, people are likely to acquire implicit biases for members of that group.

To handle such biases at the individual level, one could perhaps disconnect from media. But that's a way of combating bias with ignorance. More helpfully, one could disconnect from especially distorting media, such as Fox News and other media controlled by Rupert Murdoch. Alternatively, one could get by with a little help from one's friends in the media if they committed to covering different groups more equitably.

At this point, one might object by saying, "Don't blame Fox for their coverage! They're just reporting the news!" As stated, this objection cuts no ice. In this chapter, I described some of the ways in which implicit biases lead people to act and judge contrary to their own values. If the media cause this, and if we now know or at least have good reason to believe that they do, then the media acquire a new responsibility. It may not be legally enforceable, but after all we already decided that we were talking about moral rather than legal responsibility. And if a media outfit presents itself as morally responsible, to be effective as a corporate agent, it must at least attempt to live up to these standards.

Compare this with environmental pollution. Before people realized that industrial activity released various pollutants that harmed humans and other organisms, it made little sense to hold them responsible for their polluting activities. Once we realized that they were hurting people (often enough, themselves included), it made plenty of sense. Before people knew about implicit biases and the potential influence of media consumption on people's implicit biases, it made little sense to hold them responsible for polluting people's minds. Now that we've started to realize that the media harm people (both those in whom they instill bias and, more importantly, those against whom those biases are enacted), it makes plenty of sense.

4.3 Implications for patiency

The implications of the theories of responsibility and the empirical work on implicit bias for patiency mirror to some extent those for agency. What should the victims of implicit bias do? What should they feel? What strategies might they implement? On the one hand, it might seem that they could be understandably and rightly incensed by their own mistreatment. On the other hand, it might seem that the most effective response is not to angrily denounce people who are trying their best, despite implicit biases. However, if my arguments above are on the right track, that may be precisely what's needed, even if it ruffles a few feathers.

To bolster this argument, it's worth emphasizing the immense harm done to victims of stereotypes. In this chapter, I explored two "recipes for disaster" that seem pretty clearly to differentially harm targets of stereotypes. There are other, distinct harms that are well worth recounting. For instance, stereotyping by doctors can lead through a variety of mechanisms to systematically worse health outcomes for targets of stereotypes (Balsa & McGuire 2003; see also Mays et al. 2007 and van Ryn & Fu 2003). If biases (either explicit or implicit) lead doctors to avoid interacting with and treating members of a minority group, their health will suffer. Likewise, if implicit associations lead doctors to interpret ambiguous or uncertain symptoms differently, they will make worse diagnoses and prescribe both cures and symptomatic relief differently across groups. This is especially worrisome in connection with racial stereotypes, which tend to lead people to see blacks as experiencing less pain in the same circumstances than whites (Forgiarini et al. 2011; Trawalter et al. 2012). The surreptitious tax of implicit bias is constantly being extracted from some people's lives, taking its grim toll on their finances, their health, and their wellbeing.

5 Future directions in the moral psychology of implicit bias and responsibility

The field of implicit bias is relatively young. We don't yet know exactly how such biases work, what causes them, what prevents them, how prevalent they are in and toward various groups, and so on. We're also in the early stages of figuring out how to cope with and correct them in ourselves and others. Further empirical research may help with these questions.

In addition, we're also at the very earliest stages of learning how to cope with questions of responsibility when it comes to implicit bias. One thing should be clear at this point: the more evidence you have that you are or might be biased, the more responsibility you have to trace the exact outlines of your own biases (recall the famous Apollonian imperative: "Know thyself!") and develop strategies and tactics for counteracting them.

The question of transitive responsibility is harder to resolve. If, through behaviors that come naturally to me, I tend to influence others in objectionable ways, who is responsible for their behavior? On the one hand, *they're* the ones acting in biased ways. Moreover, they presumably embody their biases internally in some way. Nevertheless, they acquired their biases through my influence, and those biases might dissipate at least somewhat if not for my continued malignant influence. Perhaps our notion of responsibility needs to be revised.

Further readings

Arpaly, N. (2006). *Merit, Meaning, and Human Bondage: An Essay on Free Will*. Princeton University Press.

Darwall, S. (2009). *The Second-Person Standpoint: Morality, Respect, and Accountability*. Harvard University Press.

Dennett, D. (2003). *Freedom Evolves*. New York: Viking Press.

Fischer, J. M. (1999). Recent work on moral responsibility. *Ethics*, 110: 93–139.

Fricker, M. (2007). *Epistemic Injustice: Power and the Ethics of Knowing*. Harvard University Press.

Helm, B. (2012). Accountability and some social dimensions of human agency. *Philosophical Issues*, 22: 217–32.

McGeer, V. (2015). Building a better theory of responsibility. *Philosophical Studies*.

Scanlon, T. M. (2008). *Moral Dimensions: Permissibility, Meaning, Blame*. Harvard University Press.

Shoemaker, D. (2011). Attributability, Answerability, and Accountability. *Ethics*, 121: 602–32.

Talbert, M. (2015). *Moral Responsibility*. London: Polity.

Study questions

1 Describe a case in which you experienced, perpetrated, or witnessed what might have been implicit bias. Did everyone involved seem to think it was a case of bias? Why or why not?

2 What are the first three words that come to mind when you think of the word "woman"? What are the first three words that come to mind when you think of the word "man"? How do they differ? Why might this matter, from a moral psychological point of view?

3 What are the first three images that come to mind when you think of a black person? What are the first three images that come to mind when you think of a white person? How do they differ? Why might this matter, from a moral psychological point of view?

4 Imagine that you found out that you unconsciously flashed a look of contempt and disgust every time you saw someone writing with their left hand rather than the right hand, and that left-handed people sometimes noticed this. What would you feel? What would you do about it?

5 Is it easier to take proximal or distal control of one's own implicit biases? Why?

6 Is it easier to know about other people's or one's own implicit biases? What does your answer suggest for remedying implicit bias?

7 Have you ever avoided acquiring knowledge so that you wouldn't feel responsible to act on the basis of that knowledge? If yes, describe the case. Do you regret it? If no, have you seen someone else do so? Do you think they regret it?

8 Go to www.implicit.harvard.edu and take one of the IATs available there. Did the results surprise you? Why? Does this make you want to change your mind or behavior in any way?

3

Emotion

1 Introduction

A sudden loud noise.
Your bare foot stepping in a pile of festering shit.
Three dimly lit figures hulking towards you in a blind alley.
A hedge fund fraudster escaping justice.
Winning a prize you've long sought.
Your beloved pet dying.
A chemist making a fool of himself trying to explain Shakespeare.

How would these affect you? Let's go through them again.

A sudden loud noise. Your eyes pop out slightly. Your mouth opens, and you inhale. Your attention darts around, searching for the cause of the noise. You're poised to react quickly. Anyone who sees you naturally follows your gaze, searching – like you – for the unexpected. In a word: surprise.

Figure 3.1 Surprise

Your bare foot stepping in a pile of festering shit. You gape, wrinkling your nose and raising your upper lip. Nausea turns your stomach. You withdraw toward safety and purity. You're prepared to kick and scrape as much of the shit off your foot as possible, then rinse it – preferably with soap. Everything in your vicinity, especially anything close to the shit or your foot, starts to look foul. Anyone who sees your face immediately, if unconsciously, gapes as well. In a word: disgust.

Figure 3.2 Disgust

Three dimly lit figures hulking towards you in a blind alley. Your eyes open wide. Your face and core are tensed. Your heart is pounding. Your blood is flowing. You're prepared to flee: your attention seeks escape routes, places to hide, other potential threats. Your companions sense immediately that they are in danger and prepare themselves to flee. In a word: fear.

Figure 3.3 Fear

A hedge fund fraudster escaping justice. Your lips purse. Your eyebrows draw down and together, highlighting your glare. Your heart rate increases. Adrenaline courses through your arteries. Your muscles flex, your core tightens. You're spoiling for a fight; your attention seeks ways to inflict harm – on the hedge fund fraudster especially, but also on anything that catches your eye. Your demeanor is threatening, inspiring allies with confidence and others with fear. In a word: anger.

Figure 3.4 Anger

Winning a prize you've long sought. Your lips curl up slightly, exposing your teeth. The muscles between your eyes and your temples orbit upwards, creating crow's-feet wrinkles. Your lungs puff with air. You feel buoyant. Your companions sense this uplift, empathically joining in. In a word: joy.

Figure 3.5 Joy

Your beloved pet dying. You're visibly deflated: your lips curl slightly downwards, your eyelids droop, your gaze is unfocused hazily on the horizon. Your heart slows. Your shoulders droop. Anyone who sees you senses your loss. In a word: sadness.

Figure 3.6 Sadness

A chemist making a fool of himself trying to explain Shakespeare. Your lip curls, but only on one side. Your eyes take on a knowing disdain, perhaps looking slightly down your nose as you tilt your head back. A subtle scoff escapes your lungs. The poor chemist, who just a second ago was full of confidence in his ability to explain just about anything to just about anybody, shrinks with embarrassment. In a word: contempt.

Figure 3.7 Contempt

Emotions are complex mental states. Different theorists emphasize different aspects of them, arguing that some aspects are neces-
sary but others are just often, though not always, contingently
associated. Indeed, there is even disagreement about whether emotions should be understood as vectors in a multidimensional space
(with dimensions for, perhaps among other things, arousal, valence,
and approach/avoid) or discrete, categorically distinct mental constructs. The presentation thus far, referring to characteristic facial
expressions and terminology, fits more snugly with the latter
approach, which is known as **basic emotions** theory (Ekman 2007).
I do not, however, want to stake a claim with basic emotions theory;
although there is suggestive evidence for it, there are also dissenters
with compelling evidence of their own (Elfenbein and Nalini 2002;
Russell et al. 2003). In particular, the more extreme version of basic
emotions theory, according to which there is a small subset of basic
emotions with characteristic facial expressions, intertranslatable terminology, and non-human analogues, seems to exaggerate to some
extent the degree to which culture inflects both the expression and
the recognition of emotions.[1] By the same token, the opposite
extreme, according to which there is no overlap whatsoever between
the experience, expression, and recognition of emotions across cultures, exaggerates differences. A more tempered position is represented by Cameron et al. (2015), who argue that there are no
one-to-one correspondences between discrete emotions and specific
moral contents; they opt instead for a constructionist account
according to which affect and conceptualization are flexibly integrated to produce the full palate of emotions. I will not try to adjudicate such debates about the nature of emotions here. Instead, I
will describe all the potential constituents or correlates of emotion,
setting the stage for their role in moral psychology in the next
section.

Emotions have *phenomenological* components.[2] "**Phenomenology**" refers to what it feels like to have a given experience or be in
a given state. The phenomenology of pain is aversive. The phenomenology of lust is compelling attraction. The phenomenology of
hunger and thirst are well known to everyone. Like these states,
emotional states have phenomenal character. There's something it
feels like to have an emotion – the more intense the emotion, the
stronger the characteristic feeling. At a very basic level, they almost
all have a valence: joy is positive, disgust negative. Additionally,
they often have a felt degree of agency (ranging from intense
approach through inaction to intense avoidance): the angry person

feels ready to act, the sad one less so. These phenomenological components are connected to states of both the **nervous system** (both **central** and **peripheral**) and the **bodily periphery**. We feel the nausea of disgust in our viscera. We feel the fluttering of fear in our hearts. We feel the condescension of contempt in our sneers.

Emotions have *perceptual* components. We perceive with our senses. For instance, you might see fluffy clouds scudding across the sky, and you might hear a chainsaw ripping through the trunk of a tree. More cognitively, you can perceive *that* something is the case. You read the sum "3 + 4" and immediately perceive that it's 7. You watch your cat pawing at the door and perceive that she wants to be let outside. Emotions, too, are ways of perceiving. Surprise is our way of perceiving novelty: events and phenomena that run counter to our expectations are surprising. Disgust is our way of registering impurity; fear is our way of seeing threats; anger is our way of registering offenses; sadness is our way of perceiving loss; and so on. In addition, emotions put us in a frame of mind that facilitates noticing and construing things as relevant to the emotion while ignoring (to some extent) all else. Someone in the grip of contempt is quick to spot further embarrassing things about his victim – and of others. Someone in the throes of joy is somewhat immune or oblivious to losses and offenses.

Emotions have *evaluative* components. We can evaluate things by judging that they are good or bad, right or wrong. Like judgments, emotions involve evaluation. To be joyful over something is, among other things, to evaluate it as good. To feel contempt toward someone is, among other things, to evaluate him as bad.

Emotions have *motivational* components. This should be unsurprising, since evaluative judgments typically motivate action. An angry person feels the urge to put things right, to throw down the perpetrator; this seems to be connected with both social and neuroendocrinological aspects of anger, especially the secretion of testosterone and cortisol in the face of unstable social hierarchies (Denson et al. 2013; Hamilton et al. 2015). A disgusted person is driven to cleanse herself and expunge the offending object or person. A fearful person feels the need to flee, or – if that's impossible – to fight or freeze in place.

Emotions have *representational* components. These representations connect the perceptual components with the motivational components (among others). Fear is the perception of a threat; by representing the threatening object, the agent is able to direct her motivation to flee from it in particular. Disgust is the perception of impurity or corruption; by representing the corrupt object, the agent is able to direct her desire to purify or expunge it in particular. Representations may not always succeed in this task, leading an angry person to kick his dog rather than oppose the fraudster, but in many normal circumstances they facilitate smooth connections between perception and motivation.

Emotions have *functional* components. They prepare us to act more effectively in the way that they motivate us in the first place. Heart rate increases during fear, which mobilizes glucose and oxygen to muscle tissue. This enables the fearful person to run away faster and potentially to escape. The gaping expression characteristic of disgust is identical to the first stage of vomiting, helping the disgusted person to eject impurities from their mouth.

Finally, emotions have *communicative* components, a special case of their functionality. This is clearest from the facial expressions associated with them. I described these expressions briefly above. They're perhaps easier just to see, as figures 3.1 through 3.7 illustrate. Expressions for these basic emotions are nearly universal (Ekman et al. 1987). People from around the world and very different cultures express the same emotions in very similar ways (perhaps with additional culturally inflected add-ons).[3] This may be because, although emotional expressions can be mimicked and hammed up, the gross contours are evolutionarily adaptive. For example, the facial expression characteristic of fear enlarges the visual field, speeds up eye movements during target localization, and increases nasal volume and air velocity while breathing in; by contrast, the facial expression characteristic of disgust does the opposite (Susskind et al. 2008). Furthermore, it's hard to suppress the facial expression of an emotion that you occurrently feel, and mimicking the facial expressing tends to induce at least a twinge of the emotion itself. People from around the world and very different cultures recognize – usually automatically and empathically – these expressions for what they are (perhaps having more difficulty with some than with others).

2 The role of emotions in moral psychology

Because emotions are so complex, they have many roles to play in moral psychology. For theories of the emotions formulated by psychologists themselves, see especially Rozin et al.'s (1999) contempt-anger-disgust model, Haidt's (2001) social intuitionist model, Graham et al.'s (2009) moral foundations theory, and Gray et al.'s (2012) harm hypothesis. Briefly, these models seek to explain most or all moral judgment by reference to some privileged set of emotions. According to the contempt-anger-disgust model, contempt tracks violations of social hierarchy, anger tracks harms, and disgust tracks violations of purity. According to the social intuitionist model, people's automatic, emotional reactions determine whether they judge something morally right or wrong, and they then tend to confabulate reasons after the fact to justify or rationalize these judgments; the main way in which moral judgments change is through socio-emotional contagion, not reasoning. Moral foundations theory expands on the contempt-anger-disgust model by positing five main foundations, which are differentially tracked by distinct emotions: care/harm, fairness/cheating, loyalty/betrayal, authority/subversion, and sanctity/degradation. Finally, according to the harm hypothesis, the prototype of all moral situations is an agent–patient dyad in which the former harms the latter. In this section, I explore just some of the roles that emotions can play in moral psychology.

2.1 The role of emotions in patiency

Thus far, I have discussed only basic emotions identified by Ekman (2007) and those following in his research program: surprise, disgust, fear, anger, joy, sadness, and contempt.[4] These emotions are arguably basic because they are culturally universal, in the sense discussed in the previous section. One thing to notice about them immediately is that only one is clearly positive (joy) and only one is clearly neutral (surprise). The other five are arguably negative or at least ambivalent.[5] Why should human animals have more negative than positive basic emotions? It's hard to say, but one promising answer is that there are many ways for things to go badly, but only a few ways for them to go well. Joy manifests when the agent sees that things are going well; different negative emotions manifest when they're going poorly in one way or another.

One role for emotions in patiency, then, is to register successes and failures (pride in success, disappointment in failure), improvements and decrements in the world independent of one's agency (joy in improvements, sadness at decrements), and potential improvements and potential decrements (hope for potential improvements, fear of potential decrements). To the extent that someone's emotions are functioning well, they reliably tell her how well things are going for her, her friends and family, her interests, and what she cares about.

Since emotions have this perception-like connection with value, they can be more or less accurate, and one's dispositions to token them can be better- or worse-attuned. For instance, someone who's too-easily angered doesn't track offenses well, and someone who lacks fear of great and imminent dangers doesn't track threats well. Aristotle thought that how one is emotionally affected is indicative of one's character, and how one is *disposed to be emotionally affected* (among other things) is constitutive of it. The basic idea is that you're virtuous to the extent that you are disposed to feel the appropriate emotion in response to eliciting situations. A pure person is disgusted by corrupt things (and not much else). A courageous person feels fear toward genuine threats (and not much else). A just person gets angry about violations of justice, fairness, and liberty (and not much else). A virtuous person feels joy when genuinely good things happen or are promoted or protected (and not otherwise). Someone with good character is attached to good and important things, and hence tends to experience sadness when (and only when) something good and important is lost. Someone with good taste has nothing but scorn for the contemptible, but does not feel this emotion otherwise. This model is sometimes referred to as the doctrine of the golden mean (in the arithmetic sense of "average"), which says that the virtuous person is disposed (among other things) to feel the right emotion, at the right time, toward the right object, with the right intensity, and so on. This doctrine has never explicitly been connected with psychological research, but it's natural to draw the lines, since Aristotle himself argues that courage is (among other things) the disposition to fear the right thing, at the right time, with the right intensity, and so on. If this is on the right track, how one is (and is disposed to be) emotionally affected is partially determinative of one's moral character.[6]

This exploration of Aristotle might seem to miss the point. Isn't there a more obvious way in which emotions are relevant to patiency – namely, their role in determining wellbeing? If you spend two-thirds of your day angry, doesn't that mean your life is going poorly? If you spend even a third of your day disgusted, doesn't that mean you're in bad shape? If you have the occasional bout of sadness but tend to spend your days in neutral and joyous states, doesn't that mean that (at least from your own point of view) your life is going well? Surely, one's life is better to the extent that one experiences positive emotions and fails to experience negative emotions. More robustly, isn't one's life better to the extent that one is modally disposed to experience positive and not to experience negative emotions (Haybron 2008)?

These rhetorical questions seem to be tracking an important feature of emotions and wellbeing. On the one hand, if you experience a great loss and fail to feel sadness, that means you're dissociated from the things you care about – surely a problem. On the other hand, if you're to some extent immune to the suffering caused by such losses, your day is more pleasant, you're better able to cope, and you may even have more perspective on the world. Conversely, if you thoroughly and unabashedly enjoy making cutting, sarcastic remarks that leave your victims – some of them deserving, but many of them innocent – feeling wounded and vulnerable, you may be morally disconnected but your pleasant emotions are undeniable.

Presumably, a life of many joys and few sorrows (and angers and disgusts) in a context that warrants joy would be ideal. And when things are good, it's clear that the agent needn't endure frequent negative emotions. But when things start to go badly, we encounter a fork in the moral psychological path. To the left: negative emotions that correctly register what's going on. To the right: positive or neutral emotions that fail to do so. In a sufficiently pernicious environment or society, this may be the choice someone faces – a predicament explored in detail by Lisa Tessman (2005). For instance, in a misogynistic society, a moral agent seems to be confronted with the unenviable choice between protracted, intense, and potentially misdirected rage and a more pleasant but less effective and less perceptive acquiescence. As Tessman puts it:

> [I]f one chooses to be angered only in a measured way, then one must endure the degradation of oneself or of others on whose behalf one acts, but if one chooses to develop a fully angered/enraged disposition in response to the vast injustice one is fighting, then the anger can become consuming. (2005, pp. 124–5)

As I pointed out above, emotions tend to be promiscuous, which can make them apt to misfire. When you feel disgust at X, you're more likely to feel disgust at Y – even if Y isn't disgusting and, in a different frame of mind, you'd realize that. Likewise, when you feel rage at X, you're more likely to be enraged by Y – even if Y isn't a worthy target of anger and, in a different frame of mind, you'd realize that (Goldberg et al. 1999). Thus, emotions have a variety of important, sometimes contrary, implications for patiency.

2.2 *The role of emotions in agency*

Emotions also have implications for agency. As I pointed out above, emotions have motivational components. When you're green-eyed with envy, you want to take for yourself what someone else has. When you're overcome with guilt, you want to apologize and make reparations or amends. When you're filled with wonder, you want to stare and drink in the object of wonder.

Hence, just as preferences are crucial to understanding the moral psychology of agency because they lead us to act in some ways rather than others, so emotions are important to agency because they lead us to engage in some behaviors rather than others. When we evaluate both our own actions and the actions of others, we pay attention not just to their preferences but to the fine-grained emotions that did (or didn't) motivate them. If someone donates a large sum to a worthy charity such as www.givedirectly.org, we can infer immediately that they will produce good consequences. But we might also want to know more about why exactly they donated. Was it a way of easing a guilty conscience? Of expressing pity for the poor and unlucky? Of seeking prestige and praise? These different emotional motivations may make the agent more or less praiseworthy as an agent.

Gray & Wegner (2011) argue that just these two aspects of moral emotions are sufficient to explain the bulk of moral assessment. On the one hand, there are moral agents and moral patients. On the other hand, the relations between them can be either helpful or harmful. When we focus on a moral agent who helps, we tend to experience inspiration or elevation. When we focus on a moral patient who is helped, we tend to experience relief or happiness. When we focus on a moral agent who harms, we tend to feel anger or disgust. Finally, when we focus on a moral patient who is harmed, we tend to experience compassion or sadness. While these distinctions are helpful, I suggest in the next section that the full complexity of moral emotions can only be understood by introducing the concepts of sociality, reflexivity, and temporality.

2.3 The role of emotions in sociality, reflexivity, and temporality

Emotions also have implications for sociality, reflexivity, and temporality. Just as there are higher-order desires, so there are **higher-order emotions**: emotions that are directed at other emotions, thus exhibiting the nested structure that's cropped up elsewhere in this book (figure 3.8).[7]

Many of the emotions that are especially interesting in the domain of moral psychology are higher-order. Roberts (2013) explores the ways in which emotions and emotional feedback loops strengthen and desiccate such relationships as friendship, enmity, civility, and incivility. For example, he considers a sister who generously and in a spirit of friendship gives her brother her own ticket to a concert that he would like to attend. Her brother feels the emotion of gratitude for this gift, which he expresses with a token of thanks. Satisfied that her generosity has hit its mark, his sister is "gratified by his gratitude....And he may in turn be gratified that she is gratified by his gratitude" (2013, p. 137). Despite the fact that this is a tiny schematic example, it plausibly contains a fourth-order emotion (he is gratified that she is gratified that he is gratified that she was generous).[8] Such episodes of emotional ping-pong are, in Roberts's view, constitutive of friendship and other normative personal relationships (2013, pp. 140–1; see also Alfano forthcoming). Constructive feedback loops strengthen positive personal relationships but aggravate negative relationships such as enmity (leading enemies to hate, despise, or contemn each other all the more); destructive feedback loops, by contrast, undermine positive relationships (introducing distrust, contempt, or other

Figure 3.8 Recursively embedded emotions

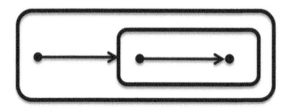

negative emotions into extant friendships) but ameliorate negative relationships (introducing sympathy, respect, or even admiration into extant enmities).

Indeed, Adam Morton (2013b, p. 132) convincingly argues that what distinguishes moral emotions from garden-variety emotions is that the former essentially involve feeling a higher-order attitude toward a point of view from which a lower-order emotion is projected. Higher-order emotions can be directed at one's own lower-order emotions (in which case they're reflexive) or at another person's (in which case they're social). For instance, guilt is a reflexive, second-order emotion because it is compounded out of imagining another person – usually someone you respect, your innocent victim, or an impartial observer – feeling (or potentially feeling) anger at an action you've performed. Likewise, shame is a reflexive, second-order emotion because it is compounded out of emotionally identifying with a point of view from which contempt (or perhaps disappointment) is directed at yourself or your action. In the same vein, moral revulsion is an irreflexive, second-order emotion because it is compounded out of emotional approval for a point of view from which disgust is directed at some person, action, or situation.

Temporality also enters here. For instance, like guilt, remorse is reflexive, but the two differ on the temporal dimension. You can feel guilty but not remorseful about what you're currently doing or plan to do. This is because remorse is a second-order emotion that essentially involves emotionally identifying with a point of view from which your past behavior – which is now irrevocable – is emotionally condemned. There are also prospective second-order emotions. For instance, moralized hope (as we might call it) is compounded out of emotional approbation for a point of view from which hope is directed at a future action or situation.

We can see the importance of the communicative components of emotions most easily in the context of sociality. Expressing an emotion often signals that others are meant to feel particular emotions too – sometimes the same emotion, sometimes other ones. For example, I cut the queue that you're waiting in. You glare at me in anger (figure 3.9).

Figure 3.9 Your anger at me

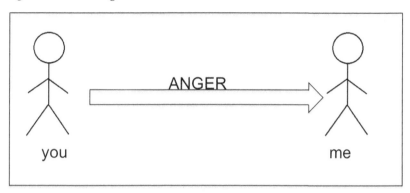

The next stage has both second-person and third-person streams. In the second-person stream, your anger prompts me to feel guilty (to emotionally identify with your anger toward me – a reflexive, second-order emotion).[9] One way I might react is by feeling and expressing guilt (figure 3.10), which would in turn prompt you to feel and express forgiveness.

Figure 3.10 Anger and guilt

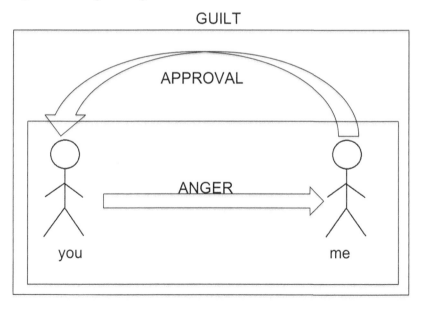

In the third-person stream, your anger prompts those around you to feel indignation (to emotionally identify with your anger toward me – an irreflexive, second-order emotion; figure 3.11), which would again prompt me to feel and express guilt. If I do, their indignation might melt away. It won't be the same as your forgiveness, since only you can forgive me for my offense to you. It might be a kind of vicarious forgiveness on your behalf, as discussed in Norlock (2008). Arguably, what distinguishes the moral domain from related domains (e.g., the prudential) is that moral attitudes are valid targets for such higher-order emotional identification.

Figure 3.11 Anger and indignation

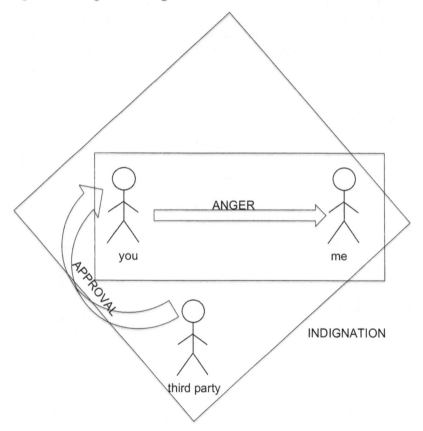

As mentioned above, reflexive higher-order emotions are directed at one's own lower-order emotions. They involve, as it were, taking a social perspective on oneself. One way in which emotions contribute to (im)moral agency, then, has to do with our higher-order emotional relation to our own first-order emotions. Roberts (2013, p. 127) plausibly argues that the status of an otherwise morally good action is undermined if the agent emotionally repudiates the first-order emotion that motivated it (e.g., feeling guilty for acting from pity, as Huck Finn does in the novel by Mark Twain).[10] In the same vein, it would seem that a base-level good action is morally enhanced if the agent emotionally endorses or at least accepts her first-order emotional motivations (e.g., feeling proud of one's resolve in the face of temptation), that a base-level bad action is ameliorated if the agent emotionally repudiates her first-order emotional motivations (e.g., feeling regret over acting from anger), and that a base-level bad action is aggravated if the agent emotionally endorses it (e.g., feeling glee over acting from greed).

3 The neuroscience of emotions

We've already seen some of the relevant scientific research on emotions. There's research on the facial expressions characteristic of emotions, including both the biological fitness (e.g., gaping in disgust to expel poisons and pathogens) and the communicative effectiveness (e.g., flashing anger to signal that you are not to be trifled with) of such expressions. There's research on the bidirectional feedback between central and peripheral aspects of emotions. For instance, when you feel proud, you adopt an upright posture, but adopting the posture independently can make you feel proud (Stepper & Strack 1993).[11] There are breathing patterns distinctive of someone who is experiencing joy, anger, fear, and sadness, yet intentionally adopting such breathing patterns induces the relevant emotion (Philippot et al. 2002).

Such research is fascinating and relevant to the moral psychology of emotion. However, I simply don't have space to cover everything that's relevant here. In this chapter, I'm instead going to focus on the *neuroscience* of emotion – a field that has grown by leaps and bounds in recent years. While it's not obvious that brain data should be more determinative than data about, for instance, behavior, this area of research is clearly relevant. Scanning people's brains gives us a "look under the hood," as it were. We can't say in advance whether what we find there will be encouraging, discouraging, or shrug-worthy, but according to some philosophically engaged scientists, such as Joshua Greene, neuroscientific findings should undermine our trust in our emotions. Let's see why.

3.1 A tale of two systems

Legend has it that, in the bad old days of philosophy, a stark and invidious distinction was made between *reason* on the one hand and *emotion* (or *passion* or *sentiment* or what have you) on the other. Reason was the higher, rational faculty that separated humans from other animals. It was pure and noble, but fragile – easily overwhelmed by the dank, fetid, embodied swarm of emotions. The heroic contingent of computation, principles, and clarity versus endless drives, feelings, and affects.

Like all legends, the tale of reason versus emotion was almost entirely false. As we've already seen, Aristotle thought that reason could and ideally would harmonize with emotions and affects. Plato, who in the *Republic* divided the soul into a reasoning part, a desiring part, and a spirited part, likewise conceived of virtue as harmony – not simply domination – among these parts; likewise, in *Laws* 2.653b–c, Plato claims that "virtue is this general concord of reason and emotion." Even the Stoics, who are notorious for their wholesale rejection of emotions, took up this position, not because emotions were sullied and spoiled but because they were almost always *mistaken cognitions* (i.e., not because they weren't cognitions *at all*). As we saw earlier in this chapter, emotions have multiple rational components. In addition to their phenomenology, they have perceptual, evaluative, motivational, representational, functional, and communicative aspects. Fear can get it wrong. Joy can be vile. Anger can motivate too little or too much. Disgust can proliferate wildly, attaching not just to corruption but to just about anything. Contempt can spread through an in-group quickly and without anyone even realizing it. There is no fundamental opposition between reason and emotion (Haidt 2012, p. 45; Railton 2014).

That said, like at least some legends, the old tale of reason versus emotion contained a kernel of truth. An explicit, effortful, rule-following *deduction* that something poses a threat is a distinct process from fluently *feeling* its threateningness as fear. Emotions often deliver their perceptual, evaluative, motivational, and representational upshots more quickly than explicit reasoning. Robert Zajonc

(1984) famously showed that the neural correlates of affective responses sometimes activate before the non-affective correlates. For instance, fear can register the presence of threat before the person even knows what's going on (Öhman & Mineka 2003). Stimuli can elicit emotional reactions even when we know full well that they aren't real: witness fear and disgust at a model tarantula in a secure enclosure. Stimuli can elicit emotional reactions even when we know full well that the emotion isn't fitting: witness fear while riding a well-maintained rollercoaster. We're better at knowing *that* we're experiencing an emotion (though not necessarily *which* emotion) than *why* we're experiencing it. To the extent that emotions share some aspects (e.g., the arousal of fear and the arousal of sexual attraction), people are apt to mistake an experience of one for an experience of the other (Dutton & Aron 1974). Mere exposure to something tends to induce positive affect toward it (Zajonc & Markus 1982). People are less attracted to gambles where they have a 7/36 chance of winning $9 and getting nothing otherwise than they are to gambles where they have a 7/36 chance of winning $9 and losing $.05 otherwise, because the $9 gain *feels* bigger when compared to a tiny loss than when there's nothing to compare it to (Slovic et al. 2002). Assessments of both risks and potential benefits associated with technology are influenced by affect. If you feel positively toward something, such as nuclear power, you'll tend to judge that its benefits are greater and that risks associated with it are lower; if you feel negatively toward it, you'll tend to judge that its benefits are negligible and that the risks associated with it are higher (Finucane et al. 2000). This is of course irrational. In the real world, risk and reward are negatively correlated because we rarely engage in highly risky behaviors that have little potential benefit. Affect and emotion tell us otherwise – especially the hybrid emotion of dread (Fischhoff et al. 1978). In addition, some emotional responses seem to be incorrigible in the face of, or at least resistant to, evidence that they are not appropriate (Haidt 2001).

In recent years, scientists have begun to explore the brain basis for these and related phenomena, in a field referred to as affective neuroscience. One popular framework, which is sometimes called *dual-process theory*,[12] distinguishes between fast, automatic, affective, effortless, unconscious, incorrigible processes (e.g., emotions) and slow, deliberative, effortful, conscious, agentic processes (e.g., deducing the square root of 169). System 1 is the fast system. It evolved to help us deal with situations our evolutionary ancestors often faced (or that our cultural ancestors faced and were able to solve in a way that could be automated and passed along, or that we ourselves have often faced and developed automatic strategies for coping with), and can be remarkably effective and efficient in responding to such situations even in the twenty-first century (Nesse & Ellsworth 2009). It can also go wildly astray when it is removed from evolutionarily (or culturally, or personally) typical situations. System 2 is the slow system. It evolved to help us cope with novel and complicated situations in which system 1 either failed to produce a response or produced a maladaptive response.[13] Recently, neuroscientific evidence has begun to emerge that vindicates the distinction between system 1 and system 2. Many of the neural correlates of system 1 processes tend to occur in particular parts of the brain, such as the amygdala, insula, orbitofrontal cortex, and anterior cingulate cortex. System 2 processes seem to occur more typically in the dorsolateral prefrontal cortex (dlPFC) and related regions. The neural correlates of system 1 processes often activate earlier than the neural correlates of system 2 processes (Decety & Cacioppo 2012).

Naturally, the two systems interact in various ways. It's a dual-*system* approach, not a dual-*person* approach. But they can and do come into conflict in various ways. If the deliverances of system 1 and system 2 (or separate deliverances of distinct system 1 processes, which seem to be pretty disparate) point in different directions, the conflict has to be adjudicated. In a now-famous study of moral decision-making, Greene et al. (2001) argued that evidence from functional magnetic resonance imaging (fMRI) suggested that regions of the brain associated with emotional system 1 processes tend to produce Kantian/deontological judgments, while regions associated with slower system 2 processes tend to produce consequentialist judgments.[14] Greene and his colleagues used fMRI to scan people's brains while they read vignettes in which the protagonist faces a tradeoff between saving five lives and sacrificing one, or failing to save five but not sacrificing one. The two best-known versions of these cases, which are due to Philippa Foot (1967), are the *switch* and *footbridge* variants of the "trolley problem." In the *switch* version, the protagonist can pull a switch that will turn a runaway trolley away from five people trapped in its path, sending it down a spur track where it will instead crush a different, lone person. In the *footbridge* version, the protagonist can push a large man off a footbridge in front of the runaway trolley, impeding its forward momentum enough to save the five innocents but killing him in the process. Perhaps unsurprisingly, most people say it would be appropriate to pull the switch, but most people also say it would be inappropriate to push the large man.[15]

On the face of it, this looks inconsistent. After all, in both *switch* and *footbridge*, the protagonist faces a choice in which one person's life can be sacrificed to save the lives of five others. The fates of the lone individuals will be gruesome and fatal regardless of the exact details. The fact that, in *footbridge*, the five would be saved by physically pushing someone rather than pulling a switch doesn't seem to make a moral difference. Some have argued that the crucial difference is that, in *switch*, the death of the lone person is merely a foreseen side-effect of saving the five, whereas in *footbridge*, his death is a means to that end. This is the famous **doctrine of double effect**, which holds that, sometimes, it's morally worse to produce a bad event (e.g., harming an innocent person) as a means to some goal than as a foreseeable side-effect of achieving that goal. People the world over make moral judgments that accord with the doctrine of double effect, though in most cases they could not state the doctrine explicitly (Mikhail 2011; see also Nichols et al. forthcoming).[16] The question then moves a stage back: even granting, for the sake of argument, that people are sensitive to the distinction between harming someone as a means to an end and harming them as a side-effect of pursuing that end, why should *that* make a difference? In other words, does the doctrine of double effect track an important moral distinction, or does it make people sensitive to morally irrelevant differences?

Greene wanted to demonstrate, using neuroscientific evidence, that the doctrine of double effect doesn't track an important moral distinction. Why put people in an fMRI machine while they answer questions about the trolley problem? What could that possibly tell us? Greene wanted to show that characteristically deontological intuitions (*don't push the large man – he has an inviolable right to life!*) were differentially associated with fast, affective, system 1 brain regions, specifically the ventromedial prefrontal cortex (vmPFC), while characteristically consequentialist intuitions (*pull the switch – one death is much less bad than five!*) were differentially associated with slow, cold, system 2 brain regions (dlPFC). If this is right, we might worry that such deontological judgments are suspect because they are here being produced in circumstances for which evolution, culture, and personal experience could hardly have prepared people. In other words, because the deliverances of system 1 are reliable in some kinds of situations but not others, and because we have reason to think that they aren't reliable in *footbridge*-like situations, we should discount our deontological intuitions about *footbridge* and similar cases. This would mean abandoning the doctrine of double effect and the moral relevance of the distinction between means and ends, among other things.

Let's break this down a bit, since there are a lot of moving parts. Greene's argument depends on a number of distinct premises:

1 Deontological intuitions about *footbridge* and similar scenarios, but not *switch* and similar scenarios, differentially activate vmPFC (and related areas, such as insula and amygdala).
2 Brain processes associated with activation of vmPFC (and related areas, such as insula and amygdala) deliver emotional system 1 intuitions.
3 Emotional system 1 intuitions are unreliable in situations of type S (lack of evolutionary, cultural, or personal preparation).
4 *Footbridge* and related situations are of type S.

From these claims, Greene infers that deontological intuitions about *footbridge* and related situations are unreliable, and hence that we should discard the doctrine of double effect. This is why he went to the trouble of scanning people's brains in the fMRI scanner. There is, in his words, a "central tension" between characteristically deontological judgments, which are "preferentially supported by automatic emotional responses," and characteristically consequentialist judgments, which are "preferentially supported by conscious reasoning and allied processes of cognitive control" (Greene 2014).

One thing that Greene is emphatically *not* claiming is that emotions or affective processes or system 1 processes are always or even typically unreliable. As he makes clear (2014; see also 2013), the claim is that automatic, emotional, system 1 processes are typically terrific (fast, efficient, reliable[17]) for decisions that the agent is prepared for (by evolution, by culture, or by extensive personal experience) but terrible for other sorts of decisions. This more modest and plausible claim nevertheless motivates surprising claims about the relative plausibility of deontology and consequentialism. These major normative theories agree about the vast majority of cases, but (says Greene), *when they disagree*, the deontological intuitions are almost always unreliable. Trusting such intuitions amounts to "point and shoot morality" (letting the fastest, most affective intuitions rule the day), abandoning careful reasoning when a moral "alarm bell" rings.

3.2 Brains and emotions

Since Greene's master argument has four premises, one could object to it by objecting to any of the premises or by objecting to the validity of the inference itself. In this section, I'll explore objections to premises 1 and 2. Together, these objections spell serious trouble for the master argument, though they point to a more modest argument that targets not emotion as such but disgust in particular.[18]

Premise 1 can be split into distinct claims about vmPFC, on the one hand, and insula and amygdala on the other. This distinction turns out to be important because the fMRI data primarily support the activation of vmPFC in *footbridge*-like scenarios, but are more ambiguous about insula and amygdala. In other words, 1a is supported, but 1b is dubious:

1a Deontological intuitions about *footbridge* and similar scenarios, but not *switch* and similar scenarios, differentially activate vmPFC.[19]

1b Deontological intuitions about *footbridge* and similar scenarios, but not *switch* and similar scenarios, differentially activate insula and amygdala.

If premise 2 were correct, this might not be a problem. However, premise 2 is false. Although it would be convenient for researchers if activation of a single region of the brain were associated with emotional processes, such a phrenological supposition is manifestly unsupported by the data.[20] Although there is some evidence that fear (especially intense fear of a near and looming threat) is associated with amygdala activation (Mobbs et al. 2010) and that disgust (especially intense, visceral disgust) is associated with insula activation (Calder 2003), the most recent meta-analysis of the brain basis of emotion found that intuitive distinctions between basic emotions are not generally respected by the brain (the same brain regions are associated with multiple emotions), and even that the distinction between *emotion* and other categories of mental state is not generally respected by the brain (Lindquist et al. 2012). Although Greene et al. (2004) point to regions other than vmPFC, such as insula and amygdala, as hotbeds of emotional system 1-processing, their primary case depends on vmPFC. In other words, 2a is unsupported, though 2b is supported:

2a. Brain processes associated with activation of vmPFC deliver emotional system 1 intuitions.

2b. Brain processes associated with activation of insula and amygdala deliver emotional system 1 intuitions.

If 1a and 2a were both supported, there would be no problem. If 1b
and 2b were both supported, there would be no problem. Unfortunately for Greene et al., 1a and 2b are supported, but not 1b
or 2a.[21]

Why do Greene et al. think that vmPFC is implicated in emotion?
Following Damasio (1995), they adhere to the general principle that
ventral (vertically lower) parts of the brain are more involved in
emotion than dorsal (vertically higher) parts. This is of course a
gross overgeneralization, but there are reasons to accept it (as such
a generalization). In general, parts of the brain closer to the brainstem (ventral and posterior / bottom and back) are evolutionarily
older and therefore shared with more species, including even non-
mammals. Higher and more forward (dorsal and anterior) parts are
evolutionarily more recent and therefore are more closely associated with the human lineage, which unarguably involves a massive
brain capable of long-term, highly social planning.[22]

As I pointed out above, the mapping from brain regions to functions is not one-one (each region performing a specific function, as
the phrenologists and various famous philosophers such as Hegel
1807/1976 held) but many-many (most regions being recruited for
multiple functions, and most functions recruiting multiple regions).
While vmPFC does seem to be implicated in processing some emotions, it does so not (like amygdala and insula) as their originator,
but as the area in which diverse value inputs from various parts of
the brain (including emotional inputs, but also many others) are
transformed into a common currency and integrated into a value
signal, which guides decision-making. Ironically, this process resembles expected-utility calculation – the very form of reasoning that
Greene (2013) contends is *not* associated with vmPFC.[23] If this is
right, vmPFC is involved in calculating the best possible outcome
even in footbridge, using a continuous value function, not a categorical distinction between prospects that trigger "alarm bells" and
those that don't.

3.3 Selective debunking: the case of disgust

If these criticisms of Greene et al.'s premises 1 and 2 are on the right
track, then their attack on "point and shoot morality" arationally

driven by "alarm bells" falls flat. On closer examination, this should be unsurprising. Although Greene (2013) compares the *footbridge* scenario to the Stroop task, arguing that deontological intuitions about pushing the man are deliverances of fast, emotional, system 1 processes, the timescale is clearly wrong. In a classic Stroop task, the participant is asked to name, as quickly and accurately as possible, the color of the font in which various words are printed. This isn't particularly hard, but it's trickier when the color of the font is, for instance, blue, but the word itself is "red." People have to slow down to get this right because a fast system 1 process (reading) is pitted against a more controlled system 2 process (naming colors, which is not a task that most people have done often enough to have habituated it into their system 1). As Huebner (forthcoming; see also 2011) points out, "studies examining *moral judgments* move at a glacial pace relative to the speed of neural processing." Reading *footbridge* can typically take participants more than twenty seconds, and responding to the question whether the protagonist's action was morally acceptable takes roughly eight seconds. Amygdala activation occurs as early as 122 milliseconds after seeing an emotional image, with vmPFC activation occurring 60 milliseconds later (Decety & Cacioppo 2012). Furthermore, the violence and graphical imagery of commonly used variants of *footbridge* tend to be much higher than for variants of *switch*; when violence and imagery are matched, *both* tend to produce emotional reactions, with almost no difference between the two (Horne & Powell 2013). In Horne and Powell's words, Greene's results have nothing to do with deontological alarm bells; what he did was make the "unremarkable observation that graphic descriptions of harmful acts are emotionally salient – an altogether trivial finding" (forthcoming). I should note that, although I'm here critical of Greene, I agree with him in spirit when he says "*Science can advance ethics by revealing the hidden inner workings of our moral judgments, especially the ones we make intuitively. Once those inner workings are revealed we may have less confidence in some of our judgments and the ethical theories that are (explicitly or implicitly) based on them*" (2014; emphasis his).

Is there then no interesting connection between emotion and moral judgment? That would be too quick an inference. As we've seen, *emotion* is a diverse category. Different emotions have different evolutionary histories, different cultural histories, different functions, different constellations of brain regions associated with their tokening, and so on. While it may be overbroad to claim, with Greene, that when emotional intuitions and reasoned responses differ, the intuitions are typically unreliable, there is room for more targeted revaluations of specific emotions in specific contexts.

In this section, I'll briefly explore one such targeted revaluation: selective debunking arguments about the moral relevance of disgust.[24] We can here give something back to Greene, who admirably explains Kant's moral disapprobation of masturbation:

> Kant, being an uptight Eighteenth Century Prussian, is uncomfortable with masturbation, but he's not content simply to voice his distaste. He wants to *prove from first principles* that masturbation is immoral, and he's got a pretty clever idea about how to do it: Masturbation is wrong because it involves *using oneself as a means*. (2014, p. 718)

This rings true. Kant had an emotional reaction of disgust towards masturbation, which led him to seek rationalizations for condemning it not merely as a matter of taste or etiquette, but as a matter of moral principle. Even if Greene is wrong about the role of emotion *in general* in distinguishing the *footbridge* and *switch* versions of the trolley case, he may be right about the role of the particular emotion of *disgust* in generating and sustaining negative moral judgments that, on reflection, seem to lack normative force.

Disgust, which takes a unique form in human animals, involves characteristic bodily, affective, motivational, evaluative, cognitive, and neural patterns. For instance, someone who feels disgusted typically makes a gaping facial expression, withdraws slightly from the object of disgust, undergoes a slight reduction in body temperature and heart rate, and feels a sense of nausea and the need to cleanse herself. In addition, she is motivated to avoid and even expunge the offending object, experiences it as contaminating and repugnant, becomes more attuned to other disgusting objects in the immediate environment, is inclined to treat anything that the object comes in contact with (whether physically or symbolically) as also disgusting, and is more inclined to make harsh moral judgments – both about the object and in general – when confronted with the object experienced as disgusting.

The disgust reaction is difficult to repress, is easily recognized, and – when recognized – empathically induces disgust in the other person.[25] There are certain objects that almost all normal adults are disgusted by (feces, decaying corpses, rotting food, spiders, maggots, physical deformities). But there is also considerable intercultural and interpersonal variation beyond these core objects of disgust, including in some better-studied cases cuisines, sexual behaviors, out-group members, and violations of social norms. Unlike other emotions, disgust is also differentially associated with insula activation – especially anterior insular cortex (Wicker et al. 2003; Wright et al. 2004).

Kelly (2011) argues that this seemingly bizarre combination of features is best explained by two theses. The universal bodily manifestations of disgust evolved to help humans avoid ingesting toxins and other harmful substances, while the more cognitive or symbolic sense of offensiveness and contamination associated with disgust evolved to help humans avoid diseases and parasites. According to the *entanglement thesis*, these initially distinct system 1 responses became entangled in the course of human evolution and now systematically co-occur. If you make the gape face, whatever you're attending to will start to look contaminated; if something disgusts you at a cognitive level, you will flash a quick gape face.[26] According to the *co-opt thesis*, the entangled emotional system for disgust was later recruited for an entirely distinct purpose: to help mark the boundaries between in-group and out-group, and thus to motivate cooperation with in-group members, punishment of in-group defectors, and exclusion of out-group members. Because disgust has a flexible acquisition system (it acquires new cues extremely easily and empathically), is on a "hair trigger" (is easily triggered in the presence of acquired triggers), and "ballistic" (once set in motion, it is difficult to halt or reverse – Kelly 2011, p. 72), it was ripe to be co-opted in this way.[27]

If Kelly's account of disgust is on the right track, "disgust skepticism" (2011, p. 139), according to which the combination of disgust's hair trigger and its ballistic trajectory mean that it is extremely prone to incorrigible false positives that involve unwarranted feelings of contamination and even dehumanization, may be the appropriate response.[28] Along these same lines, Lynne Tirrell (2012) explores how such dehumanization is a prelude to and perhaps even a constitutive part of atrocity. The Nazis described Jews as vermin. During the Rwandan genocide, Hutu Power called Tutsis cockroaches and snakes. In February 2014, President Yoweri Museveni of Uganda defended new anti-homosexuality laws by saying that gay people are "disgusting." While other emotions, such as indignation and guilt, may be morally informative, if Kelly is right, "the fact that something is disgusting is not even remotely a reliable indicator of moral foul play," but is instead *"irrelevant* to moral justification" (2011, p. 148; see also Bloom 2013, p. 156).[29] Note that this kind of targeted skepticism is importantly different from Greene's global emotion-skepticism. It does not rely on falsified claims about neuroscience, and it is consistent with thinking both that non-disgust emotions are morally relevant and that even disgust can be appropriate outside the moral domain (e.g., in prudential decision-making).

This view of disgust sits in a somewhat uneasy relation to Haidt's social intuitionist model and moral foundations theory. On the one hand, Haidt contends that this is just how (at least disgust-based) moral judgment works, and that we do ourselves no favors by trying to contend with the automaticity of our own reactions, which are difficult to control. On the other hand, as we saw in the previous chapter on implicit bias and moral responsibility, it is possible to take various more distal kinds of control of one's automatic responses. Perhaps in-the-moment suppression of disgust reactions is ill-advised, but this leaves it open whether conscious reappraisal and even more distal efforts at top-down cognitive control of disgust reactions is possible. The extent to which disgust reactions resist top-down cognitive control may be somewhat overstated. For instance, Gross (2001) argues that intentionally *reappraising* otherwise disgusting stimuli reduces both behavioral expression and physiological symptoms of disgust, whereas *suppressing* one's reaction after initially experiencing disgust reduces only the behavioral expression and in fact exacerbates the physiological symptoms of disgust. Even more worrisome is the fact that suppression also exacerbates the physiological symptoms of social partners; in other words, trying to hide your disgust from someone you're dealing with makes things even worse than just expressing it directly, and much worse than expressing the reappraised emotion you feel when you prompt yourself to think differently to begin with.[30] If this is on the right track, it suggests that the strategies most useful for obviating and neutralizing racial and gender biases may also prove effective in obviating and neutralizing unwanted biases due to automatic disgust reactions.

4 Philosophical implications of the cognitive and affective neuroscience of emotion

What does all of this evidence from the cognitive and affective neuroscience of emotion suggest?

4.1 Implications for agency, patiency, and reflexivity

Are we more authentically ourselves when we judge and act from emotion, or do emotions ring "alarm bells" that bypass reasoning? Are the "passions" well named because we passively endure them? If the discussion in the previous section is on the right track, the answer is neither an unqualified "yes" nor an unqualified "no." Strong emotions can overpower us, making us judge and act against our better judgment. This is nearly a platitude – certainly not something discovered by recent neuroscience. Yet, despite Greene's arguments, it looks like many emotional reactions feed through a fine-grained subjective value calculation, not a categorical, unreasoning "No!" Such affects don't bypass reasoning; they serve as *inputs* to it.[31] Of course, as they say: garbage in, garbage out. If an emotional input is sensitive to something that's morally irrelevant, then the emotion's influence on moral decision making will be pernicious. The neuroscientific evidence gives us no reason to think that emotions in general or moral emotions in particular typically provide garbage inputs. As I pointed out above, Greene doesn't go so far as to say that all emotions are irrelevant, but he does claim that when emotional reactions support deontological over utilitarian decisions, they are morally irrelevant. Even that more modest claim now seems suspect.

That said, if we do the work of distinguishing among the various emotions (to the extent that they can be individuated at all, and disgust does seem to have a distinctive neural, behavioral, and communicative signature), it might be possible to single out some that are more morally reliable, and others, such as disgust, that are less so. Being a moral agent would then involve monitoring one's emotional reactions, trusting them when they're reliable, engaging in conscious reappraisal when they're inappropriate, and taking distal control of them when possible. Being a moral patient would involve resisting them when they're likely to be moral garbage.

4.2 Implications for sociality and temporality

Disgust seems to be especially problematic in connection with sociality and temporality. It leads people to draw unfair and invidious distinctions between their in-group and out-groups. It leads us to dehumanize out-groups. It is transmitted automatically, unconsciously, and empathically. It severs potential empathic connections with victims. It seems to be involved in the perpetration and justification of atrocity and genocide. Modern militaries use it in their training to overcome soldiers' resistance to killing enemy soldiers, but it sometimes (indeed, far too often) leads to horrible attitudes and actions toward foreign civilians and even domestic civilians (Trivigno 2013).

Of course, just as it's not a simple and straightforward thing to take responsibility for one's implicit biases (see chapter 2), so it's not a simple and straightforward thing to gain control over one's disgust reactions. To the extent it can be accomplished at all (Tybur et al. 2013), it takes time.[32]

5 Future directions in the moral psychology of emotion

Future research on the moral psychology of emotion could go in many directions. One promising avenue is to stop talking about "emotion" and "affect" as monolithic categories, and to start thinking through the many differences among emotions. For instance, to date, there is almost no empirical research that takes the distinction between first-order and higher-order emotions into account. Although operationalizing higher-order emotions would be difficult, doing so may help to move the field forward.

Such differentiation may also prove useful in sentimentalist metaethics, an area of research I haven't been able to cover in this chapter. For instance, Prinz (2005) argues that something is morally good (bad) for an agent just in case she is disposed to have a positive (negative) moral sentiment toward it upon careful reflection. Since it's logically and probably also psychologically possible to direct both joy and disgust at the same thing (Du et al. forthcoming), it follows that sentimentalists like Prinz are committed to the same thing's sometimes being both good and bad (Alfano 2009). Perhaps Prinz can escape this contradiction by differentiating more carefully among positive and (especially) negative sentiments and the emotions they give rise to.

Further readings

Bell, M. (2013). *Hard Feelings: The Moral Psychology of Contempt*. Oxford University Press.

Ekman, P., Campos, J., Davidson, R., & de Waal, F. (2003). *Emotions Inside Out: 130 Years After Darwin's The Expression of the Emotions in Man and Animals*. New York Academy of Sciences, vol. 1000.

Elster, J. (1985). *Ulysses and the Sirens: Studies in Rationality and Irrationality*, rev. edn. Cambridge University Press.

Frank, R. (1988). *Passions Within Reason: The Strategic Role of Emotions*. New York: Norton.

Greene, J. (2013). *Moral Tribes: Emotion, Reason, and the Gap Between Us and Them*. New York: Penguin.

Haidt, J. (2012). *The Righteous Mind: Why Good People are Divided by Politics and Religion*. New York: Pantheon.

Nichols, S. (2004). *Sentimental Rules: On the Natural Foundations of Moral Judgment*. Oxford University Press.

Nummenmaa, L., Glerean, E., Hari, R., & Hietanen, J. (2014). Bodily maps of emotions. *Proceedings of the National Academy of Sciences*, 111(2): 646–51.

Price, C. (2015). *Emotion*. Cambridge: Polity.

Prinz, J. (2004). *Gut Reactions: A Perceptual Theory of Emotion*. Oxford University Press.

Roberts, R. (2003). *Emotions: An Essay in Aid of Moral Psychology*. Cambridge University Press.

Shargel, D., & Prinz, J. (forthcoming). Philosophy of the emotions. In M. Lewis, J. M. Haviland-Jones, & L. F. Barrett (eds.), *Handbook of the Emotions*, 4th edn. New York: Guilford Press.

Study questions

1 Are there any basic emotions that it's always morally good – or at least never morally bad – to feel? Are there any basic emotions that it's always morally bad – or at least never morally good – to feel? Which? Why?

2 Are there any nested emotions that it's always morally good – or at least never morally bad – to feel? Are there any nested emotions that it's always morally bad – or at least never morally good – to feel? Which? Why?

3 Are there any basic emotions that it's always prudentially good – or at least never prudentially bad – to feel? Are there any basic emotions that it's always prudentially bad – or at least never prudentially good – to feel? Which? Why?

4 Are there any nested emotions that it's always prudentially good – or at least never prudentially bad – to feel? Are there any nested emotions that it's always prudentially bad – or at least never prudentially good – to feel? Which? Why?

5 How do explanations and predictions that appeal to the target's emotions differ from explanations and predictions that appear to the target's preferences?

4

Character

1 Introduction

On October 13, 2011, Wang Yue, a 2-year-old toddler in Foshan, China, wandered out into a busy street while her caretaker was doing the laundry. Hu Jun, the driver of a minivan, accidentally hit her, knocking her to the ground and crushing her beneath the van's front right tire. He stopped momentarily, then proceeded – crushing her again with the van's rear right tire. Over the next seven minutes, eighteen bystanders passed by her tiny, stricken body. In the closed-circuit video that captures the incident, it is clear that she is still alive – bleeding, moaning, crying, and thrashing her arms and legs.[1] Some of the passers-by are on foot, others ride on motorcycles, still others drive larger vehicles. Some of them seem not to see her, others deliberately skirt around her body, even pausing to look down at her before moving on. The driver of a second vehicle runs her over with both front and rear right tires, seemingly without even noticing that she's there. Eventually, a trash scavenger by the name of Chen Xianmei stops to move her out of the street toward safety. Wang Yue survived in the hospital for eight days before succumbing to her injuries. The driver of the minivan turned himself in, was convicted of involuntary homicide, and was subsequently sentenced to three and a half years in prison. Afterwards, there was a deluge of editorials and posts on social media praising Chen Xianmei for her compassion and decrying the bystanders for their apathy, callousness, and cold-heartedness.[2]

On September 2, 1945, World War II ended when Mamoru Shige-mitsu and Yoshijiro Umezu signed the Japanese Instrument of Sur-render aboard the United States battleship *Missouri*. It was nearly four years since the surprise attack on Pearl Harbor and less than a month after the Americans had dropped atomic bombs on Hiroshima and Nagasaki, killing between 150,000 and 250,000 people – the vast majority of them civilians. As part of the surrender agreement, Japanese soldiers were ordered to stand down. Most did, but a few, who came to be known as "holdouts" (*Zanryū nipponhei*), refused – some out of a sense of honor, others out of nationalist zeal, still others out of ignorance that their own government had in fact surrendered. Some holdouts lasted a few months, some a few years. Hiroo Onoda lasted longer. He had enlisted in the Japanese military in 1944 at the age of 20, trained as a commando, and received orders never to surrender or commit suicide, even if captured. Sent to the Philippines, he was isolated from direct communications from the Japanese military. Although he saw leaflets announcing the end of the war in 1945, he concluded that they were Allied propaganda. Together with a few other holdouts, he undertook what he thought was sabotage of the Allied war effort – killing local fisherman and engaging the local police in several gun battles. One member of his holdout cell surrendered in 1950. Another was killed by gunfire in 1954. The last was killed in 1972. Onoda survived two more years on his own, when he was discovered by Norio Suzuki, a Japanese tourist. Suzuki convinced the Japanese government to send Onoda's former commanding officer, Yoshimi Taniguchi, to the Philippines to personally relieve him of his duties. By that time, he had been a holdout for twenty-nine years. His gun was still in working order. He received a hero's welcome in a Japan that he barely recognized. He died in 2014 at the age of 91. In his *New York Times* obituary, he is praised for his perseverance, grit, and sense of duty.

2 The role of character in moral psychology

How can we explain the behavior of the eighteen bystanders in Foshan? How can we explain the fact that, by the time he surrendered, Onoda had been a holdout for more than half his life? Would you predict that, in other situations, Chen Xianmei would behave differently from the eighteen people who didn't help Wang Yue? Would you predict that, after he was repatriated to Japan, Onoda displayed more perseverance and grit than the ordinary person, even in non-military contexts? To be sure, Chen Xianmei did a good thing, but in addition to praising her action, should we praise her as a person? Likewise, what the eighteen bystanders did (or failed to do) was bad, but does that make them bad people? Some think so, as evidenced by the fact that some of the bystanders have reported to the media that they've since been subject to crank calls and other forms of harassment.

2.1 The role of character in agency

These questions concern not only the explanation, prediction, and evaluation of particular actions or behaviors, but also the explanation, prediction, and evaluation of moral agents. What the eighteen bystanders *did* certainly looks apathetic, callous, and even cold-hearted. Does that make them (or make it more likely that they are) apathetic, callous, and cold-hearted *people*? What Chen Xianmei *did* was compassionate. Does that make her (or make it more likely that she is) a compassionate *person*? What Onoda *did* certainly seems to exemplify perseverance, grit, and a sense of duty (as well as remarkable ruthlessness, which can be easy to forget while telling his tale). Does that make him (or make it more likely that he was) a persever ant, gritty, dutiful, and ruthless *person*? What's the point of explaining, predicting, and evaluating not only at the level of the individual act but at the level of the whole agent? Does this provide us additional moral psychological purchase?

Virtue ethicists certainly think so. Some go so far as to say that what it means to act well is that one acts from virtue or at least acts as a virtuous person would act in your circumstances. Naturally, there are almost as many theories of virtue as there are theorists of virtue. That said, some prominent theories connect virtue with moral agency. For instance, some nearly universally acclaimed virtues are **executive** rather than **substantive**.[3] A substantive virtue aims at, and reliably succeeds in, promoting or pursuing a particular good or end. For instance, the benevolent person aims to promote the wellbeing of other people, and does so somewhat reliably. The curious person aims to discover the truth even if it hurts, and does so somewhat reliably. By contrast, an executive virtue has no particular aim. Instead, it helps its bearer achieve whatever aims she may independently have. For instance, courage helps someone face down threats in various domains: social, moral, physical, financial, and otherwise.[4] She might do so in pursuit of a morally good aim, such as bringing justice to the finance industry. Conversely, she might do so in pursuit of a morally bad aim, such as tear-gassing angry protesters against police violence. Either way, executive virtues make someone more effective *as an agent*.

Character plays a role in the virtue-ethical framework for moral psychology, as I explain below. But, as I also point it, it matters in every prominent normative theory. Other major normative theories typically make room for talk of character, even if they don't give it pride of place. A utilitarian holds that what makes a state of affairs good has nothing to do with the character of the people involved and that what makes an action right has nothing to do with whether the person who committed the action was virtuous, vicious, or neither.[5] Nevertheless, even a committed utilitarian will naturally admit that her theory needs to be *implemented* in some way. Arguably, this will involve cultivating and acting from (or at least in accordance with) various utility-promoting character traits, which the utilitarian would therefore count as virtues.[6] Likewise, Kantians hold that what makes an action right depends solely on the agent's intention in action, but that doesn't mean they can't also say that certain sorts of people tend to have right-making intentions, which would mean that whatever distinguishes those people would count as Kantian virtues. Similar points could be made about care ethics. Recognizing this led Bernard Williams to remark that objecting to the concept of moral character amounts to "an objection to ethical thought itself rather than to one way of conducting it" (1985, p. 10, n. 7).

2.2 The role of character in patiency

As we saw in the previous chapter, emotions are complex mental states that involve (among other things) being affected by one's situation in characteristic ways. A person who is typically affected in a given way can be said to have a relevant character trait. Aristotle famously argued that a virtue is a mean or average – in respect of emotion and action – between two vices. For example, courage is meant to be a mean between rashness and cowardice. This approach to virtues – enumerating them and then elucidating them by explaining which emotions and behaviors relate to them – can be fruitful. Presumably, if we have a word for a trait, that trait has had some importance in human history, even if, like "sinister" and "dexterous," that importance has largely abated.[7]

Moving in the other direction (from emotions to virtues, rather than from virtues to emotions), may be more useful because we have a firmer grasp on what the emotions are than on what the virtues are. The idea here is to start from emotions or emotionally motivated behavior and then figure out what the relevant virtue would be. In the chapter on emotions above, I argued that we have good reason to recognize at least seven basic emotions: surprise, fear, disgust, contempt, anger, joy, and sadness. One of these basic emotions is familiar from Aristotle's *Nicomachean Ethics*: fear. He argues that courage involves, among other things, the disposition to fear the right thing at the right time for the right reason in the right way with the right intensity, and so on. The vice of excess is cowardice (fearing too intensely, too many things, for too many reasons, etc.); the vice of deficiency is rashness (fearing not intensely enough, too few things, for too few reasons, etc.). When it functions well, fear tracks threats. So the person with well-functioning fear is good at tracking and responding to threats and is a candidate for courage.

What about the other six basic emotions – anger, disgust, contempt, surprise, sadness, and joy?

Aristotle claims that the virtue with respect to anger is good-temper, and that the vices are irascibility and unirascibility. I disagree. Following the literature in feminist and antiracist ethics of anger (Bell 2009; Cogley 2014; Tessman 2005), I contend that the virtue with respect to anger is justice, and that anger tracks harms. Someone who gets angry at the right things for the right reasons at the right time to the right degree and so on is someone whose sense of injustice is well-tuned. By contrast, someone who witnesses injustice and feels not a tinge of anger seems morally suspect. On the flipside, someone who's prepared to be outraged at the most minor (perceived) infraction is vicious in the other direction.[8] On this view, if someone reacted with anger to genuine offenses (and not to much else), she would be a candidate for being a just person. The source of the disagreement between Aristotle, on the one hand, and Bell, Cogley, and Tessman, on the other, lies primarily in their background presuppositions about the amount of injustice in society, as well as who is a legitimate author of moral emotions. Aristotle restricts his theory to adult male citizens in a polity built around satisfying their and only their needs. For such people, injustices are bound to be rarer than for people in oppressed groups. When such privileged citizens do experience an offense, they are likely to have the power and perceived authority to make their

Figure 4.1 Target domains, relevant emotions, and attendant virtues, vices of deficiency, and vices of excess

	Target domain: Purity Emotion: Disgust	
Vice of deficiency: Corruption	Virtue: Purity	Vice of excess: Prudishness
	Target domain: Quality Emotion: Contempt	
Vice of deficiency: Bad taste	Virtue: Good taste	Vice of excess: Snobbishness
	Target domain: Novelty Emotion: Surprise/Awe	
Vice of deficiency: Jadedness/Cynicism	Virtue: Curiosity/Wonder	Vice of excess: *Naïveté*
	Target domain: Loss Emotion: Sadness	
Vice of deficiency: Apathy	Virtue: Care	Vice of excess: Fragility
	Target domain: Goodness Emotion: Joy	
Vice of deficiency: Anhedonia	Virtue: Attachment	Vice of excess: Overenthusiasm

anger acknowledged and the fault redressed. They have the luxury to be good-tempered. Someone who systematically faces injustices and whose anger about them is ignored, dismissed, or met with further injustice is in a very different position. For them, being or appearing good-tempered may even contribute to their oppression, since it suggests that nothing is seriously wrong.

I don't have the space to consider the other five basic emotions in detail here, but figure 4.1 illustrates a schematic picture of them and the emotions related to them. These categorizations are only first guesses. One useful direction for moral psychology of character would be to explore what it means (and if it's even possible) to be virtuously (and viciously) disposed to feel disgust, contempt, surprise, sadness, and joy.[9]

2.3 The role of character in sociality, reflexivity, and temporality

The role of character in the remaining central moral psychological concepts will be clearer after we go through some of the empirical

evidence. A few things can already be said, though. First, traditionally, philosophers have argued that someone's character must be
considered longitudinally. Whether you're honest or not depends
not just on how you act today but how you act over the course of
weeks, months, and even years. In other words, *having* a particular
character takes time.

In addition, *acquiring* a particular character also takes time. You
can decide to do a honest thing right now, but you can't just decide
to *be* honest right now. That doesn't mean that you can't decide
right now to set out to become honest, but, to paraphrase T. S.
Eliot, between the idea and the reality, there's a gap. How is character acquired? One orthodox answer associated with Aristotle and
neo-Aristotelian virtue ethics is that character is acquired through
habituation. You become honest by performing a string of honest
actions. Over time, you accustom yourself to performing such
actions; it just comes naturally. Additionally, you also come to see
the value of your own and others' honest behavior, thought, and
motivation. And you learn to see the disvalue of your own and
others' dishonest behavior, thought, and motivation. The same
story is told about vicious and mixed character traits: you become
narrow-minded by performing a string of narrow-minded actions.
Over time, you accustom yourself to performing such actions; it
just comes naturally. Additionally, you also come to value your
own and your allies' narrow-minded behavior, thought, and
emotion (though presumably not under that description – perhaps
you call it not "narrow-minded" but "pure" or "respectable" or
"conservative").

According to this model, then, the acquisition of character also
involves reflexivity. Most explicitly, you could set out on a long-
term project of *self*-cultivation and *self*-improvement, which requires
that you have a concept of self and care about the character of your
future self. Less explicitly, you could at least pay attention to how
you're becoming habituated, steering yourself toward (what you
take to be) good habits and away from (what you take to be) bad
habits. Naturally, parenting and peer influence begin the process of
cultivating and monitoring the development of character long
before and even after people have a chance to engage in self-culti-
vation, self-improvement, and self-monitoring. This obvious fact
indicates that the moral psychology of virtue must also draw on
resources in developmental psychology (e.g., Bloom 2013; Masten
et al. 2013a, 2013b).

How can you tell whether a habit is good or bad? How can you tell whether it's genuinely worth cultivating or avoiding? Naturally, you will to some extent rely on your own gut reactions, as well as your more reflective judgments. But gut reactions, as we saw in the chapter on emotions, are fallible – sometimes extremely so. Reflective judgments may be better than gut reactions, at least in some contexts, but they too are fallible. Indeed, in some contexts reflection seems only to further entrench people in whatever positions they already hold, guided by the phenomenon of **confirmation bias** (Nickerson 1998). For these reasons, theorists of virtue typically hold that good character is most easily (and perhaps necessarily) cultivated in an appropriate social context. What exactly counts as a good context is subject to more controversy, but some general points are clear. It's easier to be and become virtuous among other people who care about your wellbeing and your character. It's easier to be and become virtuous among other people who encourage you to do the right thing and challenge you – in a spirit of friendship, but nevertheless aggressively – when you do what they think is wrong. It's easier to be virtuous among people who embody a diversity of viewpoints and values, so that you can avoid groupthink and confirmation bias. It's easier to be and become virtuous among other people who are themselves at least somewhat virtuous. Below, I'll argue that sociality may be even more deeply implicated in character, suggesting that others' expectations and attitudes may be not just causally but constitutively implicated in your character.

3 The person-situation debate in personality and social psychology

Two branches of psychology that I've been drawing on throughout this book are social psychology and personality psychology. During the twentieth century, these fields didn't always see eye to eye. Indeed, practitioners engaged in what's come to be known as the person-situation debate. According to an extreme **personist**, the sole or at least the primary driver of behavior is personality. If you want to know why someone did something, what you need to know is whether she's an extrovert or an introvert, neurotic or emotionally resilient, conscientious or unconscientious, and so on. If you want to predict how someone will behave, what you need to know is whether she's open or closed to new experiences, agreeable or disagreeable, and so on. Extroverts are always and everywhere extroverts. Disagreeable people are always and everywhere disagreeable. According to an extreme **situationist**, the sole or at least the primary driver of behavior is the situation. If you want to know why someone did something, what you need to know is what possibilities for action the situation afforded, whether anyone else was watching, and so on. If you want to predict how someone will behave, what you need to know is what other people in the situation suggested or demanded, whether ambient light and sound were high or low, and so on. The same person might be extroverted in some contexts, introverted in others, and what makes the difference needn't be anything so obvious as whether a dance mix is playing. The same person might be disagreeable in some contexts, agreeable in others, and what makes the difference needn't be anything so obvious as whether he's just been insulted.

As you might expect, to the extent that personism is correct, traditional conceptions of character are empirically supported, but to the extent that situationism is correct, such conceptions are undermined. In this chapter, I argue that neither extreme personism nor extreme situationism is correct. Instead, the most plausible interpretation of the empirical literature is **interactionism**. According to interactionists, both personality and situation drive behavior, and the way in which they do so is not linear. In the history of psychology, it is hard to find published views that exemplify extreme personism or extreme situationism (though one might think that Shweder 2012 and D'Andrade 1993 at least flirted with the latter). Nevertheless, philosophical interpreters of personality and social psychology have sometimes arrived at extreme personist or situationist views (e.g., Harman 1999). Moreover, feedback loops often connect a person with her situation in such a way that an initial influence of personality changes the situation she finds herself in, and the modified situation then influences her personality, which again influences her situation, which again influences her personality, and so on. In the same way that your bodily functions and the functions of the bacteria in your gut are in constant interaction, such that the trajectory of one is literally inexplicable without reference to the other, so a person and her situation are in constant interaction, such that the trajectory of one is literally inexplicable without reference to the other. While this might sound intuitively implausible, it will become more plausible after we survey some of the relevant empirical research.

3.1 An emblematic experiment

The traditional notion of character described above assumes that character has a particular structure, that it is acquired in a particular way, and that it has particular uses for explanation, prediction, and evaluation. In this framework, both substantive and executive traits motivate behavior. Compassionate people help those who are in need, suffering, or oppressed. They do so because they're differentially and consistently sensitive to others' wellbeing, including not only their current state of mind but their sense of dignity, their health, their plans and projects, and their attachments to other people and political goals (a perceptual component of virtue). They do so because they have standing preferences or sentiments that favor helping those who are in need, suffering, or oppressed (a motivational component of virtue). They don't just mindlessly go around handing out dollar bills to people who look sad; instead, when it isn't immediately obvious to them what would do the trick, they think carefully about what would promote and protect the wellbeing of those who are in need, suffering, or oppressed (a deliberative component of virtue). Their disposition to help in this way is modally robust: they aren't easily distracted or diverted from their compassionate aims – especially not by seemingly trivial events and influences that they neither value nor disvalue. They do all these things because they've become habituated to acting compassionately by doing so over and over, often automatically but also sometimes while explicitly endorsing compassionate reasons. Because they're implicated in the explanation of their own character (they habituated themselves by acting the same way over and over), they're responsible not only for particular actions that flow from their compassion but also for their standing motivations and sensitivities – for their own character. They're responsible both for what they do and for who they are.

How plausible is this picture? Does psychological research suggest that this is how people's ongoing dispositions to think, feel, deliberate, and act work? Does it suggest that this is how their ongoing dispositions to think, feel, deliberate, and act are acquired? Does it suggest that this is how behavior, cognition, and motivation are best explained and predicted? There are reasons to worry.

Think again about Chen Xianmei, Wang Yu's rescuer, and the eighteen people who failed to help. She's been praised for acting compassionately (which she clearly did) and for being a compassionate person. The bystanders have been blamed for failing to act compassionately (which they clearly did) and for being apathetic, callous, and cold-hearted people. How much of their behavior is explicable in personist terms? How much of it is best explained in some other way? We don't know enough about these nineteen individuals to confidently say anything about them, but there is relevant research on how people tend to behave in similar circumstances. One illustrative experiment is John Darley and Daniel Batson's (1973) Good Samaritan study, which was conducted with participants from the Princeton Theological Seminary. These participants filled out a questionnaire to determine whether they saw religion as a means, an end, or a quest. They were then asked to prepare a talk either on job prospects for seminarians like themselves or on the New Testament parable of the Good Samaritan, in which a robbed and beaten man is ignored by a priest and a Levite but helped by a lowly Samaritan. The moral of the parable, which Jesus tells in response to being asked "Who is my neighbor?" is that everyone – even a stranger – is your neighbor and therefore a fitting object of compassion. The audience is meant to admire and want to emulate the compassionate Samaritan, not the sanctimonious clergy. Presumably the seminarians knew this.

To test whether they would act in accordance with this moral lesson, which some of them were about to teach and with which all of them surely were familiar, Darley and Batson arranged for each of them to encounter a distressed confederate slumped on the ground along the path to the building where they were to speak. Before they headed out, some were told that they had time to spare, others that they were just on time, and still others that they were running late. The experimenters covertly observed whether the participants stopped to help like the Good Samaritan or walked by without helping. Before reading the next paragraph, ask yourself: how did the three measured variables influence their behavior? Were they more likely to help when they were about to preach about the Good Samaritan? Were they more likely to help when they were unhurried? Were they more likely to help when they saw religion as an end or a quest?

If you predicted that their view of religion made the difference, you favor personist explanations and predictions – a common view, and one that is most amenable to traditional virtue theory. People act compassionately because they explicitly endorse compassionate religious values over a long time and habituate themselves to acting from those values – for instance, by going to divinity school. If you predicted that their degree of hurry made the difference, you favor situational explanations and predictions. People act compassionately not because of anything enduring and deep within them but because they find themselves in conducive circumstances.

3.2 *Methodological interlude*

If you predicted that the subject of their talk (job prospects for people like themselves or the Good Samaritan parable) made the difference, it's a bit more complicated. On the one hand, what someone is just about to do isn't a deep aspect of their character; it may have nothing to do with what they're habituated to doing, thinking, or feeling. On the other hand, how circumstances affect your behavior is indicative of your character. Suppose you've come into some money and are planning to open your first investment account. Your advisor gives you three options: a standard portfolio that includes some stocks of companies in morally fraught but highly profitable industries (military manufacturing, tobacco, finance), a "dirty" portfolio with only such stocks, and a "clean" portfolio with none of them. The most direct indication of your character is what you would choose without anyone emphasizing particular values to you.[10] But a secondary indication is what you would choose when particular values are made salient. For instance, if you have pacifist and anti-exploitation leanings but don't often think about them, then presumably being reminded that, by opting for the dirty portfolio, you'd be supporting the profitable military manufacturing and finance industries would lead you to choose one of the other two portfolios. By contrast, if you deeply believe that the only moral and social responsibility of a business is to maximize profits, then being reminded of the same thing should make you more likely to choose the dirty portfolio. And if you don't care one way or the other about the military-industrial complex, the finance industry, or business ethics, being reminded of this should have no effect.

In other words, the situational intervention of making a particular value salient may not have a univocal effect on people's decision-making. People who embody one constellation of values will be influenced in one direction. Those with a different constellation of values will be influenced in the opposite direction. Those with neither will be uninfluenced. Statisticians would say that, in this example, someone's values function as a **moderator variable**, influencing the impact of the reminder on their decision-making.[11] The reminder doesn't have the same effect on everyone. Instead, it has a different effect depending on the level of a different variable – the person's antecedent values. You may not always be sensitive to all the things you care about; there's a lot to keep track of. But when it's made clear how something relates to your values, they become engaged.

If this is right, then how the seminarians were influenced by the topic of their speech might interact with their religious personalities. This would be a secondary indicator of their characters. For instance, if you view religion as a means to other ends and have been prompted to talk about job prospects for people like you, perhaps you will be more likely to self-servingly ignore an injured person in order to complete your task more efficiently. By contrast, if you view religion as an end in its own right or as a quest, and you've been prompted to talk about the parable of the Good Samaritan, perhaps you will be more likely to stop and help the injured person.

3.3 Back to the Good Samaritan experiment

In this experiment, neither participants' religious values nor the topic of their speech had a significant effect on their behavior. In other words, seminarians who viewed religion as an end in itself were neither more nor less inclined to help the confederate. And seminarians who were explicitly primed to think about the parable of the Good Samaritan were neither more nor less disposed to help the confederate. The only significant effect was produced by the degree of hurry. Of the seminarians in the low hurry condition, 63 percent offered some form of help; 45 percent of those in the medium hurry condition offered some form of help; only 10 percent of those in the high hurry condition helped. This way of reporting the data transforms the outcome (helping) into a **categorical variable**: participants either helped or didn't. In fact, Darley and Batson measured helping on a **continuous** scale ranging from failing to notice the victim (0) through noticing but not helping (1) all the way to stopping to help and then taking the victim to another place, such as the infirmary (5). The average response of those in the low hurry condition was 3.0: stopping and asking the victim if he needed help. The average response of those in the medium hurry condition was 1.8: not stopping, but helping indirectly. The average response of those in the high hurry condition was 0.7. Moreover, the interaction between view of religion and topic of speech was not statistically significant. In other words, even reminding people who explicitly thought of religion as an end in itself about what that requires of them did not produce more helping behavior than prompting them to think about their personal goals.[12]

3.4 *Evidence for situationism*

This is of course just a single experiment. As I pointed out in chapter 2, the results of any given study may be a false positive (indicating, for instance, that degree of hurry matters when it doesn't), or a false negative (indicating, for instance, that religious values don't matter when they do), or even both. One very useful way to deal with this drawback is to refer to meta-analyses, which combine the results of all relevant studies to come up with a best guess about the true effects. The precise details of the Good Samaritan study have not be replicated (after all, it's hard to find 40 seminarians who haven't heard about it), but a closely related line of research is even more directly related to the case of Wang Yue: the unresponsive bystander effect.

In situations where a participant knows that multiple people can intervene, helpful responses to emergencies are less frequent than in situations where the participant believes that only she can intervene. From an extreme personist point of view, this phenomenon is quite strange. One would expect the probability that someone helps to increase monotonically with the number of potential helpers. In fact, however, it monotonically *decreases*. John Darley and Bibb Latané (1968) hypothesized that the presence of other potential helpers reduces the probability that at least one of them comes to the victim's aid for two reasons. First, the presence of other people leads to a "diffusion of responsibility." Each person feels only partially responsible for what happens because he is in a position to know that others could intervene instead, and to know that others know that he knows they could intervene. Second, when bystanders are able to observe each other, they rely on what they perceive others to think in construing ambiguous stimuli. When someone sees that others don't intervene, he tends to infer that they have evidence indicating that the situation in fact is not an emergency, or that it would be wrong or dangerous to intervene even if it is an emergency. Everyone mistakenly takes everyone else's inaction as expressing knowledge that action is unnecessary, so everyone concludes that action is unnecessary.

Darley and Latané (1968) found that 75 percent of solitary bystanders in a simulated fire emergency intervened, while only 10 percent did so when two impassive confederates were present. Latané and Rodin (1969) similarly found that 70 percent of solitary bystanders intervened when they heard what sounded like a bookshelf collapsing on someone in the adjacent room, whereas only 7 percent helped when a phlegmatic confederate sat beside them. These results are robust. Latané and Nida (1981) conducted the first successful meta-analysis of the effect. More recently, Fischer et al. (2011) reviewed more than forty years of studies involving nearly 8,000 participants and found an overall effect size of $g = -.35$. Although there are subtle differences between them, the g statistic is comparable to Cohen's d, making this a large effect.

The Wang Yue incident occurred on a busy street, with many bystanders who could have potentially intervened. Ironically, this may have been one of the reasons why it took so long for someone to help. If the first bystander had been alone, it's much more likely that he would have helped. Research like this supports the situationist position. One of the main determinants of whether people will show compassion is a fleeting, temporary aspect of their situation: how many other people are around. If you want to explain what happened to Wang Yue, you need to look at context, not character.

Of course, compassion isn't the only virtue in the philosopher's stable, and bystander intervention isn't the only empirical research relevant to compassion. Philosophers such as John Doris (1998; 2002), Gilbert Harman (1999), Christian Miller (2013; 2014), and Mark Alfano (2012a; 2013) draw on a wide range of social psychological studies to argue that many traditional virtues are empirically suspect. What often explains and predicts whether someone will behave in a compassionate, honest, non-maleficent, or fair way are features of their situations that have little or nothing to do with virtue.

Research on bystander intervention (along with many other lines of research) thus provides positive support for situationism. The best-support model of situational influences in social psychology seems to be the "Situational Eight DIAMONDS" model (Rauthmann et al. 2014), which stands for:

- *Duty*: a job must be done, as in the Good Samaritan study;
- *Intellect*: the situation affords a chance to demonstrate one's intellect, drawing out such behavior;

- *Adversity*: one reacts either prospectively or retrospectively to blame;
- *Mating*: one modulates one's behavior because potential romantic partners are present;
- *pOsitivity*: the situation is potentially enjoyable;
- *Negativity*: the situation is potentially unenjoyable or anxiety-provoking;
- *Deception*: it is possible to deceive someone; and
- *Sociality*: social interaction is possible.

Together, these eight kinds of situational influences account for a large amount of the variance in people's behavior (24–74 percent), much more than trait dimensions (3–18 percent).

A second, negative source of support for situationism comes from studies that suggest that extreme personism is false. We already saw that seminarians' religious values completely failed to predict whether or how much they would help. More broadly, situationists are fond of pointing to Walter Mischel's (1968) landmark monograph *Personality and Assessment*. Mischel systematically reviewed the literature in personality psychology in an attempt to determine how well measures of personality predict measures of behavior; he found that correlations between such measures tend to be as low as .20 or even .10, and that they rarely exceed .30.[13] The rule of thumb for interpreting correlations is that the square of a correlation tells you how much of the variance in one variable is explained by another variable. Following this rule, what Mischel showed was that measures of personality tend to explain at most 9 percent of the variance in behavior, and that they often explain as little as 1 percent.

Together, the positive argument for situationism from research like the bystander intervention paradigm and the negative argument against personism from the "Mischel ceiling" of .30 are pretty impressive. Extreme personism is empirically untenable.

3.5 *Evidence for personism*

Extreme personism, however, is a bit of a caricature. Almost no one has held this view, and contemporary personality psychologists almost uniformly reject it. Naturally, then, less extreme personists have provided evidence both for their more modest view and against extreme situationism.

In favor of personism, several impressive arguments are made. First, credible stories of people who displayed extreme levels of various traits are undeniable. Hiroo Onoda was a holdout for decades. He had countless opportunities to surrender or just melt back into the local civilian population. He didn't. Not only did he refuse to surrender; he also actively maintained a commitment to his mission, engaging in firefights with local police and sabotaging local crops. As I mentioned above, his pistol was still in working order when he finally accepted orders to stand down. Surely there must have been something about him that enabled him to hold out for so long. It would be odd if people's personalities explained *none* of their behavior.

Second, as virtue theorists independently argue, what kind of person someone is depends not just on how they act in a particular situation but how they act and are disposed to act over the long term. If you want to explain or predict a particular action, that's one thing; if you want to explain or predict a pattern of actions, that's another. The philosophical conception of character is more closely tied to the latter than the former, so research on one-off actions, such as the Good Samaritan study, is only indirectly relevant. After all, it's possible that the few people who helped in the Good Samaritan experiment could also have helped in bystander intervention cases and other tests of compassion. Unless we track people over time in a variety of contexts, we can't know whether the people who do the virtuous thing in some cases are typically the people who do the virtuous thing in other cases. The implications of this are complicated. On the one hand, if it turned out that 5 percent of people consistently did the virtuous thing, that would be encouraging. At least *some* of us live up the ideal of good character. But that would mean that the other 95 percent rarely did so, so what's the point of encouraging them to be virtuous? Presumably most of them are already trying. Normative ideals should be achievable, or – at the very least – perceived as potentially achievable by the people who strive for them (Flanagan 1993). If praising virtue is like praising nearly unachievable norms of athletic performance or fitness, the discourse of virtue might be as damaging for ordinary people as conventional fitness norms are for ordinary people, who often give up at satisficing when they realize they can't achieve the ideal. On the other hand, if practically no one consistently behaved compassionately – sometimes acting well, sometimes not, depending on seemingly trivial and normatively irrelevant situational influences

– then we might worry that the very idea of a robust, cross-situationally consistent trait like a virtue is empirically untenable.

The current state of research is insufficient to tell us whether virtue theorists face either of these problems, but there is encouraging work on the so-called "aggregation solution" (Fishbein & Ajzen 1974; Epstein 1979, 1983). The basic idea here is to use measures of personal dispositions to predict and explain not individual actions but patterns of behavior. Although Epstein (1983) admits that predicting particular actions is "usually hopeless," patterns of behavior are quite predictable. Although the correlation between a trait measure and a measure of an individual behavior is usually between .10 and .20, and seldom above .30, the correlation between a trait measure and a measure of aggregate behavior can be as high as .90. This doesn't mean that all patterns are virtuous (or vicious), but it is a remarkable improvement.

From a virtue theoretic point of view, aggregation is only a partial victory. As Doris (2002) points out, some virtues seem to require perfect or near-perfect consistency. If you abstain from sexual abuse of children and murder 364 days a year, it seems preposterous to say that you have relevant virtues. Jayawickreme et al. (2014, p. 19) acknowledge this point but contend that it may apply to some virtues but not others. Which? They don't provide a criterion, but place "everyday moral traits such as fairness and honesty" on one side of the divide (for which aggregation works) and sexual fidelity and homicide-avoidance on the other. Adams (2006, p. 124) suggests that the relevant criterion is whether the behavior in question relates to a duty of perfect obligation (e.g., not killing, not lying, not cheating) or a duty of imperfect obligation (e.g., giving to charity). Accordingly, he would say that fairness and honesty, like sexual fidelity, require perfect or near-perfect consistency. In Alfano (2013, p. 31), I argue that the distinction between perfect and imperfect duties isn't the right way to sort virtues. For one thing, it's a categorical distinction, but intuitively the level of consistency required by a given virtue is on a sliding scale. For instance, you could reliably fail to do the creative thing when the opportunity arises, but still qualify as creative if you do so often enough; creativity is hard to muster up, even for remarkable individuals. Virtues seem to be distributed along a dimension between very low-fidelity traits like creativity through very high-fidelity traits like chastity. Low-fidelity virtues include (I suggest) charity, diligence, friendliness, generosity, industriousness, magnanimity, mercy, tact, and tenacity;

high-fidelity virtues include chastity, fairness, honesty, justice, and trustworthiness.[14]

Fleeson (2001) and Fleeson & Gallagher (2009) provide highly suggestive evidence that most people's patterns of behavior are, though predictable, at best candidates for low- or medium-fidelity traits (virtues, vices, or neither). Some traits predict extremely important and valuable long-term outcomes. For example, people who score low in Propriety – a dimension of the "Big Six" personality model formulated by Saucier (2009) – are much more likely to, at least once in their lives, engage in such morally questionable behaviors as drunk driving, bar brawls, shoplifting, vehicle theft, assault, and delinquent gang activity (Simms 2007). Along these lines, Jayawickreme et al. (2014) and Noftle & Fleeson (2010) contend that the Agreeableness and Conscientiousness dimensions of the "Big Five" personality model are associated with such low-fidelity virtues as compassion, prudence, and reliability.[15]

While these considerations hardly establish extreme personism, they do show that any plausible theory of human behavior – including moral behavior – must make significant room for the influence of personality. In addition to this positive evidence for personism, there is also evidence against (extreme) situationism. The most compelling is a *tu quoque* response to Mischel's (1968) demonstration, which I discussed above, that personality measures tend to correlate with measures of individual behaviors at best around .30. Funder & Ozer (1983) showed that correlations between situational factors (e.g., presence of bystanders, as in the studies discussed above) and particular behaviors tend not to be much greater than .30. In other words, just as situationists showed that knowing someone's traits isn't enough, on its own, to explain and predict their particular behaviors, so personists showed that knowing someone's situation isn't enough, on its own, to explain and predict their behaviors.[16]

3.6 Interactionism and factitious virtue

Where does this leave us? The most plausible alternative to both extreme personism and extreme situationism is interactionism. Personality and context both contribute to the explanation and prediction of behavior – including moral behavior. And they often do so in a nonlinear way, as I explained in section 3.2 above. This suggests that character should be recast in interactionist terms, as partly due to features of the agent, partly due to features of the situation, and partly due to the interaction between the two.

For instance, there is suggestive empirical evidence – much of which I canvass in my (2013) book – for the phenomenon of *factitious* virtue. A factitious virtue simulates its neo-Aristotelian counterpart through the stabilizing influences of self-concept and social expectation-signaling. Someone may not be disposed to think, feel, and act as a generous person would think, feel, and act *except insofar* as she both thinks of herself as generous (self-concept) and knows both that others think of her as generous and that they know that she knows that they think of her as generous (social expectation-signaling).[17] When this happens, she does not have the trait of generosity construed in neo-Aristotelian terms, but she does have factitious generosity.

This dialectical conception of virtue fits nicely into the framework developed by Darley and Fazio (1980, p. 868; see also Cantor & Kihlstrom 1987), which I quote at length:

(1) Either because of past observations of the other or because of the categories into which he or she has encoded the other, a perceiver develops a set of expectancies about a target person. (2) The perceiver then acts toward the target person in a way that is in accord with his or her expectations of the target person. (3) Next, the target interprets the meaning of the perceiver's action. (4) Based on the interpretation, the target responds to the perceiver's action, and (5) the perceiver interprets the target's action. At this point, the perceiver again acts toward the target person and so can be regarded as reentering the interaction sequence loop at Step 2. … After acting toward the perceiver, the target person interprets the meaning of his or her own action. Ordinarily, of course, the interpretation will be that the action was the appropriate one and was "caused" by the perceiver's action to which it was the response. However, other possibilities do exist. From his or her action, the individual may infer something new about himself or herself. As a result, the individual's self-concept may be modified.[18]

This framework for understanding the virtues partially offloads them onto the environment. If someone is disposed to think, feel, and act generously, that will be explained not only by reference to narrow features of herself but also to features of her social context, which interact with her personality (especially her identity or self-concept[19]) through ongoing feedback loops.

Naturally, self-fulfilling and self-sustaining prophecies are not the only way in which character is developed and manifested. Recent work by Lee Jussim (1991) on the "reflection-construction model" suggests that, while such effects do have a real and important influence on behavior, they must be understood in the context of other drivers of behavior, such as personality traits traditionally conceived and stray situational pressures (for instance, as described in the DIAMONDS model), as well as other strategies, such as situation-selection (choosing to be in environments that draw out one's strengths), specialization (developing one's strengths over time), and situation-manipulation (designing one's environment to make it a more congenial niche). These sources of influence fit with the more distal models of control discussed in chapters 2 and 3.

4 Philosophical implications of personality and social psychology

What does this interactionist approach to character mean for the moral psychology of character?

4.1 *Implications for agency*

Executive virtues such as courage, prudence, and grit enhance their bearer's agency. Executive vices such as cowardice, imprudence, and fecklessness undermine it. If the interactionist, factitious approach to executive virtues is on the right track, then your agency might better be enhanced by fine-tuning your self-concept and the social expectations directed at you. If you think of yourself as hard-working and industrious, and you know that other people think of you as hard-working and industrious, that may be more of an inducement to action than trying to habituate yourself – as neo-Aristotelians would recommend.[20] I say "if" because we currently lack evidence one way or the other about which virtues are characterized by the factitious, interactionist framework. There is some evidence that it works for tidiness (Miller et al. 1975), charity (Jensen & Moore 1977), cooperativeness and competitiveness (Grusec et al. 1978), helpfulness (Grusec & Redler 1980), eco-friendliness (Cornelissen et al. 2006), and scholastic motivation (Rist 1973; Spitz

1999). These are all substantive rather than executive virtues. Clarkson et al. (2010) found that telling people that they *currently* had or lacked self-control produced a self-confirming effect. To date, no one has investigated whether attributing self-control as a trait rather than a state has the same effect, a stronger effect, or something else. It would be unsurprising, though, if attributions of executive virtues did function, like attributions of substantive virtues, as self-fulfilling prophecies.

4.2 Implications for patiency

If virtue involves, among other things, the emotions one feels and is disposed to feel, then the interactionist, factitious approach to virtue forces us to pay special attention to emotional contagion and what I called, in the previous chapter, emotional ping-pong. Which emotions you're disposed to feel, to what degree, toward which objects, and so on are a function of (among other things) the emotions signaled by those around you, especially people who are part of your in-group. This does not mean that you always and only mechanically re-express whatever emotions you perceive, but it does mean that your emotional dispositions are partly determined by what goes on in your social environment. And, of course, it also means that how others are disposed to react emotionally is in part a function of how you emote.

4.3 Implications for temporality, reflexivity, and sociality

The implications for agency and patiency point us toward the implications for temporality, reflexivity, and – most importantly – sociality. After all, if your agency is enhanced or undermined by ongoing social influences, then it's partially a function of temporality and sociality. And if the degree to which you embody virtuous patiency is partially determined by the emotional signals sent to you by other people, especially by your close associates, then once again it's partially a function of sociality.

There's much more to be said than I can squeeze into these pages, so I'll limit myself to one paragraph about each moral psychological concept. Regarding temporality, the interactionist, factitious approach to virtue suggests a different method of acquisition from the orthodox Aristotelian model. According to Aristotle and neo-Aristotelians, virtue-acquisition takes time, and the *reason* it takes time is that becoming virtuous requires continuous practice and habituation. For the majority of virtues, this was never particularly plausible. Habituation involves systematically putting oneself in, or allowing others to put one in, ever more challenging situations that require acting skillfully from or in accordance with the habit to be acquired. For instance, habituating oneself to shooting field goals in basketball involves systematically putting oneself in a position to attempt shooting free throws from different parts of the court, with different reaction times and obstructions. Becoming habituated to honesty, on this model, would involve systematically putting oneself in a position to feel and overcome a wide variety of temptations to dishonesty that involve different reaction times and moral obstructions. Has anyone ever done this? Successfully? If they did, was it a good idea? I think not. I would suggest instead that, typically, virtues (or at least factitious virtues) are acquired over time not through habituation but through social signaling and the entrenchment of self-concept. In other words, you become honest by becoming more and more certain that other people see you as honest, and knowing that you are certain of that, and knowing that you know that they know that you are certain of that. And you become honest by becoming more and more certain that you are honest, and knowing that you're certain, and knowing that you know that you're certain.

It might seem that this criticism of the traditional method of virtue cultivation misses the mark because it caricatures the account of habituation. After all, someone who is cultivating, for example, honesty, is bound to encounter plenty of circumstances in which honesty is called for even if she doesn't seek them out. This rejoinder fails to distinguish two importantly different kinds of virtue: those for which it is contrary to the virtue to want to encounter the virtue's eliciting conditions and those for which it is not contrary to the virtue to want to encounter its eliciting conditions. The eliciting condition for courage is danger or threat, but the courageous person does not want there to be threats and does not unnecessarily seek them out. The eliciting condition for honesty is the temptation to lie, cheat, or steal, but the honest person does not seek out such temptations. By contrast, the eliciting condition for generosity is having resources that could benefit another person; there is nothing inconsistent about the generous person's seeking out such conditions. And here's the rub: virtue is meant to be a form of moral expertise, and both Aristotelian virtue theory and contemporary research on the acquisition of expertise (e.g., Ericsson et al. 1993; Ericsson & Lehmann 1996; Feltovich et al. 2006) agree that expertise is acquired only through reliable feedback, deliberate practice, concentration, and effective metacognition. If someone encounters threats only in a haphazard way, without deliberately practicing at responding to them with the aid of reliable, real-time feedback, there's little reason to think that they will acquire the expertise involved in courage. If someone encounters temptations to lie, cheat, and steal only in a haphazard way, without deliberately practicing at responding to them with the aid of reliable, real-time feedback, there's little reason to think they will acquire the expertise involved in honesty. Such deliberate, guided practice might be possible for traits like generosity, but it's hard to imagine how it would be implemented for courage and honesty, let alone chastity (assuming that chastity is a virtue).

Regarding reflexivity, the main implication has to do with self-concept. According to an intuitive, Aristotelian conception of character, you're first disposed to think, feel, and do certain things, and then you realize – to some extent or other – that that's how you're disposed to think, feel, and act. The factitious virtue model flips this around. Instead of thinking that you're, for instance, loyal *because you are* loyal, you're loyal *because you think so*. Without thinking of yourself in a certain way (and caring about how others think of you and what they expect of you), you can't be factitiously loyal.

Finally, there are clear and important implications for sociality. On the factitious virtue model, virtue inheres "in the interstices between the person and her world. The object that possesses the virtue [is] a functionally and physically extended complex comprising the agent, her social setting, and her asocial environment" (Alfano 2013, p. 185; see also Wong 2014). As I mentioned above, there is indirect support for this view from one-off studies of particular behaviors and even patterns of behaviors over the short term. It's difficult (and expensive and time-consuming) to study this kind of interaction longitudinally, as it ought to be investigated. Although *virtue* has not been considered in exactly this way, *being a supportive romantic partner* has.[21] In one astonishing study, Srivastava et al. (2006) found that the trait-optimism of one partner in a dating relationship had important and positive effects in the short term and also after an entire year. People who scored high in optimism and partners of such people reported greater support from their partner. People who scored high in optimism and partners of such people reported greater satisfaction with their relationship. People who scored high in optimism and partners of such people saw themselves and each other as more positively engaged during conflicts. People who scored high in optimism and partners of such people reported that conflicts were better resolved a week after talking about it in the experimenters' lab. Relationships involving male optimists were more likely to survive after a year than those involving male pessimists. Most impressive of all, these effects were multiply mediated: optimists and their partners resolved their conflicts more successfully *because* they engaged in them more positively; they engaged more positively *because* they perceived greater support; and they perceived greater support *because* at least one of them was optimistic.[22]

This study dealt with romantic relationships, but the variable that supplied the "glue" for the relationship had nothing to do with romance: what mattered were optimism and perceived support, which are of course relevant to parent–child relationships and friendships just as much as to romantic partnerships.[23]

5 Future directions in the moral psychology of character

Of all the moral psychological themes covered thus far in this book, character is the most difficult to study and the most complicated. This is because character involves all the other themes. What sort of person you are is in part a function of what you prefer and disprefer (chapter 1). What sort of person you are is in part a function of how you handle your responsibilities and take control of yourself and your situation (chapter 2). What sort of person you are is in part a function of the emotions you're disposed to feel, toward whom you're disposed to feel them, how intensely you're disposed to feel them, and so on (chapter 3). What sort of person you are depends on all of these things not just in the short term but in the long term, making character much more difficult, time-consuming, and expensive to study well. Character is – if interactionism and the factitious virtue model are on the right track – constitutively social, making it much harder to study in a controlled way. On the one hand, this all means that any conclusions we might want to draw about character will be even more tentative than conclusions we might draw about other moral psychological phenomena. On the other hand, it also means that there is a lot of room for creative speculation and collaboration between philosophers, psychologists, and others.

Further readings

Annas, J. (2009). *Intelligent Virtue*. Oxford University Press.
Battaly, H. (2015). *Virtue*. Cambridge: Polity.
Doris, J. (2015). *Talking To Ourselves: Reflection, Ignorance, and Agency*. Oxford University Press.
Miller, C. (2013). *Moral Character: An Empirical Theory*. Oxford University Press.
Onoda, H. (1999). *No Surrender: My Thirty-Three Year War*. Annapolis, MD: Naval Institute Press.
Ross, L. & Nisbett, R. (1991). *The Person and the Situation*. Cambridge University Press.
Zagzebski, L. (1996). *Virtues of the Mind*. Oxford University Press.

Study questions

1 Is it easier to tell that someone has bad character than that they have good character? Why?
2 If one person's virtue constitutively depends on another person, then the former bears less responsibility while the latter bears more responsibility for that trait. Does this raise or lower the moral standards for virtue?
3 Which provides better evidence about someone's character – ordinary circumstances or extraordinary circumstances? Why?
4 If it turned out that being virtuous was extremely difficult for everyone and impossible for some, would that be a problem for virtue theory? Why?
5 Which matters more when deciding whether someone has a particular virtue – their behavior or their internal states (emotions, beliefs, desires, perceptions)? Why?
6 Does it ever make sense to seek out situations that challenge your own virtue? If yes, when? If not, why not?
7 Are there some virtues that are only appropriate for certain types of people, depending on (for instance) their gender, age, culture, social position, and so on? If yes, which? If no, why not?

5

Disagreement

1 Introduction

In the *Histories*, Herodotus recounts an anecdote about Darius, the emperor of the Persia. Darius's empire spanned much of modern-day Iran, Iraq, Syria, Jordan, Lebanon, Israel, Palestine, Turkey, and Greece, making it both enormous and multicultural. According to Herodotus, Darius summoned some of the Greeks in his court and asked the price they would put on eating their fathers' bodies at death. Appalled, they responded that there was no sum large enough.[1] Greek custom at the time was to burn the dead, so such an act struck them as colossally wrong. While the Greeks watched, Darius then summoned some of the Indians in his court and asked the price they would put on burning their fathers at death. They too responded that there was no sum large enough. Among this group, the custom was to eat parents after death, so burning them instead struck them as colossally wrong. Evaluating this vignette, Herodotus remarks that the poet Pindar was right to say that "custom is king of all."

Contemporary moral disagreements across cultures may be about different topics, but the strength and depth of them doesn't seem to have diminished since the sixth century BCE. Dominant strands of Judaism hold that it is a moral violation to eat shellfish, to work on the Sabbath, or to fail to live in a hut constructed out of unprocessed vegetable matter during the week of Sukkoth. A contemporary secular atheist might find these prohibitions not only pointless but incomprehensible.

Supporters of "open-carry" firearm policies believe that it is a gross moral (and legal) violation of their rights to deny them access and permission to powerful firearms. For instance, when this book was written, the AR-15 was a popular rifle. The AR-15's capacity is 30 rounds, which can be fired off as quickly as the shooter can pull the trigger. It can be outfitted with a laser target-finder, sniper sight, and grenade launcher. Some politically libertarian Americans think not only that they should have access to such weaponry, but also that it is important for them to exercise that right by carrying their fully loaded AR-15s in shopping malls, grocery stores, and other public places. Mass murderers such as Adam Lanza, who in 2012 killed his own mother, twenty elementary schoolchildren, six teachers, and himself, also seem to have an affinity for the AR-15 and guns like it. Such outrages have led other Americans to think that possessing and brandishing weapons like the AR-15 is morally repugnant. Many others are ambivalent, wishing both that people who want to carry guns responsibly be allowed to do so and that such powerful weaponry not fall into the "wrong hands."

What are we to make of such seemingly intractable moral disagreements? Ordinarily, when two people disagree, at most one of them is right. If X says that the speed of light in a vacuum is 299,792,458 meters per second but Y says that it's 302,970,234 meters per second, they can't both be right. (In this case, X is right and Y is wrong.) If X says that there are 15 ounces in a pound but Y says that there are 17, they can't both be right. (In this case, they're both wrong: there are 16 ounces in a pound.) Are moral disagreements the same way? Darius's Greek courtiers said that it was morally repellent even to contemplate eating their parents, and his Indian courtiers said that it was repellent even to contemplate *not* eating their parents. Must it be the case that at least one group was wrong? Open-carry enthusiasts believe that it's morally good to walk around in public armed to the teeth, but gun-control advocates believe that it's morally repugnant to do so. Must at least one group be wrong?

An answer to such questions that's become more common in at least some swaths of North America and Western Europe is: no, they can both be right (or at least, not-wrong). Another is: they're neither right nor wrong; it's just a matter of taste or preference. A third is: it would be intolerant to say that another person's or group's moral beliefs are wrong. A fourth: it would be disrespectful to say that another person's or group's moral beliefs are wrong.

(Note that the last two responses are refusals to answer the question, not negative answers.)

Against this, an increasingly common view among philosophers is: *of course* at least one of them must be wrong. After all, if they *disagree*, then there must be some proposition about which they disagree. That proposition is either true or false. If it's true, then the person or group that says it's true is right and the other person or group is wrong. If it's false, then the person or group that says it's false is right and the other person or group is wrong.

This debate quickly takes us deep into a thicket of thorny problems involving psychology, sociology, anthropology, politics, applied ethics, normative ethics, and metaethics. In the opening section of this chapter, I lay out some of the key distinctions and questions. In the remainder of the chapter, I will survey some of the relevant scientific evidence and offer an interpretation of it. Unfortunately, my main conclusion will be that we do not know how much and how deeply different people and cultures disagree, and, moreover, that perhaps we *cannot* know, given the conceptual, empirical, and moral difficulties associated with investigating moral disagreement.

1.1 Retrospective interlude

As this book has progressed, we've gradually expanded our empirical, social, and temporal scales. Preferences are largely a matter of how an individual person is disposed to think, feel, act, and evaluate at a particular moment (though when they're shaped by choice blindness, they take on a social dimension, as we saw in chapter 1). They can be studied using highly controlled experiments. Responsibility can be toward oneself or one's future self, but it can also be toward other people – sometimes right now, sometimes (as I argued in chapter 2) more distally. The control and knowledge required for responsibility can be studied in the laboratory, but they must also be observed in the wild over longer periods. Through their signaling function, emotions are essentially social; furthermore, they involve attitudes and evaluations directed both at the past (e.g., remorse) and the future (e.g., hope). They can be studied in the lab, but must also be observed in the life of an individual moral agent and in whole moral communities, which are partially constituted by the joint and empathic emotional dispositions – such as trust – of their members. Character develops and plays out over time. Because it involves a disposition to engage in particular patterns of behavior, it can't easily be studied in the lab (though that doesn't mean it can't be studied at all). If my arguments in the previous chapter were on the right track, it is also essentially social, making it even harder to isolate in controlled experiments (though not impossible, as Srivastava et al. 2006 showed).

Disagreement continues this trend. Two individuals can agree, but many of the arguments in this domain also concern disagreement across *cultures*, not single individuals. Such disagreement is often between linguistic communities (e.g., the Greeks and the Indians in Darius's court) or between groups with distinct linguistic practices (e.g., southerners in the USA, who tend to be more supportive of gun rights, and their northern counterparts). Thus, in addition to the many obstacles to empirical investigation already discussed, we have to face the surprisingly difficult problem of translation. After all, if one group says that it's wrong to do something they call "Xing" and another group says that it's not wrong to do something they call "Ying", they only disagree if "Xing" in the first group's language correctly translates to "Ying" in the other's (and if "Ying" in the second group's language translates to "Xing" in the first group's). Even within a natural language, individual people can use the same term in different ways. For instance, in some parts of the United States, "Coke" refers to any carbonated soft drink, including not only Coca-Cola, but also Pepsi. If one person says of a beverage, "This is a Coke," and another says, "This is not a Coke," they might disagree, but they might not. Suppose the drink under discussion is a Pepsi. If the first person uses "Coke" to refer to any carbonated soft drink and the latter uses it to refer only to classic Coca-Cola, then they don't disagree, even though it might seem at first blush that they do. Apparent moral disagreements might involve such issues of translation.

It's very difficult to study culture experimentally. A truly experimental investigation would involve randomly assigning people to be enculturated in different ways, then testing how such assignment influenced their moral values, judgments, behavior, beliefs, and so on. Arguably, even a wildly unethical experiment involving randomization to culture would not do the job, since cultures always have histories, communities, and enemies (e.g., arguably, part of what it means to be Irish is resenting English colonization and genocide). To study culture experimentally, one would have to randomly assign people to groups of various sizes, enculturate them into those groups, randomize the groups to engage and clash with one another in particular ways, and so on. For obvious reasons, no one does this. Instead, we have to rest content with halfway measures (e.g., priming bicultural participants with one or the other of their two cultures, as in Luna et al. 2008) and correlational studies.

The best that scientists can do now – and perhaps ever – is to try to plausibly operationalize cultural belonging, then measure its relation to other variables of interest in the wild and during the "natural experiments" afforded by historical contingency. It may not be perfect, but it's not nothing either.

2 The role of disagreement in moral psychology

In this section, I first briefly describe the history of scientific and quasi-scientific investigations of moral disagreement in anthropology and philosophy. I then explore some relevant methodological issues. Because they are so densely intertwined in this context, I will not try here to separate issues related to agency, patiency, sociality, temporality, and reflexivity into distinct subsections.

2.1 Cultural anthropology of disagreement

People have long been fascinated with moral differences. Herodotus chronicled a series of bizarre practices many of which his readers would have found immoral, and philosophers such as Sextus Empiricus attempted to draw philosophical inferences (in Sextus's case, skeptical ones) from such reports. Enlightenment thinkers such as Hume, Locke, and Montaigne discussed cases of apparent moral disagreement as well. More serious investigations of moral differences came with the birth of cultural anthropology as a distinct discipline around the beginning of the twentieth century, especially under the influence of Finnish philosopher, sociologist, and anthropologist Edward Westermarck (1906/1932; 1932), American sociologist William Graham Sumner (1907), and American anthropologist Franz Boas (1955), along with his students, including Ruth Benedict (1959), Melville Herskovits (1964; 1972), and Margaret Mead (1928/1961).

These twentieth-century thinkers for the most part advocated what came to be known as descriptive (cultural, ethical, or moral) relativism. The boundaries and distinctions among the variously named theories were often vague or imprecise, and the connections between them and the empirical data were not always strong or even real.[2] By the middle of the century, philosophers had begun to engage the issues, taking a more cautious and nuanced approach. Two in particular, Richard Brandt (1954) and John Ladd (1957), did their own significant philosophico-anthropological fieldwork among Hopi and Navaho Native Americans communities, respectively.

In addition, Alasdair MacIntyre's *A Short History of Ethics* (1998), while not based on experimental research, arguably bears mention as a work in which the author attempted to treat the history of ethics from a perspective that combined philosophical discussions with an informed perspective on history proper. MacIntyre's subsequent work, along with that of others such as Martha Nussbaum (2001) and Taylor (1992), continued this trend to view the history of morality through the twin lenses of philosophical work and empirical scholarship on history. J. L. Mackie (1977) drew an antirealist (he called it *skeptical*) conclusion about morality based on abductive inference from vaguely referenced anthropological knowledge with a brief but influential discussion of "the argument from relativity." A few years later, naturalist moral realist Nicholas Sturgeon began his seminal paper, "Moral Explanations" (1988) by pointing to his respect for the argument from moral disagreement and his recognition that it could be resolved only through "piecemeal" and "frustratingly indecisive" *a posteriori* inquiry. These sentiments were echoed a decade later by antirealist Don Loeb (1998), who described a version of the argument that proceeded by way of an inference from irresolvable moral disagreement – what Brandt (1967) called fundamental disagreement – to the inference that we lack moral knowledge. If our apparent knowledge of morality is our best (or even our only) reason for believing it to be a realm of fact, then an argument for moral skepticism is also indirectly an argument for moral antirealism, he claimed, since it is not epistemically responsible to believe in things for which we lack good evidence. The question, he thought, was *how much* moral disagreement (and agreement, for that matter) would remain if various explanatory alternatives were exhausted. Brian Leiter (2014), drawing on remarks by Friedrich Nietzsche, makes a similar argument based on disagreement not across cultures, but between alleged moral experts (moral philosophers).

In an important paper, John Doris and Alexandra Plakias (2008) turned their attention to the question Loeb had posed, referring to the alternative explanatory strategies mentioned by Loeb and others as *defusing* explanations. Doris and Plakias considered an experiment suggesting that a so-called "culture of honor" is much more prevalent in the Southern United States than in the North, and described an unpublished study that suggested that East Asians react differently to "magistrate and the mob" scenarios than do Westerners. In both cases, they argued, no good defusing explanation for the moral disagreement seems available, and thus this evidence seems to support moral antirealism.[3] In the remainder of this chapter, I cast a critical eye on such arguments.

2.2 Sweet charity

As I mentioned above, translation and interpretation across and even within languages makes it difficult to know whether people genuinely disagree about anything, be it morality or other matters. Following in the path paved by Quine (1960) and Davidson (2001b), philosophers who investigate moral disagreement, such as Moody-Adams (1997) and David Wong (2006), have argued that much apparent moral disagreement evaporates or is at least understandable when people's moral utterances and beliefs are interpreted charitably.[4] Just as it would be uncharitable to treat the person who says "This is a Coke" as disagreeing with the person who says "This is not a Coke" if they use the word "Coke" differently, so it would be uncharitable to treat the person who says "Xing is morally wrong" as disagreeing with the person who says "Xing is not morally wrong" if they use the word "Xing" (or '"morally" or "wrong") differently.

The basic idea here is that, in interpreting the utterances of another person, we are obligated to apply a **principle of charity**.[5] Early discussions of the principle of charity treated it as monolithic, involving in the first instance an attempt to render true as many as possible of another person's utterances. If you pour me a Pepsi while remarking, "Here's a Coke for you," the charitable interpretation is that you are not lying or making a mistake, but that you use the word differently. When reconstruing the intended reference of terms doesn't do the trick, the charitable interpreter is enjoined to attribute only errors that make sense from the speaker's point of view, given best guesses about her perceptual and cognitive capabilities. People do make mistakes, after all, but they tend not to make obvious mistakes such as directly contradicting themselves or claiming to use a word in one way when in fact they use it in a very different way. Further reflection on the nuances and competing desiderata involved in charitable interpretation led David Rosenthal (2009) to distinguish three potentially competing levels at which to apply the principle of charity: reference, truth, and consistency. At the level of reference, you attempt to interpret someone who seems to be speaking the same language as you as using words to refer in the same way that you do. At the level of truth, you attempt to interpret someone who seems to be speaking the same language as you as saying things that are true (by your lights). As we've already seen, these injunctions can conflict. When someone says of a Pepsi, "This is a Coke," you have to choose whether to interpret them as using the word in the same way that you would but saying something manifestly false, or as using the word in a way you would not but saying something true.

Rosenthal points out that there is a third level at which charity can be applied: consistency. People's remarks are typically not just a catalogue of randomly selected assertions they consider true. They say things like "so," "therefore," "but, "hence," "on the other hand," "if...then...," "however," and so on. Such logical and quasi-logical connectives indicate the inferential relations the speaker takes to hold among the things she's saying. Someone who says "BLAH, so BLERG," doesn't just assert that "BLAH" and "BLERG" are true; she indicates that BLERG *follows from* BLAH (deductively, inductively, or abductively). Someone who says "BLAH, but BLERG," doesn't just assert that "BLAH" and "BLERG" are true; she indicates that this is surprising, perhaps because BLAH makes it less likely that BLERG. Suppose someone says, "I have Pepsi and rum, so I can make you a rum and Coke." She's indicating that she thinks that it *follows* from the fact that she has Pepsi and rum that she can make a rum and Coke. Does it? If you interpret her use of the phrase "rum and Coke" compositionally, such that the meaning of the larger phrase is determined by the meanings of the words that make it up, it might seem that she's making a mistake. Here, reference is pitted against both truth and consistency. Probably the most charitable interpretation (and one that most people would make automatically and intuitively, without conscious reasoning) is that by "rum and Coke" she means something like *rum and Coke-or-other-similar-soft-drink*. Responding, "No you can't; you can only make me a rum and Pepsi" would be at best a fatuous and obnoxious joke.

More generally, even when someone isn't indicating explicitly the inferential relations she takes to hold among her remarks, it's generally charitable to interpret her as saying things that are relevant to and consistent with each other, or at least aren't obviously irrelevant and inconsistent. Suppose that someone says, "Einstein failed high school physics. The greatest physics genius of the twentieth century started off as a failure in his own discipline." In this case, truth is pitted against reference and consistency. Despite the oddly persistent myth, Albert Einstein was an outstanding student of physics in high school. Simple truth-maximizing charity would force the interpreter to render both claims made by the speaker as true, and hence to reconstrue the speaker's use of "Einstein" (or "fail") as highly non-standard. Alternatively, the interpreter could construe the speaker as using the definite description "the greatest physics genius of the twentieth century" to refer to someone other than Einstein. A better and more charitable interpretation is that the speaker uses terms in the usual way and has consistent beliefs, but that her beliefs are simply and straightforwardly mistaken.

Rosenthal's development of the principle of charity was intended to aid in charitable interpretation of utterances generally, not specifically to help adjudicate alleged moral disagreement. Moody-Adams (1997) and Wong (2006) have argued that, especially when dealing with moral disagreements, a fourth level at which charity should be applied is *valuation*. Not only should the interpreter try to render the speaker's words as having their usual meaning and reference; not only should the interpreter try to render the speaker's claims as true; not only should the interpreter try to render closely connected utterances as logically consistent and relevant to one another; in addition, the interpreter should try to render the other's speech (and action) as motivated by familiar or at least understandable values.

Wong points out that making sense of other people isn't done in a hermetically sealed doxastic vacuum. As I pointed out in chapter 1, we tend (rightly) to assume that people typically act in such a way as to bring about the best outcome they think they can achieve, and to offer reasons that support undertaking the actions they are in fact disposed to perform. This involves imputing not only beliefs but also desires, values, and intentions. In Wong's words:

> To make sense of the actions of others, we construe these actions as stemming from intentions, which in turn stem from certain patterns of beliefs, desires, and values. Some patterns

make others intelligible to us, and others don't. However, such ways of making sense of others do not prevent us from attributing to them some desires, values, and intentions that are different from ours. (2006, p. 14)

Moody-Adams sails closer to the wind, arguing that

a judgment or belief can be a moral judgment or belief only if it fits into a complex of beliefs and judgments that, to a substantial degree, resemble one's own moral beliefs and judgments. The interpretation of unfamiliar moral practices is possible only because "ultimate" or "fundamental" moral disagreement is not. (1997, pp. 55–6)

The basic point here is that if another person's actions and utterances are sufficiently different from the interpreter's moral actions and judgments, the interpreter has no reason to treat them as *moral* in the first place. As David Cooper (1978) has argued, if another person's allegedly moral belief or value has nothing to do with welfare, happiness, suffering, security, the good life, and perhaps a few other phenomena, there seems to be no reason to construe it as moral. In a different context, Adam Morton (2004) argues that – despite our self-serving and self-righteous protestations to the contrary – we can understand the actions even of evil people such as Adolf Eichmann and Hannibal Lecter as springing from beliefs, desires, values, and emotions not all that different from our own.

Exactly how aggressively to push this line of argument is a tricky question. Moody-Adams seems a bit quick in inferring *a priori* that charity rules out the very possibility of ultimate or fundamental disagreement. Empirical investigation might yield that conclusion as an *a posteriori* inductive or abductive result of many, many successful interpretations of past and present cultures' values. I'll argue in the remainder of this chapter that we lack the evidence to say one way or the other whether Moody-Adams or Wong is correct. Wong seems to be confident that anthropological and philosophical investigations have already substantiated that, while there is a great deal of substantial agreement across cultures, there are unresolvable disagreements about exactly how much weight to give to different fundamental values, such as freedom, security, social cohesion, and so on.

2.3 Shallows and depths of disagreement

The discussion has gotten a bit ahead of itself. Moody-Adams claims that there can be no fundamental moral disagreements. Wong claims there can, but not too many. Cultural anthropologists and philosophers impressed by anthropologists' findings claim not only that there can be such disagreements but also that they're common. The disputants are using the same words, but are they using them in the same way? Charity is needed in understanding philosophical (dis)agreement too. As we've seen, Moody-Adams and Wong follow Brandt (1967, p. 76) in distinguishing fundamental from non-fundamental moral disagreement. We can help adjudicate this dispute by assessing moral agreements on three dimensions: *psychological depth, modal robustness,* and *defusability*.

Start with defusability. To defuse a disagreement is to show that at least one party to the disagreement is not arguing in good faith or is otherwise suspect. According to Brandt (1967), a fundamental moral disagreement between two people occurs only when they attribute all and only the same non-moral properties to an action, person, principle, or value, but attribute opposed moral properties (e.g., permissibility and impermissibility, goodness and badness, courage and cowardice). If this condition does not hold, Brandt plausibly argues, any apparent moral disagreement might simply be an upshot of underlying non-moral disagreement. To this already quite stringent requirement, other philosophers have added further conditions on fundamentality. Sturgeon (1988) and Moody-Adams (1997, p. 101) correctly point out that beneficiaries of oppression find it immensely easy to fail to notice or appreciate the suffering of the people whose oppression redounds, however indirectly, to their benefit. If a particular disagreement is explicable in terms of at least one of the party's self-serving (potentially affected) ignorance, once again we do not have a case of fundamental disagreement. If social dominance theory (Sidanius & Pratto 1999; Pratto & Stewart 2012) is on the right track – and it certainly seems that it is – then such defusing explanations of moral disagreements are bound to be common. Finally, Shafer-Landau (1994, p. 331; 2003, p. 218) has argued that if either of the parties to the disagreement is being irrational by allowing an emotional response to influence their judgment, the disagreement is not fundamental. As stated, this criterion is harder to accept, especially in light of the discussion of emotions in chapter 3. *Pace*

Greene and Shafer-Landau, emotions are often rational responses. Moreover, disqualifying all emotional reactions as somehow automatically morally irrelevant is unmotivated. That said, we can sometimes tell that someone is being irrational. When they are, it seems reasonable not to count any disagreement they're party to as fundamental.

Next, consider robustness. Suppose you've mixed up Costa Rica and Panama, and so you think that Panama is an island. You nevertheless remember that there is such a thing as the Panama Canal. I, by contrast, happen not to have mixed them up. We agree that Panama has a canal through it, but you think it's an island while I think it's an isthmus. Your other beliefs about Panama are, let's stipulate, all correct, as are mine. It's not in your interest to think that Panama is an island, nor are you irrational (though you are mistaken) to think it's an island. Everyone makes mistakes of memory. Jumping directly to impugning someone's rationality simply because they've innocently mixed up a couple of countries is too extreme. In this example, we have a disagreement that looks fundamental by the criteria just discussed. We agree about all other relevant properties of Panama. Neither of us gains by holding onto our positions. And neither of us is being irrational. Our disagreement, though, hardly seems fundamental. Suppose that, were we to find out that we disagreed about Panama's island-hood, I'd say, "But look, you know that Panama has a canal through it. Why would anyone bother to build a canal through an island?" At that point, you'd probably say, "Oh, right. I mixed it up with Costa Rica. Oops." Any disagreement in which one party is disposed, given the right evidence, to back down immediately, shrug, and say "Oops" shouldn't count as fundamental. Fundamental disagreement needs to be *modally robust*.

How robust? There is a spectrum of relevant options. At the weak end of the spectrum, one party would immediately revise their view after the disagreement became explicit. At the strong end, neither party would back down even after sustained, open-minded, respectful, and meticulous argument by both parties. In between, there are more and less robust disagreements, in which the disagreement isn't argued for very long, one or both of the parties is less than fully open-minded, one or both of the parties isn't fully respectful of the other, or one or both of the parties is less than fully meticulous. Such faults in a disagreement needn't indicate faults in the interlocutors, of course. Life is short. We rarely have the time and energy to follow through with arguments to this extent, preferring either to just go our separate ways, agree to disagree, flip a coin, or impose one party's view more or less forcefully on the other.

It's unclear how close to the modally robust end of the spectrum a disagreement needs to be to count as fundamental. Descriptive cultural relativists are fond of saying that people from very different cultures live in different worlds. For instance, Evans-Pritchard claims that

> were a Zande [a member of a tribe in central Africa] to give up faith in witch-doctorhood he would have to surrender equally his belief in witchcraft and oracles...In this web of belief every strand depends upon every other strand, and a Zande cannot get out of its meshes because this is the only world he knows. (1937/1976, pp. 194–5)

"Cannot" is awfully strong. If this is what it takes, disagreement must be maximally modally robust to count as fundamental. It's unclear whether advocates of fundamental disagreement need Evans-Pritchard to be right, but the closer to full modal robustness disagreements are, the better their case is.

Turn now to psychological depth. I once had a disagreement with someone who insisted that Panama was an island with a canal through it. I walked her through the silliness of building a canal through an island when boats could just sail around it. I showed her the entry for Panama in Wikipedia. I got everyone else who happened to be in the room to say that they agreed with me. She wouldn't budge. Did she live in a different world from me? Were her other beliefs, actions, and values so utterly foreign that she was incomprehensible? Hardly. She had a recalcitrant, idiosyncratic, false belief, but she was otherwise an ordinary person. No one's perfect. If moral disagreements meet the criteria for defusability and modal robustness, they might still resemble this idiosyncratic, peripheral factual disagreement. It would be silly to infer from such evidence that moral disagreements can be fundamental. To count as fundamental, a disagreement should be about something deep. Indeed, the metaphor of being *fundamental*, deriving from the Latin for *foundation*, presupposes exactly this.

We can distinguish several levels of depth: judgments about particular actions, moral heuristics, moral principles, values, and meta-ethical commitments. I'll consider each of these in turn.

Judgments about particular actions. X and Y witness Z, a parent, distributing three treats between his two children. Z gives each child one treat and discards the third. X says that this is wasteful, and therefore wrong. Y says that it's fair, and therefore right.[6] X and Y talk it over meticulously and at length. Each engages respectfully and open-mindedly. X quickly convinces Y that Z's action was wasteful. Y quickly convinces X that Z's action was fair. They agree that wanton wastefulness is generally wrong, as is wanton unfairness. In the end, they continue to disagree about the appropriate all-things-considered judgment about Z's action. Let's stipulate that this is because they place slightly different weights on efficiency and outcome-based distributive justice. Is this a fundamental disagreement? Hardly. Disagreement about particular moral judgments – even if it satisfies the defusability and modal robustness conditions – on its own seems insufficiently deep to count as fundamental.

Moral heuristics. A heuristic is a rule of thumb for decision-making (Gigerenzer 2008). Since we make many moral decisions in a given day, quite quickly and without the opportunity for reflection, we often rely on such heuristics, which are arguably among the system 1 processes discussed in chapter 3. For instance: *Do what feels right. Don't lie. Don't steal. Don't hit people. Don't insult people.* These are of course just heuristics. Sometimes, the morally right thing feels terrible. Sometimes (Kant to the contrary), the right thing is to lie. Sometimes, it would be wrong not to steal. Sometimes striking another person is the only way to prevent a much more serious wrong. Sometimes the best way to cut a bully down to size or provoke someone into rethinking their dogmatism is an insult. As Keynes (1933) put it, "Words ought to be a little wild, for they are the assaults of thoughts on the unthinking." Still, these are exceptions. Generally following heuristics that forbid such actions even if you recognize that there may be exceptions is perfectly rational.

Suppose X and Y disagree about a moral heuristic. X has made a habit of giving a dollar to every panhandler who asks him for money. He reasons that, since he's fairly affluent, it doesn't hurt him to engage in such small acts of kindness. And even if the panhandlers might be better served in other ways or if his money could be put to better use helping someone else, it's unlikely that, all things considered, his small donations will harm them. Y, by contrast, has made a habit of never giving money to panhandlers. She tallies up the times she's asked for money and donates a proportional amount to a political advocacy group that promotes legislation aimed at systematically helping the homeless and preventing homelessness in the first place. She figures that the political advocacy group, even after accounting for its operating costs, will do more good with her donations than would be done by her giving directly to the homeless. X and Y discuss their moral heuristics with each other meticulously and at length. They do so in an open-minded and respectful way. X points out that someone who feels snubbed after asking for money may in turn feel disrespected as a person. He points out that political advocacy groups that aid the homeless sometimes don't do a great job. He points out that it's easy for Y to self-servingly diminish her tally. Y recognizes all of these points. She points out that individual citizens' giving of money to panhandlers makes it easier for the state to shirk its responsibilities. She points out that someone living on the street becomes a target for assault and theft if they're carrying cash. She points out that it's a real possibility that a panhandler will spend donations on drugs that might hurt him rather than on something, like food, that would benefit him. The relevant reasons point in different directions. Both X and Y recognize that the issue is complicated, but also that the monetary sums involved are unlikely to make a substantial difference one way or the other. After talking things through, X insists that the better thing to do is to follow his heuristic. Y disagrees, sticking with her own heuristic. They both realize that following their own heuristic will lead to no small number of mistaken decisions, but they both feel that, on balance, it's the best rule of thumb for a busy person, and that the other should follow it too. Do they fundamentally disagree? Again, it seems clear that they don't.

There's a general conclusion to be drawn here: disagreement about *how to implement* the same or nearly identical values is not fundamental moral disagreement. Consider a variant of the story of Darius from the start of this chapter: suppose that Barack Obama, the current president of the United States (a large, multicultural, imperial power like Darius's Persia) summoned an Englishman and a Frenchwoman to the White House. First, he asked the French-woman how much she would ask to be paid to drive henceforth on the left side of the road. She looked at him in astonishment and said there was no amount great enough. He then asked the Englishman how much he would ask to be paid to drive henceforth on the right side of the road. The Englishman gasped in shock and replied that there was no sum great enough. Obama then summarized the inter-action by remarking that Pindar was right in saying that "custom is king of all." A member of his cabinet then responded, "Oh, grow up. The point is that they don't want to crash into people and get killed." If Emperor Darius had had a courtier who wasn't a sycophant, perhaps he would have heard, "Oh, grow up. The point is that you have to treat your parents' dead bodies respectfully. Some people think that respect entails burning; others think that it entails eating. One or both of them might be wrong, but their disagreement is superficial." What would count as a *deep* or *fundamental* disagreement has to be more profound than this. To have a fundamental moral disagreement, people have to disagree not just about how to implement shared or mostly shared values, but about what's valuable in the first place.

Moral principles. Unlike moral heuristics, moral principles as I understand them in this context are meant to be exceptionless. For this reason, a given person can endorse only a few of them, lest they conflict. Indeed, one might think that having more than one moral principle puts one in a potentially practically inconsistent situation, and that one should therefore endorse at most one principle. Kantians endorse the categorical imperative, the three (or four?) formulations of which are meant to be either consistent or even synonymous. Consequentialists endorse the injunction to produce the best possible consequences. It seems that they disagree. But how much do they really disagree? Their principles point them in the same practical direction in the overwhelming majority of cases. Because their principles are so general, they have to implement them by employing a variety of moral heuristics. In many tricky cases, the deliverances of one or both of their principles will be difficult, if not impossible, to determine. Is that a fundamental disagreement?

Why do they hold to these principles in the first place? If the principles are just different ways of implementing still-deeper shared values, they don't fundamentally disagree. Even if the principles aren't meant to implement shared values, the fact that they almost always point in the same direction makes it hard to see why their disagreement counts as fundamental. This should be unsurprising; after all, ethicists often test their moral principles by whether they agree with common intuitions. If (nominally) distinct moral principles mostly agree, that's probably because they were designed to be consistent with the same or nearly identical sets of moral intuitions.

Things start to get more troubling when people disagree about values as such. Following Tiberius (2008), I understand a value as a relatively robust pro-attitude or con-attitude that the valuer takes to "generate reasons for action and furnish standards for

Figure 5.1 Slightly different weightings of shared values

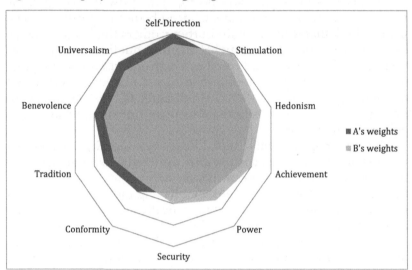

evaluating" how their life is going.[7] People's values can differ in various ways and to various degrees. We've already seen that disagreement about exactly how to weight shared values, as in figure 5.1, generally doesn't constitute a fundamental moral disagreement. Perhaps if the weightings differ wildly, with one person or group giving almost no weight to value V while another person or group gives nearly decisive weight to V (and the defusability and modal robustness conditions are met), that would constitute a fundamental disagreement. It may depend on the details of the case and the extent to which the different weightings simply lead people to go their separate ways or instead lead them to political or violent conflict. The goods promoted and protected by moral values are pretty different from one another. It should therefore come as no surprise that, when forced to put them on a single scale, people come up with different weightings. As Stich (2006) pertly puts it, and as we should expect if my discussion of different emotions in chapter 3 was on the right track, morality is a "kludge."

A more extreme version of disagreement about values involves one person or group valuing V and another person or group giving it no value at all, though both parties to the dispute agree about other values, if not their exact weightings. This is represented in figure 5.2. Such a disagreement would involve not just different

Figure 5.2 Very different weightings of mostly shared values

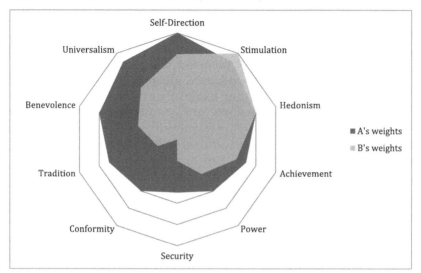

weightings of shared values, but incomprehension by one party of the other party's values. Such a disagreement would probably constitute a fundamental disagreement, though given the injunction to charitably interpret, it would be hard to establish that such a disagreement genuinely held (especially one that met the defusability and modal robustness criteria). Still, even a disagreement this stark might not constitute a fundamental disagreement if it simply led the parties to go their separate ways rather than to engage in practical conflict.

A yet more extreme version of axiological disagreement involves one person or group actively *de*valuing something that's positively valued by the other person or group. Such disputes are harder to find than you might think. For instance, when the Frenchwoman and the Englishman disagree about which side of the road to drive on, it's because they share the deeper values of safety and security. A disagreement of the sort I'm envisioning here would not involve different ways of implementing shared values but outright contradiction in basic values (which therefore can't be represented in the sorts of figures I used above, since they don't have negative axes). One potential example that I've managed to find is this statement from William Donohue, President of the American Catholic League, during an interview on MSNBC:

Hollywood likes anal sex. They like to see the public square without nativity scenes. I like families. I like children. They like abortions. I believe in traditional values and restraint. They believe in libertinism. We have nothing in common.

Even if Donohue is right that there is a disagreement between him and the culture of Hollywood, how deep is that disagreement? Presumably Hollywood, to the extent that it can be said to value anything, doesn't value anal sex and abortion fundamentally, but only as they play a role in loving relationships and women's control over their own bodies. The so-called culture wars in the United States may be a lot shallower than some of their disputants would be inclined to admit. Donohue and his alleged opponents in Hollywood both value deep and longstanding attachments to significant others. They both value love. They both value tradition (though perhaps different traditions or similar traditions construed in different ways). They both value families (though not necessarily families of the same size and configuration). Despite Donohue's claim to the contrary, it's highly unlikely that anyone values abortion as such. It's nearly unimaginable to think that people who believe abortion should be legal and not lead to shaming of a woman who has an abortion think that the more abortions there are, the better. For them, abortion serves a purpose that would have been better served (in terms of pain, hassle, emotional turmoil, termination of potential life, etc.) by prophylactics. In general, when it seems that one person or group intrinsically values V and another person or group intrinsically disvalues V, it's useful to ask whether the disagreement can't be explained in more mundane terms.

The same point holds even more obviously for even starker disagreements in values. Beyond disagreement about a particular value paired with general agreement about other values, disagreement could involve mostly disjoint values (i.e., X's values are mostly unrecognized by or devalued by Y, and Y's values are mostly unrecognized by or devalued by X) or utterly disjoint values (i.e., X's values are all unrecognized by or devalued by Y, and Y's values are all unrecognized by or devalued by X). Such a disagreement is represented in figure 5.3. In the next section, we'll see that there is little reason to believe that such disagreements are common (or even extant, after the defusability and modal robustness criteria are met).

Metaethical commitments. A somewhat quixotic literature has sprung up recently not about first-order folk moral judgments and

Figure 5.3 Completely disjoint values

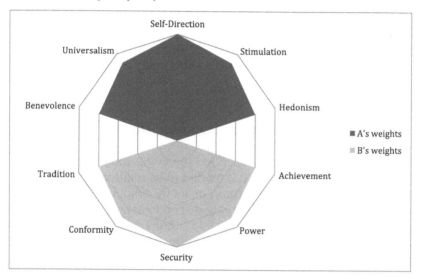

values, but about folk *meta*ethical judgments.[8] The idea here is not to find deep (dis)agreements about what people intrinsically value, how much they value it, or how they balance their various potentially conflicting values, but to explore disagreements about the nature of moral beliefs, judgments, and utterances. It's unclear precisely what such higher-order folk intuitions indicate. In our moral lives, we rarely ascend to meta-disagreement by arguing about what sort of disagreement we're even having, let alone the meta-meta-disagreement or the meta-meta-meta-disagreement sometimes explored in this and related literatures.[9] As should be evident from the previous chapters, I tend to think that we should avoid "going meta" as long as possible, given how much there is to learn just at the first-order level.

3 The science of cross-cultural disagreement

As I described above, prominent cultural anthropology of the last century has tended to support descriptive cultural relativism. Some philosophers have taken anthropologists' summaries and interpretations of their own findings uncritically at face value (e.g., Mackie 1977; Harman 1977). Others, such as Moody-Adams and Wong, have engaged more critically with the science. In addition to anthropology, other disciplines such as sociology, psychology, and behavioral economics have produced interesting and relevant evidence. In this section, I'll briefly critique the anthropological evidence that's typically adduced by those who argue for fundamental moral disagreement. I'll then turn to the other fields, focusing primarily on recent work in psychology.[10]

3.1 Beyond anthropology's synthetic a priori

The anthropological work described so far was mostly from the first half of the twentieth century. It tended to be relativist in orientation – often as a working assumption or methodological principle, not as a result of empirical observation. For instance, Benedict (1934) described the word "morality" as just "a convenient term for socially approved habits." On this understanding, since what's approved in some societies differs from what's approved in others, morality is relative to culture. It's an awfully quick and awfully bad argument. Let's explore some of its flaws.

For one thing, this argument erases even the possibility of moral error. If a society ceases to approve of a habit, the members of the society can't, on Benedict's account, say, "We were wrong to approve of that," even when *that* was chattel slavery, female genital mutilation, coercive pederasty, or hedge fund management.

Second, as Moody-Adams (1997) shows at length, the idea that a society or culture as such can approve or disapprove of anything is highly dubious. Cultures are made up of lots of people. Those people don't necessarily agree with each other about what's worthy of approbation and disapprobation. Talk of disagreement *between* cultures presupposes, though, that there's such a thing as a given culture's values or moral attitudes. Within a given culture, there may be a majority view, but it would be a crude oversimplification to treat the majority view as the voice of the culture. Indeed, one might think that eliminating dissent in this way falsifies the rich moral texture of a culture, which is better conceived as a cacophony of voices rather than a unanimous clarion. As Wong puts it:

> The identity of a culture is in part defined by which values are the most salient and which ones serve as counterpoints to others. A shared culture just is this dynamic configuration of values, but the configuration typically leaves a significant

degree of openness and ambiguity in how conflicts between values are to be resolved. This is one important reason why moral ambivalence exists not only across different moral traditions but also within a single moral tradition. (2006, p. 23)

On this view, what makes a culture the culture it is is (in part) the signature of variance among the culture's members in weightings of different basic values.[11]

Conceiving of culture in this way is superior to thinking of it simply in terms of majority opinion within a group. It's also superior to identifying culture naively with nationality or group membership. Someone can belong to multiple cultures (indeed, many people do). Different nations often share or nearly share cultures. Within a given nation, there are often many cultures and subcultures (as we've already seen in the difference between the America North and South on gun control, and between William Donohue and what he imagines to be the culture of Hollywood).

The myth of unanimous, impenetrable, closed cultures passing one another like ships in the night was more popular in the first half of the twentieth century than the second (or, for that matter, the twenty-first century). That said, some recent anthropologists such as Roy D'Andrade disapprove of the recent trend toward recognition of similarity, overlap, and comprehensibility. In a complaint about the new model of morality in anthropology, he says:

It is strong for equality (the escape from inequality) and freedom (the release from oppression). In my opinion these are not bad values, but they are very American. These are not the predominant values of modern Japan, India, China, the Middle East or Southeast Asia, but they are the predominant values in the United States and much of Europe. It is ironic that these moralists should be so colonialist in their assumptions about what is evil. (1993, p. 408)

As we'll see below, this is an overstatement. It may be that equality and freedom are valued less in, for instance, Singapore than they are in Western Europe, but the difference is nothing like the categorical contrast D'Andrade represents. Many sociologists have approached moral disagreement in the same spirit as the early cultural anthropologists and holdouts like D'Andrade. As Gabriele Abend remarks, typically, "Weberians do not argue for [anti-realism] but just take it for granted, perhaps as a platitude that only unreflective people are unaware of" (2008, p. 94). That notion, too, seems to be changing.

It might seem at this point that I'm dubious of all anthropology (and sociology) or that I'm dismissing the importance and difficulty of negotiating moral difference. Hardly. Anthropology has had an immensely salutary effect for tolerance, but it has often been misinterpreted – especially by philosophers, though anthropologists are partly to blame for making claims that are easily misinterpreted. My contention here is that anthropologists and many of the philosophers who read their work have tended to overplay their hands and over-interpret the evidence in pursuit of the understandable and worthy projects of opposing colonialism, undermining missionary proselytes, and debunking self-serving myths of cultural superiority. One common refrain of those who supported imperial adventures over the decades and centuries has been the idea that "we" are bringing civilization and the one correct morality to "them." This notion goes back at least to the Spanish conquest of South and Central America, and the British conquest of North America, India, and parts of Africa. It characterizes the United States doctrine of Manifest Destiny, which was used to justify and motivate the genocide of Native Americans across the continent. More recently, it's been used to justify and motivate multiple incursions by the United States and Britain into Afghanistan, Iraq, and other countries. I distinctly recall that after the September 11, 2001 terrorist attacks, some of my compatriots said – only half in jest – things like, "Hand over Bin Laden or we'll educate your women!" Many relativists are motivated to destroy such false pretenses for war, conquest, and destruction of other cultures' ways of life. As Geertz (2000, p. 45) puts it, "What the relativists, so-called, want us to worry about is provincialism – the danger that our perceptions will be dulled, our intellects constricted, and our sympathies narrowed by the overlearned and overvalued acceptances of our own society." The correct banner for such a movement, I want to suggest, is not relativism, but pluralism, cosmopolitanism, and humility.

I thus contend that relativist anthropologists have tended to pursue their otherwise worthy goals overzealously. Instead of insisting that we should remove the beams in our own eyes before attempting to remove the motes in others', they argued that it was impossible for others to have motes in their own eyes. In other words, we need to be careful to distinguish the idea *that moral questions have right answers* from the idea *that there is only one right answer, which is obvious to me but not you, so change now or else.* More recent anthropological work does this. In what amounts to a manifesto for the new cultural relativism, Richard Shweder argues that the primary aim of anthropologists' relativism is

> not to subvert the entire process of genuine moral debate by denying the existence of moral truths. By their lights their primary aims are to caution against haste (rapid, habitual, affect-laden or spontaneous information processing [i.e., system 1 as described in chapter 3]) and parochialism (assimilating all new experiences to readily available local frames of reference) and to lend credence to the general caution that one should be slow to make moral judgments about the customary practices of little-known others. (2012, p. 88)

It's hard to imagine a reasonable person disagreeing with this. More to the point, it's hard to imagine someone applying the nuanced principle of charity discussed above disagreeing with it. How should anthropologists pursue these primary aims? Shweder identifies three desiderata. First, avoid saying that there are no objective values. Second, avoid accusing those who disagree with you of being "moral cretins or barbarians who fail to understand the requirements of the one true morality, or demonic others who willfully seek to promote vice over virtue."[12] Third, avoid "assuming in advance that one's own way of life is the only possible flowering of the ideals of an objective moral character" (2012, p. 94).

As an example of this neo-relativism, Shweder contrasts the moral judgments of elite Americans in Hyde Park, Chicago with those of elite Indians in Bhubaneswar. In a well-known set of studies, Shweder and his colleagues asked these two groups to make moral judgments about the following four scenarios:

1 A poor man went to the hospital after being seriously hurt in an accident. At the hospital, they refused to treat him because he could not afford to pay.
2 In a family, the first-born son slept with his mother or grandmother until he was 10 years old. During these years he never slept in a separate bed.
3 The day after his father's death, the eldest son had a haircut and ate chicken.
4 A widow in your community eats fish two or three times a week.

Chicagoans tend to rank these scenarios in decreasing order of moral violation (refusal to treat is the worst, eating fish least bad). Hindu Brahmins tend to rank them in increasing order of moral violation (eating fish and chicken worst, failure to treat least bad). Stark, incomprehensible moral disagreement? Hardly. As Shweder explains, among Brahmins in Bhubaneswar, it's common to think that the way a son expresses respect and love for a dead father is to mourn for twelve days. Denizens of Hyde Park would have little trouble accepting such an idea. They might even think that twelve days was too short. But in Bhubaneswar, it's also common to think that *the way* a son expresses respectful mourning is by abstaining from sexual intercourse and eating meat, and that he should wait twelve days before getting a haircut. This belief is deeply tied into ideas about the transmigration of souls, moral taint, and other aspects of folk and philosophical Hinduism. Whether or not the beliefs of the Brahmins of Bhubaneswar about these further matters are correct or incorrect is beside the point. In the Chicago context, eating chicken after one's father's death is an unremarkable meal. In the Indian context, it's a "willful and horrifying renunciation of the entire project of assisting the soul of his father and places the father's spiritual transmigration in deep jeopardy" (Shweder 2012, p. 96). What Shweder shows, then, is that the reason his Indian participants make the moral judgments they do has to do with a familiar basic value: respect and love of family, especially parents. By the criteria of psychological depth, modal robustness, and defusability discussed above, the disagreement between Chicagoans and Bhubaneswarians is far from fundamental.

Following Wong (2006), Shweder calls his neo-relativism "moral pluralism," and characterizes it as "the doctrine that human reason at some point reaches a limit that allows for discretion as to which values or goods to privilege and how they should properly be applied in the light of local beliefs, interests and social facts" (2012, p. 97). What are these basic values? How diverse are the cultural signatures associated with them? I address these questions in the next section.

3.2 *Psychological and sociological convergence*

The best-supported axiological model in psychology is the Schwartz (1994) Value Survey, which identifies ten basic values:

1 Power, including social status and prestige, and control or dominance over people and resources.
2 Achievement, including personal success through demonstrating competence according to social standards.
3 Hedonism, including pleasure and sensuous gratification for oneself.
4 Stimulation, including excitement, novelty, and challenge in life.
5 Self-direction, including independent thought and action (choosing, creating, exploring).
6 Universalism, including understanding, appreciation, tolerance, and protection for the welfare of all people and for nature.
7 Benevolence, including preservation and enhancement of the welfare of people with whom one is in frequent personal contact.
8 Tradition, including respect, commitment, and acceptance of the customs and ideas that traditional culture or religion provide.
9 Conformity, including restraint of actions, inclinations, and impulses likely to upset or harm others and violate social expectations or norms.
10 Security, including safety, harmony, and stability of society, relationships, and the self.

The Schwartz Value Survey asks people to rate how important each of these is. They're arranged in a circumplex as in figures 5.1, 5.2, and 5.3 above. In this model, items adjacent to one another tend to correlate positively. For instance, someone who highly values power is likely also to highly value achievement and security. Items opposite one another tend to correlate negatively. Someone who highly values benevolence is likely to value achievement less, though not typically to actively *dis*value it.

Are these all and only the basic values of all cultures? Maybe not, but it's a very good start. In a meta-analysis of responses from 15,757 teachers and 26,024 students from 53 countries, Fischer et al. (2010) explored the degree to which patterns of responses correlated across individuals and across countries. As I mentioned above, one's culture is not identical to one's country, but it's not a terrible proxy. Countries represented in this survey were quite diverse, including Israel, Bulgaria, Germany, Slovakia, Indonesia, Hong

Kong, South Africa, Holland, Portugal, Singapore, Sweden, Mexico, Canada, Switzerland, Australia, England, Bolivia, Greece, Denmark, the United States, Japan, South Korea, Poland, Turkey, Nepal, Zimbabwe, Estonia, Georgia, France, Cyprus, China, Slovenia, India, Italy, Spain, Venezuela, Brazil, Malaysia, Finland, Hungary, New Zealand, and Taiwan. The correlation between individual students' and teachers' values was an utterly astonishing .98. The correlation between aggregated country-level values ranged between .88 and .92. In other words, in general, individuals within a country tend to agree with each other and with individuals in other countries; and countries tend to agree with other countries. Beyond this already remarkable result, Saucier (forthcoming) has further shown that ordinal *rankings* of values across individuals exhibit remarkable similarity, and that they correlate highly with rankings of values proposed by several philosophers, including Plato and Bentham.[13] Women's value-hierarchies highly correlated with those of men, and correlated better with the value-hierarchies of philosophers than men's did.[14]

In independent work, sociologists collaborating on the World Values Survey (2009) have constructed their own catalogue of basic values, which includes family, friends, leisure time, political power, work, religion, independence, conscientiousness, sense of responsibility, imagination, tolerance, thrift, perseverance, benevolence, obedience, self-expression, and trust (among others). This catalogue of values is remarkably similar to Schwartz's. The World Values Survey has been conducted for more than three decades. Agreement from country to country is typically astonishingly high. For instance, in the most recent round of surveys, responses were collected from people in Algeria, Armenia, Australia, Azerbaijan, Belarus, Chile, China, Colombia, Cyprus, Ecuador, Egypt, Estonia, Germany, Ghana, Iraq, Japan, Jordan, Kazakhstan, Kuwait, Kyrgyzstan, Lebanon, Libya, Malaysia, Mexico, Morocco, Netherlands, New Zealand, Nigeria, Pakistan, Palestine, Philippines, Poland, Qatar, Romania, Russia, Rwanda, Singapore, Slovenia, South Korea, Spain, Sweden, Taiwan, Trinidad and Tobago, Tunisia, Turkey, Ukraine, the United States, Uruguay, Uzbekistan, Yemen, and Zimbabwe. This is an extremely diverse sample of 74,044 people. In almost every country, more than 90 percent of participants rated family as "very important," the highest possible answer (the exceptions were Belarus at 88.3 percent, China at 85.7 percent, Colombia at 85.1 percent, Estonia at 88.0 percent, Germany at 77.6 percent, Lebanon at 75.1 percent, Slovenia at 88.7 percent, Sweden at 89.2 percent, and

Uruguay at 88.7 percent.). Ratings for other values are similarly shared (though not, of course, always near the ceiling).

Naturally, both the Schwartz Value Survey and the World Values Survey have their limitations. Nevertheless, their overall convergence both across individuals and across cultures is impressive, and not to be ignored. Moral foundations theory, which has cropped up above in chapter 3, holds that there are more serious divergences in people's values. This is not the place to adjudicate that disagreement, which is very much a live debate in contemporary moral psychology. Suffice it to say here that even moral foundations theorists hold that (almost) everyone shares the same foundations. The claim is not that some people are sensitive to some foundations while others categorically ignore or even reject them. Instead, the (more plausible) view is that different sorts of people are differentially more sensitive to some foundations than others. As with the disagreements already canvassed above, it is unclear whether such differences amount to *fundamental* moral disagreement. This is especially clear because the modal robustness, depth, and defusability of disagreements about foundations has barely been studied.

4 Philosophical implications and future directions of the psychology of disagreement

The neo-relativist model proposed by Shweder and the results of the Schwartz and World Value Surveys described above should make us dubious of claims that there are fundamental moral disagreements, and even more dubious of claims that such disagreements have already been found and confirmed. When people are asked not about particular actions or moral heuristics but about basic values, they tend to concur. Thus, in terms of psychological depth, most moral disagreements seem to be pretty shallow.

There is *some* disagreement about basic values, however, which suggests that Wong (2006) and Shweder (2012) might be right in advocating moral pluralism. However, even this disagreement may not reach the levels required for there to be fundamental disagreement. To date, no one has explored in a systematic way the modal robustness of moral disagreement. As I mentioned above, there is a quixotic literature in philosophy and psychology that investigates folk meta-disagreement, but such work has no direct bearing on modal robustness. What would need to be done (and what should be done by some enterprising philosophers, psychologists, sociologists, and anthropologists) is to put people in a room together and get them to talk through the differences in their value signatures. Would they converge? Crutchfield's (1955) experiments suggest that they would, at least somewhat. Kahan et al.'s (2013) more recent experiments suggest that initial differences in basic values might drive people further apart, rather than bringing them together. This is a clear future direction of research for moral psychologists.

To the extent that people didn't converge even in the scenario just envisioned, would their disagreement be defusable? Recall that moral disagreement can be defused to the extent that people disagree about other matters, argue in bad faith, fail to argue open-mindedly and respectfully, fail to argue for a sufficiently long time, or fail to argue meticulously. Such constraints are hard to enforce in an experimental setting, though they can be coded for. It doesn't help that, when people disagree morally, they often switch from open-minded debate to abuse and contempt.[15]

This point brings us back to the unanswered questions about respect and tolerance above. Isn't it intolerant to say that some other person's or culture's moral convictions are or might be wrong? Isn't it disrespectful to suggest the same? It should be clear at this point that the answer is, "not necessarily." Indeed, taking another person or culture seriously seems to involve construing their utterances and actions in such a way that, while they *might* be wrong, they are at least intelligible, given charitable interpretation. Consigning another person or culture to unintelligibility is often itself a form of disrespect and intolerance, as it suggests that nothing could possibly make sense of their speech and behavior. And when one's best interpretation of another person or culture still makes them out to be morally objectionable, the principle of charity enjoins one to pause, to engage in intellectual humility, to ask seriously whether the error lies with oneself rather than the other, and to look deeper at what might yet turn out to be shared values.

5 Future directions in the moral psychology of disagreement

Existing work on the diversity of moral judgments and values across cultures tends to focus primarily on unreflective intuitions. When these intuitions are about ultimate or intrinsic values, as the Schwartz values survey is, they seem to satisfy the depth requirement on locating a fundamental moral disagreement. It's less clear whether this kind of research satisfies the modal robustness and defusability requirements.

Recall that, for a disagreement to count as genuinely fundamental, it must be robust in the sense that the parties to the disagreement would not easily (or perhaps *at all*) find a way to reconcile their differences through concession, splitting the difference, agreeing to disagree, or reference to a deeper shared value. If one person rates security as a more important value than pleasure, while another person rates pleasure as a more important value than security, how would they respond to each other? If one would be easily convinced to shift her value-ordering, their disagreement is shallow, not fundamental. If they would both concede some ground, agreeing that the two values are roughly of equal weight, and that it's hard to say with any exactness how much emphasis to give to them, then again their disagreement is shallow, not fundamental. If, by contrast, they would hold firm in their disagreement or become even more entrenched, their disagreement is a candidate for fundamentality. Future research on the psychology of moral disagreement may help to determine the extent to which such disagreements tend to be modally robust.

Whether they're really fundamental, though, will further depend on whether disagreements are defusable. If at least one party to a moral disagreement is being insincere, their disagreement is not fundamental. If at least one of them is self-deceived, likewise, their disagreement is not fundamental. If at least one of them is expressing a self-serving bias at the expense of others, again, their disagreement is not fundamental. If at least one of them lacks crucial evidence or cognitive resources to fully understand and appreciate what's at stake, once more, their disagreement is not fundamental. The problem is that moral disagreements about deep values that exhibit modal robustness are almost always susceptible to such complaints, at least in principle – a point about which Moody-Adams (1997) is especially clear and comprehensive.

Regarding sincerity, it often seems that people exaggerate the viciousness and turpitude they see in their opponents. Recall William Donohue's claim that he had nothing in common with the culture of Hollywood because they "like abortions." Does he really think that? In his more sober moments, would he say that there are people who value terminating the lives of fetuses for its own sake? That's hard to believe. Perhaps many moral disagreements can be defused in the same way.

Regarding self-deception and self-serving bias, which often operate in tandem, consider white supremacist ideology concerning slavery or misogynistic ideology concerning the subjugation of women. One common argument leading up to the American Civil War held that slavery was a beneficial social arrangement. The master was likened to a stern but benevolent father, while slaves were likened to unruly but loving children in need of discipline. An otherwise reasonable and upstanding person in the grip of white supremacist ideology can, in retrospect, be seen to be suffering from both self-deception and self-serving bias. How convenient for him that things just naturally turn out to require him to assume a dominant position in society! What a lucky accident that the people who disagree with him ought to serve him! Likewise, a common argument both during the struggle for women's enfranchisement in many parts of the world and afterwards was that the natural role of a man is to lead and protect, while the natural role of a woman is to obey and provide comfort. An otherwise reasonable and upstanding man in the grip of misogynistic ideology can, from an outside perspective, be seen to be suffering from both self-deception and self-serving bias. How convenient for him that things just naturally turn out to require him to assume a dominant position over half of the population! What a lucky accident that the people who disagree with him ought to serve him! It's hard to overestimate how easy it is to fall into such self-serving self-deception. When moral disagreement seems deep and modally robust, we should always ask whether at least one of the parties benefits illicitly from holding onto their position and whether they might be self-deceived. This can be especially hard to assess when you are yourself one of the parties to the disagreement; self-deception is notoriously hard to detect from the inside.

On a related note, people who occupy a dominant or privileged position in society are sometimes at a systematic epistemic *dis*advantage when it comes to acquiring relevant evidence and when it comes to understanding and appreciating what's at stake in moral disagreements that they're party to. Some phenomena are best accessed and understood via direct experience. If you want to know what it's like to suffer a ruptured eardrum, you can interview people who've had that experience and employ your empathy and your imagination. But it's likely that you won't fully understand and appreciate the pain of a ruptured eardrum unless you experience it yourself. Of course, that doesn't mean you can't realize that it hurts a lot, but it does mean you're at a disadvantage. In the moral domain, the same point holds. If you want to know what it's like to suffer the humiliation of slavery (or Jim Crow, or the constant fear of being brutalized by the police) or the frustration of being a woman in a misogynistic society that systematically constrains her career prospects, you're at a severe epistemic disadvantage if you cannot (because of your race or gender) directly experience these affronts. You can interview people of color who live under the pall of police surveillance; you can interview women who've been disqualified in advance for various prestigious jobs. You can employ your empathy and your imagination to the best of your ability. But it's likely that you won't fully understand and appreciate the physical and emotional turmoil that often result unless you experience them yourself.

If these arguments are on the right track, they suggest that the appropriate attitude for a party to a moral disagreement who stands to gain from standing his ground, and who stands on ground that at least potentially makes it difficult or impossible for him to understand and appreciate the experiences of others, is intellectual humility. If you are especially likely to lack the evidence and conceptual resources required to understand a phenomenon, and if you are especially likely to be self-deceived about that phenomenon, the only epistemically responsible stance combines self-doubt and open-mindedness. This includes the designers and interpreters of research on moral disagreement. In other words, the future of the moral psychology of disagreement is a brave new world – one that calls for a diverse range of open, humble, self-critical explorers.

Further readings

Clarke, B. (2010). Virtue and disagreement. *Ethical Theory and Moral Practice*, 13(2): 273–91.

Egan, A. (2007). Quasi-realism and fundamental moral error. *Australasian Journal of Philosophy*, 85(2): 205–19.

Frances, B. (2014). *Disagreement*. Cambridge: Polity.

Fraser, B. & Hauser, M. (2010). The argument from disagreement and the role of cross-cultural empirical data. *Mind & Language*, 25(5): 541–60.

Kumar, V. (forthcoming). Moral judgment as a natural kind. *Philosophical Studies*, 1–24.

Prinz, J. (2007). *The Emotional Construction of Morals*. Oxford University Press.

Quintelier, K. & Fessler, D. (2012). Varying versions of moral relativism: The philosophy and psychology of normative relativism. *Biology & Philosophy*, 27(1): 95–113.

Sneddon, A. (2009). Normative ethics and the prospects of an empirical contribution to assessment of moral disagreement and moral realism. *The Journal of Value Inquiry*, 43(4): 447–55.

Wong, D. (2000). Moral relativity and tolerance. In C. W. Gowans (ed.), *Moral Disagreements: Classic and Contemporary Readings*. New York: Routledge.

Study questions

1 Do you *dis*value any of the basic values identified in the Schwartz Value Survey or the World Values Survey? Why?

2 Are there basic values that both the Schwartz and World surveys missed? Which? Why are they basic?

3 Are there other ways of being charitable in interpreting others' utterances and actions beyond the reference, truth, consistency, and value dimensions identified in this chapter?

4 Design an experiment to test for fundamental disagreement. Ensure that it meets the modal robustness, defusability, and psychological depth criteria. If you cannot, explain why not.

5 When moral disagreements involve urgent, one-off, high-stakes decisions, it might seem that applying the principle of charity is inappropriate. For instance, in the USA, some states still use capital punishment. If someone is going to be executed and you strongly disagree with the death penalty, it can be hard to force yourself to charitably interpret supporters of capital punishment. A similar argument could be made about disagreement about the permissibility of third-trimester abortion when the life and health of the mother are not threatened. Are such disagreements fundamental? Why or why not?

6 Imagine two people who have the following kind of peculiar moral disagreement: X believes that *getting a tattoo* is a moral decision because one's body is a temple, and to get a tattoo is to defile that temple. By contrast, Y believes that *getting a tattoo* is merely a prudential decision because having a tattoo might make it harder to get a job in certain fields (e.g., as a kindergarten teacher). In other words, X and Y disagree about the boundaries of the moral domain. Is this sort of disagreement amenable to the principle of charity? Why or why not?

Afterword

This book introduced five central concepts for moral psychology – agency, patiency, sociality, temporality, reflexivity – and explored their connection with five areas of philosophical inquiry: preferences, responsibility, emotion, character, and disagreement. Empirical evidence from psychology, sociology, anthropology, criminology, neuroscience, and experimental philosophy informed our discussion. Models, theories, and concepts from normative ethics, meta-ethics, and moral epistemology framed it. Naturally, much has been left unsaid even about the topics covered in most detail, and many topics of interest have been discussed only in passing or not at all. We can, however, summarize a few of the main conclusions and lines of argument presented above.

Although a simple model of preferences like the revealed preference model commonly used in economics is mathematically tractable and intuitively appealing, a more complex picture of human preferences and their relation to agency and wellbeing is both more consistent with the evidence and opens up interesting possibilities. People don't always follow what they take to be the best means to their own ends. Sometimes they prefer to change their own first-order preferences. They often don't know what their preferences are, instead constructing them on the fly in the face of well- or poorly framed choice architectures. If agency is at least partly a matter of acting effectively to prevent outcomes you genuinely disvalue and bring about outcomes you genuinely value, then these complications indicate that full agency may be harder to achieve than appears at first blush. If wellbeing is at least partly a matter of getting what you would want if you were well informed, then again these complications indicate that pursuing your own wellbeing or the wellbeing of people you care about may be more difficult than it might seem. Perhaps in some cases the thing to do is to shape our own or our loved ones' preferences rather than take them as given.

As with preferences, responsibility might seem at first blush like a simple moral psychological concept. You're responsible when you knowingly bring about a consequence that you have some control over. As we saw in chapter 2, things aren't so simple. We can fail to know in culpable ways. We can culpably lack control. If the empirical work on implicit bias is on the right track, coming to know what we're doing and why we're doing it may be very difficult, and taking sufficient control of our behavior even when our explicit values and moral beliefs are clear may prove challenging. In that chapter, we also started to see more clearly how moral psychological concepts are inextricably intertwined. You might lack knowledge because you antecedently lack control, or vice versa. You might gain control by acquiring knowledge. The seemingly innocuous exercise of agency by, for instance, media outlets, may influence the implicit associations of ordinary people, police officers, and would-be vigilantes. Because humans are such wildly social animals, with much of our cognitive and affective lives occurring beyond the purview of consciousness, we overestimate our direct control of our behavior and underestimate the licit and illicit influence of factors we may not approve of.

In chapter 3 on emotions, we considered the value of looking "under the hood" to help elucidate the nature and moral value of various emotions: to what extent does a neural perspective on emotions clarify their rationality, their appropriateness in various situations, and their role in agency, patiency, sociality, reflexivity, and temporality? Contrary to Joshua Greene, we saw that the dichotomous distinction between reason and emotion is hopeless, that emotions help us to implement the only kind of reason that creatures like us are capable of, and that considering a broad category like emotion as a monolithic phenomenon may be less useful than making fine-grained distinctions among different emotions.

Chapter 4 on character and virtue expanded on this insight: just as it is difficult to treat all emotions from a single theoretical perspective, so it might be difficult to think of all virtues in a unified way. We considered the differences among substantive virtues, executive virtues, and negative virtues. We explored the extent to which virtues (and vices) partake of sociality. At one extreme, one might think that if you have a virtue, it is your trait entirely and something for which you alone are responsible. Moving away from this idea, one might think that you cannot become virtuous or vicious without the causal and developmental influence of other people, but that once you've reached such a state of character, you own it. Moving even further, to the view I endorsed in chapter 4, one might think that your possession of various character traits is constitutively dependent in an ongoing way on the social feedback loops in which you're a node. This raises both philosophical and empirical problems, however. Empirically, it is very hard to study such ongoing feedback loops in a controlled laboratory environment. If part of what it means to be virtuous is to be integrated in a particular social ecology, then removing someone from their social ecology and placing them in a laboratory setting modifies their character. Philosophically, if other people are partly constitutive of your character, then you seem to be less responsible for your own character than one might think, but more responsible for the character of others than you're comfortable being.

Finally, in chapter 5 on disagreement, we further explored the difficulty of scientifically investigating phenomena that cannot be easily controlled in the lab. We saw that, while superficial moral disagreements are fairly easy to identify, modally robust fundamental disagreements between epistemically responsible agents are much harder to pinpoint. We also saw that moral disagreement often constitutes grounds for intellectual humility, openness, and self-criticism, especially for members of dominant majorities with a history of trampling the values and ways of life of others.

In the remainder of this brief afterward, I gesture at four further areas of moral psychological inquiry and recommend a few readings in each. Instructors may find this section a useful guide for personalizing their moral psychology syllabi. Students may find it helpful as they branch out into independent research.

Human evolution and analogues of morality in non-human animals. Humans share a vast amount of their genetic endowment with non-human animals, especially (in increasing order of relatedness) mammals, primates, and bonobos and chimpanzees. Frans de Waal (1996, 2006), among others, has explored the analogues of morality in our closest evolutionary relatives, with special emphasis on things like cooperation, empathy and reciprocity, distributive justice, and violence and de-escalation. It turns out that our humaneness is shared in many ways with non-human animals. To the extent that we can show morality or proto-morality in non-human animals, we can see how humans are continuous with the rest of nature, justifying confidence in naturalistic ethics and Nietzsche's goal of "translat[ing] man back into nature" (1886/1966, section 230). Many non-human animals clearly demonstrate capacities for agency, patiency, and first-order sociality. It's less clear how adept they can be at higher-order sociality, with one acting on another that's acting on another. It's also less clear how capable non-human animals are of reflexivity, though members of some species seem to be able to recognize themselves in a mirror, including elephants (Plotnik et al. 2006), chimpanzees (Gallup 1970), bonobos (Westergaard & Hyatt 1994), orangutans (Suárez & Gallup 1981), dolphins (Reiss & Marino 2001), killer whales (Delfour & Marten 2001), and magpies (Prior et al. 2008). It's also less than clear how aware non-human animals are of their own pasts and futures. Humans may be unique or at least unusual in their miserable knowledge that, someday, they will die.

Developmental psychology and the stirrings of morality in babies. On a related note, just as evolutionary biology and evolutionary psychology help us to understand the origins of morality in the past of our species, developmental psychology helps us to understand the origins of morality in each of our own natal (and neo-natal) histories. For instance, Paul Bloom (2013) addresses the development of empathy, compassion, fairness, hierarchy and the in-group/out-group distinction, and punishment. It's remarkable how even infants and young children demonstrate at least the ingredients for morality. Like non-human animals, babies seem to be capable of agency, patiency, and sociality at a very young age. Infants as young as 18 months pass the mirror test, and reflexivity remains part of our capability set until injury or dotage strips us of it.

Linguistics and the structure of action. Mikhail (2007, 2008, 2011) and Dwyer (1999, 2009), drawing on Rawls (1971), argue that the recursive structures investigated in linguistics are a useful analogy for similarly recursive structures of action and the deontological rules applied to such structures, such as the doctrine of double effect discussed in chapter 3. These investigations relate to both human evolution (which made possible the immensely complex languages that we almost all speak) and developmental psychology (which also explores how children manage to learn both language and moral rules with relatively little instruction). Without recursion, we would likely be incapable of the highly complex forms of agency and sociality that make possible long-term planning (e.g., going to class in order to learn, in order to pass the class, in order to graduate, in order to get a job, in order to have money, in order to be able to pursue intrinsically valuable ends such as supporting one's family and friends). Just how far the linguistic analogy can be pushed is an open question.

Religious psychology and ethics, especially in-group cooperation and intergroup conflict. Philosophers – especially contemporary secular philosophers – tend to downplay the relation between religion and ethics. This is in large part because we assume that there is only one interesting way for religion and philosophy to interact: God makes some things good and right, others bad and wrong by fiat. This is a (simplistic) understanding of Divine Command Theory, and the majority of philosophers agree that it is refuted by the so-called Euthyphro Problem, which was first explored in detail in Plato's *Euthyphro* dialogue. Single-minded focus on the Euthyphro Problem may have blinded philosophers to other interest connections between religion and ethics, especially religion's role in promoting in-group cooperation and sustaining intergroup conflict. These phenomena have been explored in detail by psychologists of religion like Azim Shariff (Shariff 2011; Shariff & Norenzayan 2011; Norenzayan & Shariff 2008; Shariff & Norenzayan 2007). Religious psychology thus seems to have much to say about intense and complex forms of sociality, reflexivity, and temporality.

Notes

Introduction

1 For more on mediator variables and moderator variables, see Baron & Kenny (1986). I also discuss these statistical concepts at more length later in the book.

2 Paul Krugman, March 17, 2014, on his blog, "The Conscience of a Liberal," in a post titled "Sergeant Friday was not a Fox."

3 When a term appears for the first time in **boldface**, it is a technical term that is defined in the glossary at the end of the book.

4 I am here indebted to James Wilk.

5 I am here indebted to Joshua May, who insisted that I raise this last point.

Chapter 1   Preferences

1 Values influence preferences, which in turn influence behavior, but values on their own don't do all the work (Homer & Kahle 1988). For a philosophically nuanced interpretation of the attitude of valuing, see Haybron & Tiberius (2012), who construe values as "relatively robust pro-attitudes, or clusters of pro-attitudes, that we take to generate reasons for action and furnish standards for evaluating how our lives are going" (p. 9). I would add that values sometimes include con-attitudes and clusters of con-attitudes, such as those exhibited in the "whatever it is, we're against it" opposition by Congressional Republicans to Barack Obama's political agenda during his presidency. Values are discussed in more detail in chapter 5.

2 A version of this idea was first formulated by Sidgwick (1981). Rosati (1995) argues persuasively that mere information without imaginative awareness of and engagement with that information is not enough. See also Railton (1986).

3 See Lichtenstein & Slovic (1971); Slovic (1995); Slovic & Lichtenstein (1968, 1983); Tversky & Kahneman (1981); Tversky et al. (1990).

4 See also Ariely & Norton (2008); Green et al. (1998); Hoeffler & Ariely (1999); Hoeffler et al. (2006); Johnson & Schkade (1989); Lichtenstein & Slovic (1971).

5 A social security number is a kind of national identification code: it associates each citizen of the United States with a unique, quasi-random number.

6 In the United States, this would be equivalent to flipping preferences across the conservative–liberal gap; in the United Kingdom, it would be equivalent to flipping preferences across the Conservative–Labour gap.

7 For more, see the discussion of David Wong's work in chapter 5.

8 Bentham (1789/1961, p. 31), Mill (1861/1998, p. 26), and Sidgwick (1874/1981, p. 413) all deal with the objection in this way.

9 See Berg et al. (1985); Pommerehne et al. (1982); Reilly (1982).

Chapter 2   Responsibility

1 I use these cases as examples because they were partly responsible for the development of the psychological literature on implicit bias. The reader will no doubt be able to substitute any number of more recent, analogous incidents. The *Guardian* newspaper has created a website to track police killings in the United States (http://www.theguardian.com/us-news/series/counted-us-police-killings); in the first half of 2015 alone, 47 unarmed blacks were recorded on this grim list.

2 http://fivethirtyeight.com/datalab/another-much-higher-count-of-police-homicides/.

3 I here follow Washington & Kelly (forthcoming), and – like them – remain agnostic on whether there are further conditions.

4 For more on this, see DesAutels (2004).

5 I say "in a sense," because there is another sense in which she is morally responsible. Arguably, she has a responsibility to herself (and perhaps her family and friends) to maintain her health, and so she should be praised rather than blamed for stealing the bread.

6 An alternative way of putting this point analyzes responsibility as a categorical rather than a graded concept (you're either responsible or you're not – there's no such thing as partial responsibility) but goes on to distinguish graded levels of blameworthiness and praiseworthiness. It's not clear how much hangs on this distinction. As there is an

enormous literature in social psychology on the "diffusion of responsi-bility," there at least seems to be a sense in which responsibility can be (perceived as) partial.

7 I am here indebted to Dan Kelly.

8 A related, even more extreme, notion of control is sometimes referred to as "libertarian free will." I will not discuss the debate among libertar-ians, hard determinists, and soft determinists (compatibilists) in this book.

9 Further such connections are explored in Morton (2013a).

10 Note that, according to these characterizations, bias isn't necessarily bad: the notion of bias I'm working with in this chapter is statistical. In some cases, it might be good to be biased for Xs. For instance, it's plau-sible to think that a small to substantial bias for one's family and friends – at least in some decision contexts – is not just acceptable but even laudable. Likewise, it's plausible to think that a small to substantial bias against jerks and free-loaders – at least in some decision contexts – is not just acceptable but even laudable.

11 It should be clear that the precise number of interactions and the precise probabilities are irrelevant. It should also be clear that there are other ways that implicit biases can be harmful.

12 Also, as time goes by, those facing bias (and perhaps even the fairly treated person who sees others receiving an unfair advantage) might curtail their effort and involvement out of frustration, anger, resent-ment, and some other understandable emotions. In such an eventuality, their boss could in some sense justify giving them smaller raises, though the boss would be making a decision based on behavior that was induced by his own unfair treatment in the first place. Feedback loops like this are discussed in more detail in chapter 4.

13 The equation, in case you want to explore things further, is: (salary in year n) = (initial salary)$(1 + \%$ increase per year$)^n$.

14 This is an extremely simplified model. Just one way of making it more complicated and more accurate would be to note that not everyone has the same number of potential interactions with law enforcement. Police patrol certain neighborhoods more aggressively than others, leading to more opportunities for interaction in these neighborhoods.

15 Other common measures of effect size include r, η^2, and partial-η^2.

16 The rule of thumb suggested by Richard et al. (which is only a rule of thumb) is that an effect size of .10 indicates a small effect, .20 a medium effect, and .30 or higher a large effect. Before their meta-meta-analysis, Cohen's (1988) suggestion was to treat .10 as small, .30 as medium, and .50 as large.

17 For more on this see Messick (1995, 1998), Cronbach (1990), and Camp-bell & Fiske (1959).

18 As mentioned above, explicit, virulent racism presumably also explains a lot.

19 I should note that none of this work supports or presupposes that race is a legitimate biological category. For more on this, see Zack (2002).
20 For critical discussion of this claim, see Besser-Jones (2008), Brownstein & Saul (2013), Holroyd (2012), Holroyd & Kelly (forthcoming), and Washington & Kelly (forthcoming).
21 This suggestion receives some support from Cameron et al. (2010), who found that ordinary people tend to view implicit racial bias as culpable only when it is portrayed as something the agent is aware of.
22 It might seem that there is an important disanalogy here: consciously engaging in positive affirmative action by giving stigmatized minorities preferences that might otherwise seem unfair is different from consciously increasing one's following distance on the highway. In the first case, one does what one takes to be, at least prima facie, wrong, with the understanding that things will wash out in the long run, while in the latter case, one doesn't do something that seems prima facie wrong. This objection is misguided. It can be dangerous to leave too great a following distance on the highway, since that tempts other drivers to interpose themselves in that distance, potentially leading to accidents. The point is that in both cases, one forces oneself to do something that *feels* inappropriate because one has relevant background knowledge.
23 It's also worth noting that early evidence indicates that the "oh well, everybody stereotypes after all" message may actually induce people to engage in stereotyping more often (Duguid & Thomas-Hunt 2015). This suggests that we may face a tradeoff between letting individuals off the hook and collectively encouraging worse behavior.
24 I am here indebted to Holroyd & Kelly (forthcoming). For a review of much of the relevant empirical literature, see Blair (2002).
25 I leave aside here the very important and fraught question of whether I ought to try to counteract not only my own biases but other people's. It should be obvious, at the very least, that, to the extent possible, I shouldn't engage in patterns of behavior that compound others' biases.

Chapter 3 Emotion

1 I should also note that emotions can be characteristically embodied in many ways, not just through facial expressions. Kret (2015) explores many of these, including blushing, sweating, direction of gaze and eye contact, tearing up, pupil dilation, blinking, and posture.
2 Here, and in the rest of this section, when I say that emotions have X components, I should be read as meaning that they have – at least often and according to some prominent theories – one or more of X components either essentially or contingently.
3 Even **hybrid emotions**, which result when someone has two distinct basic emotions at once, are recognizable in people's faces, though

they're naturally a bit harder to parse. For a fascinating exploration, see Du et al. (forthcoming).

4 Like everything in this field, what counts as an emotion is contentious. Some theorists reject disgust but include trust (Helm 2014). Others might be inclined to reject trust but include disgust. It's beyond the scope of this chapter to develop a comprehensive catalogue. However, you can get a taste for the variety of emotions and candidates-for-emotion from this list: anger, disgust, fear, happiness, sadness, surprise, contempt, joy, wonder, gratitude, shame, guilt, indignation, curiosity, pride, love, empathy, sympathy, regret, resentment, temptation, forgiveness, doubt, envy, ambivalence, terror, rage, grief, depression, happiness, tranquility, confidence, cruelty, pity, amusement, patience, anxiety, hope, relief, frustration, greed, hatred, irritation, boredom, despair, shock, contentment, tenderness, infatuation, jubilation, ecstasy, bitterness, loathing, agony, gloom, melancholy, remorse, homesickness, humiliation, hysteria, mortification, ambition, jadedness, satisfaction, mirth, *schadenfreude*, camaraderie, merciful, cocky, cold, vengeance, sardonic, stinginess.

5 For instance, anger is perhaps most naturally construed as negative, but there is a certain thrill and sense of empowerment in at least some episodes of wrath. Likewise, contempt may seem negative, but the sense of superiority it engenders in the person who feels it can be quite pleasant.

6 For more on this idea, see chapter 3.

7 Note also the analogy to higher-order desires explained in the previous chapter in connection with Harry Frankfurt's work on responsibility and free will.

8 This example shows that there can be not just second-, but third- and fourth-order social emotions. It's also possible to have not just second-, but third-order complex emotions in a single mind. For instance, consider someone enjoying a moment of swagger. He expresses contempt for those less fortunate than himself, but that's not all: he's also delighted at the appalled attitude directed at him from (what he takes to be) a mawkish point of view. Swagger = delighted$_a$→(appalled$_b$→contempt uous$_a$(X)), where X is something b values. Or consider an example from Strawson (1960): vicarious indignation on one's own behalf. In this emotion, you feel approval of an objective point of view from which indignation is directed at someone who's treated you badly.

9 Peter Strawson (1960) discusses this complex phenomenon, claiming that resentment calls for guilt. I suggest that resentment is more accurately construed as a response to contempt. Both contempt and resentment are importantly hierarchical: the contemptuous person looks *down* her nose at the resentful person, who stares defiantly back *up*.

10 For more on this, see Arpaly (2003).

11 Though see Ranehill et al. (2015) for a skeptical take on so-called "power poses."

12 The name is actually – and importantly – ill-chosen. There is no *theory* in dual-process theory. It's better conceived as a meta-theory or framework that specifies the sorts of entities, processes, properties, and relations that a first-order theory may and should refer to.

13 For a terrific introduction to dual-system theory, see Kahneman (2013).

14 fMRI is a real-time measure of activation of regions of the brain. The details are, of course, complicated, but the basic idea is straightforward. What fMRI measures is blood-oxygen-level dependent activation in the brain. The harder a particular part of your brain is working, the more resources, such as oxygen, it needs. Oxygenated blood alters the local magnetic field slightly more than deoxygenated blood, and that alteration can be detected in the presence of a strong magnetic field. Thus, by measuring tiny changes in the magnetic field and thus oxygenated blood flow, the researcher can indirectly measure how much activity is going on in different parts of the brain (or brainstem, or even other organs). Other methods, such as electroencephalography (EEG), are more fine-grained in terms of temporal resolution, though coarser in terms of spatial resolution. In any event, fMRI has various methodological and research-ethical advantages that have led researchers to favor it, at least for the sorts of research questions discussed here.

15 If you ask them for judgments about both cases, one after the other, an order effect tends to crop up. People who face *footbridge* first tend to say that it's not OK to push the man and then *also* tend to say that it's not OK to pull the switch. People who face *switch* first tend to say that it's OK to pull the switch but not to push the large man (Schwitzgebel & Cushman 2012).

16 They might, however, recognize it when it's explained to them and subsequently endorse it.

17 A splendid example of this, which supports the role of amygdala and insula in emotional processes, though not vmPFC, is Mobbs et al. (2010), who showed that activation of these areas reliably tracked both the proximity and the trajectory (moving closer or moving further) of an 8.6″ tarantula to the participant's feet.

18 This should not be taken to suggest that there are no *other* problems with Greene's argument. For further critique, see Berker (2009) and Bauman et al. (2014).

19 In addition, vmPFC is sometimes associated with emotion *regulation*, a paradigmatic system 2 process (Quirk & Beer 2006; Wager et al. 2008). I am here indebted to Elliot Berkman.

20 And by logic, as Elliot Berkman has emphasized to me (Poldrack 2006).

21 A separate issue is that Greene et al. have at best shown that vmPFC activates more when people contemplate *footbridge* than when they contemplate *switch*. This doesn't mean that vmPFC isn't involved in *switch* as well. To show that, one would have to compare *switch* with a non-moral control.

22 Damasio argued that vmPFC is specifically associated with emotions, drawing among other things on a tall tale from the nineteenth century: Phineas Gage. Following Damasio, Greene perpetrates the now-familiar slander that Gage, a foreman whose forehead was punctured by a railroad spike in a freak accident over a century ago, must have sustained damage to his vmPFC, which destroyed his emotional capabilities and transformed him overnight into a sociopathic drifter. Greene (2013) mentions Gage more than a dozen times, treating him as a poster boy for the implication of vmPFC in emotion processing. Unfortunately, the well-known story about Gage is a myth, as Macmillan (2002) demonstrates in his book-length investigation of Gage's life and the medical culture of the time (and since).

23 There is some controversy over whether vmPFC implements expected-utility or prospect-theoretic value calculations. For details, see Philiastides et al. (2010), Tom et al. (2007), Lebreton (2009), Zaki et al. (2014), Kim & Johnson (2015), and Berkman et al. (forthcoming).

24 For more sustained arguments along these lines, see Kelly (2011, 2014) and Kelly & Morar (2014). For a skeptical response, see Clark & Fessler (2014).

25 See Kelly (2011, esp. ch. 1) and Strohminger (2014) for recent literature reviews.

26 This is an instance of what is known as the James-Lange theory of emotion, after William James and Carl Lange, who originated it.

27 The extent to which disgust is on a hair trigger that also involves *moral* condemnation of the disgusting target or related content has been questioned by Justin Landy and Geoffrey Goodwin (forthcoming), who conducted a meta-analysis of fifty studies on incidental disgust and found that the probable effect size is between $d = -.01$ and $d = .11$. This result should not be taken to mean that people who are congenitally more sensitive to disgust do not have distinctive patterns of values and moral judgment; nor does it mean that harboring a disgusted attitude toward a particular content for an extended period of time is irrelevant to the kinds of moral judgment one tends to make about it.

28 For a defense of the moral value of disgust, see Kahan (1998).

29 This discussion is based in part on Alfano & Loeb (2014). For more on distinctions among emotions and what they're sensitive to, see Graham et al. (forthcoming) on the so-called moral foundations of care/harm, fairness/cheating, loyalty/betrayal, authority/subversion, and sanctity/degradation. The moral foundations model is a descendant of the contempt-anger-disgust model discussed in the next chapter. For a skeptical take on the fine-grained distinctions made by moral foundations theory, see Iurino & Saucier (forthcoming).

30 See also Gross (2002), Goldin et al. (2008), Poldrack et al. (2008), and Gallo et al. (2009).

31 This is sometimes referred to as the "affect as information" hypothesis, which is most associated with Paul Slovic (Slovic et al. 2002).

32 Note that these suggestions are consistent with both consequentialist and deontological normative ethics. The consequentialist can say that disgust is to be discounted because it tends to lead to horrors like genocide. The deontologist can say that disgust is to be discounted because of its dehumanizing aspect: it runs counter to treating humanity as an end in itself.

Chapter 4 Character

1 A fuller description of the incident, along with the disturbing footage, is available at http://en.wikipedia.org/wiki/Death_of_Wang_Yue.
2 Commentators have tended to connect this incident with the 1964 rape and murder of Kitty Genovese in New York City. While what happened to Genovese was clearly horrible, more recent investigations suggest that reports of apathetic bystanders to her assault were exaggerated. See http://nypost.com/2014/02/16/book-reveals-real-story-behind-the-kitty-genovese-murder/ for more details.
3 Still others, such as humility, modesty, chastity, and other virtues of innocence, are **negative**.
4 For a nuanced catalogue and discussion, see Adams (2006, ch. 10).
5 A potential exception is motive and conscience utilitarianism (Adams 1976).
6 See, for instance, Driver (2001).
7 Etymologically, "dexterous" refers to the right hand. Since most people are right-handed, military formations and infrastructure have built-in right-handed assumptions. In such contexts, being right-handed was prudentially and socially good. By contrast "sinister" refers etymologically to the left hand. This is because left-handed comrades in battle were much less effective (unless they were all in formation with other left-handed comrades, of course). We still have these words in the English language, centuries later, even though left-handedness is, at worst, only slightly stigmatized. Indeed, left-handed pitchers, quarterbacks, and other athletes are now typically prized because they have a slight advantage over their right-handed opponents. I am here indebted to Sanjay Srivastava.
8 For a dissenting voice, see Nussbaum (forthcoming).
9 For a psychologist's model of contempt, anger, and disgust as moral emotions, see Rozin et al. (1999), who argue that contempt tracks offenses against social hierarchies, anger tracks harms, and disgust tracks violations of purity. Shweder et al. (1997) argue that these three moral emotions individuate three moral domains (community, autonomy, and divinity) in cultures around the world.
10 Though see chapter 1 on preferences for some worries about whether such pristine preferences even exist.

11 A mathematically equivalent way to characterize it is that there is a **statistical interaction** between a person's values and the reminder.

12 I hasten to add, however, that because Darley and Batson had only 40 participants in this experiment, their statistical power was almost certainly too low to detect moderation. Their chance of detecting a small moderation effect was less than 10 percent, of detecting a medium-sized moderation effect less than 20 percent, and of detecting a large moderation effect less than 40 percent. Unfortunately, underpowered studies, with far too few participants, have been the norm in much of social psychology. Things do appear to be improving these days.

13 I should note, however, that the effect size of $g = -.35$ mentioned above is equivalent to a correlation of $r = -.17$, within this same range Mischel identified. I am here indebted to Sanjay Srivastava.

14 Carter & Gordon (forthcoming) question these intuitive categorizations. Further research is needed to explore this issue.

15 Though both Agreeableness and Conscientiousness also seem to be associated with greater willingness to shock an innocent stranger with up to 450 volts of electricity (Bègue et al. forthcoming).

16 For more, see Flanagan (2009).

17 This also makes some sense of the literature on choice blindness discussed in chapter 1.

18 See also Bryan et al. (2011, 2013).

19 For more on the power of self-concept, see Greenwald et al. (2002) and Swann et al. (2003).

20 And both are surely more effective than the Kantian moral catechism, in which the moral pupil memorizes a series of rote moral questions and answers in an attempt to internalize moral principles. This method is described at some length in Kant's *Metaphysics of Morals* (1797/1999), which has been critically evaluated by Suprenant (2010).

21 Related research on social scaffolding as a determinant of moral development is plentiful. See for instance Costanzo (2014).

22 See also Assad et al. (2007). See Neff & Geers (2013) for a word of warning and clarification.

23 See also Hofmann et al. (2014).

Chapter 5   Disagreement

1 The resonance with Ginges & Atran's (2013) conception of sacred values should be clear.

2 See Kluckhohn (1959) and Benedict (1959).

3 This subsection draws substantially on Alfano & Loeb (2014). For more on the "culture of honor" hypothesis, see Nisbett & Cohen (1996).

4 See also Flanagan (forthcoming) and Wiggins (2005). Enoch (2011) has also written about moral disagreement, but more dogmatically and less convincingly.

5 The nature of the obligation is complex. It's a moral obligation because failing to interpret charitably is disrespectful. But it's also an epistemic obligation because the most reliable way to figure out what someone means is to interpret them charitably. One reason among others why charity is reliable is that people typically communicate under the assumption that they will be treated respectfully and charitably, making the moral obligation a partial ground of the epistemic obligation. For more on meaning and interpretation, see Neale (2004).

6 Children tend to agree with Y (Shaw & Olson 2012).

7 This definition is comfortingly close to definitions of values in psychology and marketing. For instance, Schwartz (1994) says that a value is a belief pertaining to desirable end states or modes of conduct that transcends specific situations, guides selection and evaluation of behavior, people, and events, and is ordered in importance relative to other values.

8 See, for instance, Beebe (2014), Beebe & Sackris (forthcoming), Beebe et al. (forthcoming), and Goodwin & Darley (2008, 2010, 2012).

9 See, for example, Manne & Sobel (2014).

10 This should not be seen as a summary dismissal of sociology or behavioral economics.

11 Wong (personal communication) has informed me that he views these patterns of differentiation not as absolute but as interest-relative, depending in part on how fine-grained the analysis is. A more coarse-grained analysis might fail to turn up differences, whereas a nuanced and detailed analysis would find many.

12 This should make us dubious of recent Israeli claims that Palestinians "love death" and William Donohue's claim, quoted above, that Hollywood likes abortions.

13 Unfortunately, Saucier was unaware of the value model proposed by Nussbaum (2000), who was building on seminar work by Sen (1985). According to Nussbaum, the basic values promoted by nearly every person in nearly every culture are (1) life, (2) bodily health, (3) bodily integrity, (4) senses, imagination, and thought, (5) emotion, (6) practical reason, (7) affiliation, (8) other species, (9) play, and (10) political and material control. This catalogue is remarkably similar to Schwartz's.

14 For more psychological evidence of the overall similarity, paired with non-trivial diversity, of values across and within cultures, see Haidt (2012), Sverdlik et al. (2012), Henrich et al. (2006), and Herrman et al. (2008).

15 Anscombe (1958, p. 17) famously said of someone who disagreed with her about whether it's even open to question whether certain actions are permissible: "I do not want to argue with him; he shows a corrupt mind."

Glossary

Agency: the property of humans and other animals in their capacity as actors who more or less intentionally bring about results in the world

Bias: a systematic tendency for one variable or construct to influence another variable or construct

    Confirmation: the tendency for people to seek out and make inferences from evidence that confirms or is at least consistent with what they already believe

    Explicit: a consciously accessible tendency to associate people who belong to some particular group with certain characteristics

    Implicit: an automatic, often consciously inaccessible tendency to associate people who belong to some particular group with certain characteristics

Bodily periphery: part of the body outwith the limits of the central nervous system (brain, brainstem, spinal cord)

Care ethics: a family of normative ethical theories partly inspired by Carol Gilligan's *In a Different Voice* (1982); these theories place caring relationships between embodied individuals at the core of the ethical life

Choice blindness: a phenomenon in which people lack conscious access to their own preferences and reasons, which can lead them to accept instead the preferences and reasons that are attributed to them

Cognitive psychotherapy: the process, first articulated by Richard Brandt, for achieving a fully informed set of preferences, which involves vividly and imaginatively taking into account all knowable facts that, if you thought about them, would make a difference to your desires and tendencies to act

Con-attitude: any negative attitude towards an object, e.g., contempt, anger, disgust, hatred, disapprobation, fear, regret, guilt, shame

Consequentialism: a family of normative ethical theories that account for the moral properties of agents, actions, motives, and institutions in terms of the good and bad consequences that they do or can be expected to produce

Deontological ethics: a family of normative ethical theories that account for the moral properties of agents, actions, motives, institutions, and consequences in terms of moral rules

Doctrine of double effect: a normative principle according to which it is sometimes worse to bring about a bad effect intentionally rather than as the merely foreseen side-effect of an action

Effect size: a quantitative measure of the strength of an effect, association, or influence. In social and personality psychology, common statistics include the correlation r between two variables and Cohen's d

Emotion: a class of complex mental states that have, or typically have, phenomenological, perceptual, evaluative, motivational, representational, functional, and communicative components

  Basic: a narrow class of emotions that are expressed and recognized the same way across human cultures, have analogues in non-human species, and names in all or almost all natural languages; arguably, the basic emotions are contempt, anger, disgust, fear, joy, sadness, and surprise

  Higher-order: emotions that take other emotions as their intentional objects, e.g., guilt, shame, *schadenfreude*

  Hybrid: emotions that simultaneously involve components characteristic of at least two distinct emotions, e.g., fright (fear and surprise), horror (disgust and fear), awe (joy and fear)

Higher-order desire: a desire that takes another desire as its intentional object; higher-order desires can be social (desiring that someone else's desire either be satisfied or frustrated) or reflective (desiring that one's own desire either be satisfied or frustrated)

Implicit association test (IAT): a high-speed test of someone's quick, automatic, often affective associations between constructs; used in the study of implicit bias

Interaction, statistical: see "moderator variable"

Interactionism: a framework in personality and social psychology in which human behavior is explained not only in terms of the independent contributions of the individual and the environment, but also in terms of the ongoing feedback between the individual and environment

Interactivity: a complex form of agency in which one agent acts on or toward a second agent, while the second agent acts on or toward the first agent

Kantian ethics: see "deontological ethics"

Mediator variable: a variable that partly or fully explains the influence of an independent variable on a dependent variable; for example, decreased lung capacity (a mediator variable) explains the influence of smoking cigarettes (the independent variable) on running speed (dependent variable)

Meta-analysis: a statistical examination of all studies on a particular phenomenon, which is typically used to help researchers find a more accurate understanding of the complexities of the phenomenon

Moderator variable: a variable that determines the degree to which an independent variable influences a dependent variable; for example, the level of the hormone cortisol (moderator) determines the degree to which the presence of the hormone testosterone (independent variable) influences aggression (dependent variable)

Moral heuristic: a rule of thumb for moral decision-making, which is understood to be an imperfect but fast approximation of an ideal moral principle, e.g., "Don't lie!"

Moral principle: an exceptionless moral rule; moral principles are typically understood to be appropriate as standards of rightness but not as decision procedures because of the informational complexity required to use them in decision making

Nervous system: the parts of an animal's body that transmit sensory information and motor commands, and that coordinate action, perception, and cognition

Central: the brain, brainstem, and spinal cord

Peripheral: all parts of the nervous system other than the brain, brainstem, and spinal cord

Null hypothesis: a proposition that specifies, more or less, that there is no relationship among the variables under study

Null hypothesis significance test: a statistical test that provides as output the probability of observing data at least as extreme as those actually observed given that the null hypothesis is true; the null hypothesis is conventionally rejected (and some alternative hypothesis tentatively accepted) if the probability is below .05, .01, or .001.

Patiency: the property of humans and other animals in their capacity as beings that suffer and enjoy things happening to them

Personism: a framework in personality and social psychology in which human behavior is explained solely or primarily in terms of the contribution of the individual, their traits, and their other dispositions

Phenomenology: what it feels like to have or experience a mental state, such as an itch, a pleasure, or an emotion

Preference: a mental state that ranks two goods, outcomes, or prospects

Cardinal: an information-rich preference between x and y that specifies not only whether x is preferred to y, y to x, or neither, but *by how much* one is preferred to the other

Lexicographic: a categorical preference for any amount of one good over any amount of another good

Ordinal: a less information-rich preference between x and y that merely specifies whether x is preferred to y, y to x, or neither

Reversal: state of affairs in which someone's preferences are either synchronically or diachronically inconsistent; e.g., the agent prefers x to y, prefers y to z, but prefers z to x

Principle of charity: a basic presupposition of all interpretation, the principle of charity enjoins us to interpret others' utterances and behavior as expressing attitudes that refer to the same things we would refer with the same signs, as expressing beliefs that are true or at least likely to be true given the others' available evidence, that are consistent, and that stem from recognizable basic values, such as pleasure, security, affiliation, stimulation, etc.

Pro-attitude: any positive attitude towards an object, e.g., joy, wonder, contentment, approbation, pride, gratitude

Recursion: the logical process by which an object of a particular type is embedded in another object of the same type to generate a further, more complex object of the same type

Reflexivity: the property of humans and other animals in their capacity as individuals who are aware of, evaluate, and act with an understanding of themselves as themselves

Situationism: a framework in personality and social psychology in which human behavior is explained solely or primarily in terms of the contribution of the situation or environment

Sociality: the property of humans and other animals in their capacity as, on the one hand, agents who act on others as patients and, on the other hand, patients who are acted on by others as agents

Temporality: the property of humans and other animals in their capacity as individuals that have numerical identity over time, despite various material and psychological changes; makes possible long-term plans, friendship, regret, pride, and hope, among other diverse moral psychological phenomena

Utilitarianism: see "consequentialism"

Variable: any construct that can be measured and assigned a value

    Categorical: a variable that can be assigned values that differ but do not fall on a scale or dimension; for example, gender, race, nationality

    Continuous: a variable that can be assigned values that fall on a scale or dimension; for example, height, weight, age

Virtue ethics: a family of normative ethical theories that account for moral properties of actions, motives, states of affairs, and institutions primarily in terms of the character (virtue and vice) of the agents involved

    Executive virtues: virtues that make someone more effective as an agent, regardless of whether her other traits are traits and values are virtuous; e.g., courage, self-control, persistence

    Negative virtues: virtues that consist primarily in the lack of some (allegedly) undesirable traits or qualities; e.g., humility, modesty, chastity

Substantive virtues: virtues that primarily involve commitment to some substantive value or other; e.g., compassion, generosity, honesty, curiosity

Wellbeing: whatever is ultimately, intrinsically, or non-instrumentally good for a person; constituents of wellbeing are often thought to include pleasure, preference satisfaction, health, various forms of affiliation (e.g., friendship), and so on

References

Abend, G. (2008). Two main problems in the sociology of morality. *Theory and Society*, 37: 87–125.

Adams, R. M. (1976). Motive utilitarianism. *The Journal of Philosophy*, 73(14): 467–81.

Adams, R. M. (2006). *A Theory of Virtue: Excellence in Being for the Good*. Oxford University Press.

Alfano, M. (2009). A danger of definition: Polar predicates in metaethics. *Journal of Ethics and Social Philosophy*, 3(3): 1–13.

Alfano, M. (2012a). Expanding the situationist challenge to responsibilist virtue epistemology. *Philosophical Quarterly*, 62(247): 223–49.

Alfano, M. (2012b). Wilde heuristics and Rum Tum Tuggers: Preference indeterminacy and instability. *Synthese*, 189: S1, 5–15.

Alfano, M. (2013). *Character as Moral Fiction*. Cambridge University Press.

Alfano, M. (forthcoming). Friendship and the structure of trust. In J. Webber & A. Masala (eds.), *The Architecture of Personality and Ethical Virtue*. Oxford University Press.

Alfano, M. & Loeb, D. (2014). Experimental moral philosophy. In E. N. Zalta (ed.), *The Stanford Encyclopedia of Philosophy*. Available at: http://plato.stanford.edu/archives/sum2014/entries/experimental-moral/.

Annas, J. (2011). Practical expertise. In J. Bengson & M. A. Moffatt (eds.), *Knowing How*, pp. 101–12. Oxford University Press.

Anscombe, E. (1957). *Intention*. Oxford: Blackwell.

Anscombe, E. (1958). Modern moral philosophy. *Philosophy*, 33(124): 1–19.

Arendt, H. (1963). *Eichmann in Jerusalem: A Report on the Banality of Evil*. New York: Penguin.

Ariely, D. & Norton, M. (2008). How actions create – not just reveal – preferences. *Trends in Cognitive Science*, 12(1): 13–16.

Ariely, D., Loewenstein, G., & Prelec, D. (2006). Tom Sawyer and the construction of value. *Journal of Economic Behavior & Organization*, 60: 1–10.

Aristotle. *Nicomachean Ethics*.

Arpaly, N. (2003). *Unprincipled Virtue: An Inquiry Into Moral Agency*. Oxford University Press.

Assad, K., Donnellan, B., & Conger, R. (2007). Optimism: An enduring resource for romantic relationships. *Journal of Personality and Social Psychology*, 93(2): 285–97.

Audi, R. (2015). *Reasons, Rights, and Values*. Cambridge University Press.

Balsa, A. & McGuire, T. (2003). Prejudice, clinical uncertainty and stereotyping as sources of health disparities. *Journal of Health Economics*, 22(1): 89–116.

Baron, R. & Kenny, D. (1986). The moderator–mediator variable distinction in social psychological research: Conceptual, strategic, and statistical considerations. *Journal of Personality and Social Psychology*, 51: 1173–82.

Bauman, C., McGraw, A. P., Bartels, D., & Warren, C. (2014). Revisiting external validity: Concerns about trolley problems and other sacrificial dilemmas in moral psychology. *Social and Personality Psychology Compass*, 8/9: 536–54.

Beebe, J. (2014). How different kinds of disagreement impact folk metaethical judgments. In H. Sarkissian & J. C. Wright (eds.), *Advances in Experimental Moral Psychology*, pp. 167–87. New York: Bloomsbury.

Beebe, J. & Sackris, D. (forthcoming). Moral objectivism across the lifespan.

Beebe, J., Runya, Q., Wysocki, T., & Endara, M. (forthcoming). Moral objectivism in cross–cultural perspective.

Bègue, L., Beauvois, J.-L., Courbet, D., Oberlé, D., Lepage, J., & Duke, A. (forthcoming). Personality predicts obedience in a Milgram paradigm. *Journal of Personality*.

Bell, M. (2009). Anger, virtue, and oppression. In L. Tessman (ed.), *Feminist Ethics and Social and Political Philosophy: Theorizing the Non-Ideal*, pp. 165–83. Springer.

Benedict, R. (1934). Anthropology and the abnormal. *Journal of General Psychology*, 10: 59–82.

Benedict, R. (1959). *Patterns of Culture*. Boston: Houghton Mifflin.

Bentham, J. (1789/1961). *An Introduction to the Principles of Morals and Legislation*. Garden City, NY: Doubleday.

Berg, J., Dickhaut, J., & O'Brien, J. (1985). Preference reversal and arbitrage. In V. Smith (ed.), *Research in Experimental Economics*, pp. 31–72. Greenwich, CT: JAI Press.

Berker, S. (2009). The normative insignificance of neuroscience. *Philosophy and Public Affairs*, 37(4): 293–329.

Berkman, E., Kahn, L., & Livingston, J. (forthcoming). Finding the "self" in self–regulation: The identity-value model.

Besser-Jones, L. (2008). Social psychology, moral character, and moral fallibility. *Philosophy and Phenomenological Research*, 86(2): 310–32.

Blackorby, C., Bossert, W., & Donaldson, D. (1995). Intertemporal population ethics: Critical-level utilitarian principles. *Econometrica*, 63(6): 1303–20.

Blair, I. (2002). The malleability of automatic stereotypes and prejudice. *Personality and Social Psychology Review*, 6(3): 242–61.

Bloom, P. (2013). *Just Babies: The Origins of Good and Evil*. New York: Crown Publishers.

Boas, F. (1955). *Primitive Art*. New York: Dover.

Bostic, R., Herrnstein, R., & Duncan, L. (1990). The effect on the preference-reversal phenomenon of using choice indifferences. *Journal of Economic Behavior and Organization*, 13: 193–212.

Brandt, R. (1954). *Hopi Ethics: A Theoretical Analysis*. University of Chicago Press.

Brandt, R. (1967). Ethical relativism. In P. Edwards (ed.), *Encyclopedia of Philosophy*, vol. 3. New York: Macmillan and Free Press.

Brandt, R. (1972). Rationality, egoism, and morality. *Journal of Philosophy*, 69(20): 681–97.

Brandt, R. (1983). The real and alleged problems of utilitarianism. *The Hastings Center Report*, 13(2): 37–43.

Brown, J. & Langan, P. (2001). Policing and homicide, 1976–98: Justifiable homicide by police, police offers murdered by felons. US Department of Justice Office of Justice Programs Bureau of Justice Statistics.

Brownstein, M. & Saul, J. (forthcoming). *Implicit Bias and Philosophy*. Oxford University Press.

Bryan, C., Adams, G., & Monin, B. (2013). When cheating would make you a cheater: Implicating the self prevents unethical behavior. *Journal of Experimental Psychology: General*, 142(4): 1001–5.

Bryan, C., Walton, G., Rogers, T., & Dweck, C. (2011). Motivating voter turnout by invoking the self. *Proceedings of the National Academy of Sciences*, 108(31): 12653–6.

Calder, A. (2003). Disgust discussed. *Annals of Neurology*, 53: 427–8.

Cameron, C. D., Lindquist, K., & Gray, K. (2015). A constructionist review of morality and emotions: No evidence for specific links between moral content and discrete emotions. *Personality and Social Psychology Review*: 1–24.

Cameron, C. D., Payne, B. K., & Knobe, J. (2010). Do theories of implicit race bias change moral judgments? *Social Justice Research*, 23: 272–89.

Campbell, D. & Fiske, D. (1959). Convergent and discriminant validation by the multitrait-multimethod matrix. *Psychological Bulletin*, 56(2): 81–105.

Cantor, N. & Kihlstrom, J. F. (1987). *Personality and Social Intelligence*. Englewood Cliffs, NJ: Prentice-Hall.

Carter, J. A. & Gordon, E. (forthcoming). Openmindedness and Truth. *Canadian Journal of Philosophy*.

Clark, A. (2007). Soft selves and ecological control. In D. Spurrett, D. Ross, H. Kincaid, & L. Stephens (eds.), *Distributed Cognition and the Will*, pp. 101–22. Cambridge, MA: MIT Press.

Clark, J. & Fessler, D. (2014). The role of disgust in norms, and of norms in disgust research: Why liberals shouldn't be morally disgusted by moral disgust. *Topoi*. DOI 10.1007/s11245-014-9240-0.

Clarkson, J. J., Hirt, E. R., Jia, L., & Alexander, M. B. (2010). When perception is more than reality: The effects of perceived versus actual resource depletion on self-regulatory behavior. *Journal of Personality and Social Psychology*, 98(1): 29–46.

Cogley, Z. (2014). A study of virtuous and vicious anger. In K. Timpe & C. Boyd (eds.), *Virtues and Their Vices*, pp. 199–224. Oxford University Press.

Cohen, J. (1988). *Statistical Power Analysis for the Behavioral Sciences*, 2nd edn. New York: Academic Press.

Cooper, D. (1978). Moral relativism. *Midwest Studies in Philosophy*, 3: 97–108.

Cornelissen, G., Dewitte, S., Warlop, L., Liegeois, A., Yzerbyt, V., & Corneille, O. (2006). Free bumper stickers for a better future: The long-term effect of labeling techniques. *Advances in Consumer Research*, 33: 284–85.

Correll, J., Park, B., Judd, C., & Wittenbrink, B. (2002). The police officer's dilemma: Using ethnicity to disambiguate potentially threatening individuals. *Journal of Personality and Social Psychology*, 83(6): 1314–29.

Costanzo, P. (2014). Conscientiousness in the life course context: A commentary. *Developmental Psychology*, 50(5): 1460–4.

Cronbach, L. (1990). *Essentials of Psychological Testing*. London: Harper Collins.

Crutchfield, R. (1955). Conformity and character. *American Psychologist*, 10: 191–8.

Czopp, A., Monteith, M., & Mark, A. (2006). Standing up for change: Reducing bias through interpersonal confrontation. *Journal of Personality and Social Psychology*, 90(5): 784–803.

Damasio, A. (1995). *Descartes' Error: Emotion, Reason, and the Human Brain*. New York: Avon.

D'Andrade, R. G. (1993). Moral models in anthropology. *Current Anthropology*, 36: 399–408.

Darley, J. & Batson, C. D. (1973). "From Jerusalem to Jericho": A study of situational and dispositional variables in helping behavior. *Journal of Personality and Social Psychology*, 27: 100–8.

Darley, J. & Fazio, R. (1980). Expectancy confirmation processes arising in the social interaction sequence. *American Psychologist*, 35: 867–81.

Darley, J. & Latané, B. (1968). Bystander intervention in emergencies: Diffusion of responsibility. *Journal of Personality and Social Psychology*, 8: 377–83.

Davidson, D. (2001a). *Essays on Actions and Events*. Oxford: Clarendon.

Davidson, D. (2001b). *Inquiries into Truth and Interpretation*. Oxford: Clarendon.

Decety, J. & Cacioppo, S. (2012). The speed of morality. *Journal of Neurophysiology*, 108(11): 3068–72.

Delfour, F. & Marten, K. (2001). Mirror image processing in three marine mammal species: Killer whales (*Orcinus orca*), false killer whales (*Pseudorca crassidens*) and California sea lions (*Zalophus californianus*). *Behavioral Processes*, 53(3): 181–90.

Denson, T., Mehta, P., & Tan, D. (2013). Endogenous testosterone and cortisol jointly influence reactive aggression in women. *Psychoneuroendocrinology*, 38(3): 416–24.

DesAutels, P. (2004). Moral mindfulness. In P. DesAutels & M. U. Walker (eds.), *Moral Psychology: Feminist Ethics and Social Theory*, pp. 69–81. New York: Rowman & Littlefield.

Devine, P., Forscher, P., Austin, A., & Cox, W. (2012). Long-term reduction in implicit bias: A prejudice habit-breaking intervention. *Journal of Experimental Social Psychology*, 48(6): 1267–78.

de Waal, F. (1996). *Good Natured: The Origins of Right and Wrong in Humans and Other Animals*. Harvard University Press.

de Waal, F. (2006). *Primates & Philosophers: How Morality Evolved*, ed. S. Macedo & J. Ober. Princeton University Press.

Donner, W. (2011). Morality, virtue, and aesthetics in Mill's art of life. In B. Eggleston, D. Miller, & D. Weinstein (eds.), *John Stuart Mill and the Art of Life*. Oxford University Press.

Doris, J. (1998). Persons, situations, and virtue ethics. *Noûs*, 32(4): 504–40.

Doris, J. (2002). *Lack of Character: Personality and Moral Behavior*. Cambridge University Press.

Doris, J. & Plakias, A. (2008). How to argue about disagreement: Evaluative diversity and moral realism. In W. Sinnott-Armstrong (ed.), *Moral Psychology: The Cognitive Science of Morality: Intuition and Diversity*, pp. 303–32. Cambridge, MA: MIT Press.

Driver, J. (2001). *Uneasy Virtue*. Cambridge University Press.

Du, S., Tao, Y., & Martinez, A. (forthcoming). Compound facial expressions of emotion.

Duguid, M. & Thomas-Hunt, M. (2015). Condoning stereotyping? How awareness of stereotyping prevalence impacts expression of stereotypes. *Journal of Applied Psychology*, 100(2): 343–59.

Dutton, D. & Aron, A. (1974). Some evidence for heightened sexual attraction under conditions of high anxiety. *Journal of Personality and Social Psychology*, 30(4): 510–17.

Dwyer, S. (1999). Moral competence. In K. Murasugi & R. Stainton (eds.), *Philosophy and Linguistics*, pp. 169–90. Boulder, CO: Westview Press.

Dwyer, S. (2009). Moral dumbfounding and the linguistic analogy: Implications for the study of moral judgment. *Mind and Language*, 24: 274–96.

Ekman, P. (2007). *Emotions Revealed, 2nd edition: Recognizing Faces and Feelings to Improve Communication and Emotional Life*. New York: Henry Holt.

Ekman, P., Friesen, W., O'Sullivan, M., Diacoyanni-Tarlatzis, I., Krause, R., Pitcairn, T., Scherer, K., Chan, A., Heider, K., LeComplte, W., Ricci-Bitt,

P., Tomita, M., & Tzavaras, A. (1987). Universals and cultural differences in the judgments of facial expressions of emotion. *Personality Processes and Individual Differences*, 53(4): 712–17.

Elfenbein, H. & Nalini, A. (2002). On the universality and cultural specificity of emotion recognition: A meta-analysis. *Psychological Bulletin*, 128(2): 203–35.

Enoch, D. (2011). *Taking Morality Seriously*. Oxford University Press.

Epstein, S. (1979). The stability of behavior: On predicting most of the people much of the time. *Journal of Personality and Social Psychology*, 37: 1097–126.

Epstein, S. (1983). Aggregation and beyond: Some basic issues in the prediction of behavior. *Journal of Personality*, 51: 360–91.

Ericsson, K. & Lehmann, A. (1996). Expert and exceptional performance: Evidence of maximal adaptation to task constraints. *Annual Review of Psychology*, 47: 273–305.

Ericsson, K., Krampe, R., & Tesch-Roemer, C. (1993). The role of deliberate practice in the acquisition of expert performance. *Psychological Review*, 100: 363–406.

Evans-Pritchard, E. (1937/1976). *Witchcraft, Oracles, and Magic among the Azande*. Oxford University Press.

Fehr, E. & Fischbacher, U. (2004). Third party punishment and social norms. *Evolution and Human Behavior*, 25: 63–87.

Feldman, R. (2008). Modest deontologism in epistemology. *Synthese*, 161(3): 339–55.

Feltovich, P. J., Prietula, M. J., & Ericsson, K. A. (2006). Studies of expertise from psychological perspectives. In K. Ericsson, N. Charness, P. Feltovich, & R. Hoffman (eds.), *The Cambridge Handbook of Expertise and Expert Performance*, pp. 41–68. Cambridge University Press.

Finucane, M. L., Alhakami, A., Slovic, P., & Johnson, S. M. (2000). The affect heuristic in judgments of risks and benefits. *Journal of Behavioral Decision Making*, 13: 1–17.

Fischer, J. M. & Ravizza, M. (1999). *Responsibility and Control: An Essay on Moral Responsibility*. Cambridge University Press.

Fischer, P., Krueger, J., Greitemeyer, T., Vogrincic, C., Kastenmüller, A., Frey, D., Heene, M., Wicher, M., & Kainbacher, M. (2011). The bystander effect: A meta-analytic review on bystander intervention in dangerous and non–dangerous emergencies. *Psychological Bulletin*, 137(4): 517–37.

Fischer, R., Vauclair, C.-M., Fontaine, J., & Schwartz, S. (2010). Are individual-level and country-level value structures different? Testing Hofstede's legacy with the Schwartz value survey. *Journal of Cross-Cultural Psychology*, 41: 135–51.

Fischhoff, B., Slovic, P., Lichtenstein, S., Reid, S., & Coombs, B. (1978). How safe is safe enough? A psychometric study of attitudes towards technological risks and benefits. *Policy Sciences*, 9: 127–52.

Fishbein, M. & Ajzen, I. (1974). Attitude towards objects as predictors of single and multiple behavioral criteria. *Psychological Review*, 81: 59–74.

Fishkin, J. (1982). *The Limits of Obligation*. Yale University Press.

Fishkin, J. (1986). *Beyond Subjective Morality: Ethical Reasoning and Political Philosophy*. Yale University Press.

Flanagan, O. (1993). *Varieties of Moral Personality: Ethics and Psychological Realism*. Harvard University Press.

Flanagan, O. (2009). Moral science? Still metaphysical after all these years. In D. Narvaez & D. Lapsley (eds.), *Personality, Identity, and Character*, pp. 52–78. Cambridge University Press.

Flanagan, O. (forthcoming). *The Geography of Morals*. Oxford University Press.

Fleeson, W. (2001). Toward a structure- and process-integrated view of personality: Traits as density distributions of states. *Journal of Personality and Social Psychology*, 80: 1011–27.

Fleeson, W. & Gallagher, P. (2009). The implications of Big Five standing for the distribution of trait manifestation in behavior. Fifteen experience-sampling studies and a meta-analysis. *Journal of Personality and Social Psychology*, 97: 1097–114.

Foot, P. (1967). The problem of abortion and the doctrine of double effect. *Oxford Review*, 5: 5–15.

Foot, P. (1978). *Virtues and Vices and Other Essays in Moral Philosophy*. Oxford: Blackwell.

Forgiarini, M., Gallucci, M., & Maravita, A. (2011). Racism and the empathy for pain on our skin. *Frontiers in Psychology*, 2: 108.

Frankfurt, H. (1971). Freedom of the will and the concept of a person. *The Journal of Philosophy*, 68(1): 5–20.

Frankfurt, H. (1992). The faintest passion. *Proceedings and Addresses of the American Philosophical Association*, 66(3): 5–16.

Funder, D. & Ozer, D. (1983). Behavior as a function of the situation. *Journal of Personality and Social Psychology*, 44: 107–12.

Gallo, I., Keil, A., McCulloch, K., & Rockstroh, B. (2009). Strategic automation of emotion regulation. *Journal of Personality and Social Psychology*, 96(1): 11–31.

Gallup, G. (1970). Chimpanzees: Self-recognition. *Science*, 167(3914): 86–7.

Garcia, J. L. A. (2004). Three sites for racism: Social structures, valuings and vice. In M. Levine & T. Pataki (eds.), *Racism in Mind*, pp. 36–55. Cornell University Press.

Geertz, C. (2000). Anti-anti-relativism. In *Available Light: Anthropological Reflections on Philosophical Topics*, pp. 42–67. Princeton University Press.

Gigerenzer, G. (2008). Moral intuition = fast and frugal heuristics? In W. Sinnott-Armstrong (ed.), *Moral Psychology: The Cognitive Science of Morality: Intuition and Diversity*, pp. 1–26. Cambridge, MA: MIT Press.

Gilbert, D. (2007). *Stumbling on Happiness*. New York: Vintage.

Gilligan, C. (1982). *In a Different Voice: Psychological Theory and Women's Development*. Harvard University Press.

Ginges, J. & Atran, S. (2013). Sacred values and cultural conflict. In M. J. Gelfand, C. Y. Chiu, & Y. Y. Hong (eds.), *Advances in Culture and Psychology*, pp. 273–301. Oxford University Press.

Goldberg, J., Lerner, J., & Tetlock, P. (1999). Rage and reason: The psychology of the intuitive prosecutor. *European Journal of Social Psychology*, 29: 781–95.

Goldin, P., McRae, K., Ramel, W., & Gross, J. (2008). The neural bases of emotion regulation: Reappraisal and suppression of negative emotion. *Biological Psychiatry*, 63(6): 577–86.

Goodwin, G. & Darley, J. (2008). The psychology of meta-ethics: Exploring objectivism. *Cognition*, 106(3): 1339–66.

Goodwin, G. & Darley, J. (2010). The perceived objectivity of ethical beliefs: Psychological findings and implications for public policy. *Review of Philosophy and Psychology*, 1: 161–88.

Goodwin, G. & Darley, J. (2012). Why are some moral beliefs perceived to be more objective than others? *Journal of Experimental Social Psychology*, 48(1): 250–6.

Graham, J., Haidt, J., & Nosek, B. (2009). Liberals and conservatives use different sets of moral foundations. *Journal of Personality and Social Psychology*, 96: 1029–46.

Graham, J., Haidt, J., Koleva, S., Motyl, M., Iyer, R., Wojcik, S., & Ditto, P. (forthcoming). Moral foundations theory: The pragmatic validity of moral pluralism. *Advances in Experimental Social Psychology*.

Gray, K., Waytz, A., & Young, L. (2012). The moral dyad: A fundamental template unifying moral judgment. *Psychological Inquiry*, 23(2): 206–215.

Gray, K. & Wegner, D. (2011). Dimensions of moral emotions. *Emotion Review*, 3(3): 258–60.

Green, D., Jacowitz, K., Kahneman, D., & McFadden, D. (1998). Referendum contingent valuation, anchoring, and willingness to pay for public goods. *Resources and Energy Economics*, 20: 85–116.

Greene, J. (2013). *Moral Tribes: Emotion, Reason, and the Gap Between Us and Them*. New York: Penguin.

Greene, J. (2014). Beyond point-and-shoot morality: Why cognitive (neuro) science matters for ethics. *Ethics*, 124(4): 695–726.

Greene, J., Nystrom, L., Engell, A., Darley, J., & Cohen, J. (2004). The neural bases of cognitive conflict and control in moral judgment. *Neuron*, 44: 389–400.

Greene, J., Sommerville, R., Nystrom, L., Darley, J., & Cohen, J. (2001). An fMRI investigation of emotional engagement in moral judgment. *Science*, 293: 2105–08.

Greenwald, A., McGhee, D., & Schwartz, J. (1998). Measuring individual differences in implicit cognition: The Implicit Association Test. *Journal of Personality and Social Psychology*, 74: 1464–80.

Greenwald, A., Oakes, M., & Hoffman, H. (2003). Targets of discrimination: Effects of race on responses to weapons holders. *Journal of Experimental Social Psychology*, 39: 399–405.

Greenwald, A., Poehlman, T., Uhlmann, E., & Banaji, M. (2009). Understanding and using the implicit association test: Meta-analysis of predictive validity. *Journal of Personality and Social Psychology*, 97(1): 17–41.

Greenwald, A. G., Banaji, M. R., Rudman, L. A., Farnham, S. D., Nosek, B. A., & Mellott, D. S. (2002). A unified theory of implicit attitudes, stereotypes, self–esteem, and self-concept. *Psychological Review*, 109(1): 3–25.

Gross, J. (2001). Emotion regulation in adulthood: Timing is everything. *Current Directions in Psychological Science*, 10(6): 214–19.

Gross, J. (2003). Emotion regulation: Affective, cognitive, and social consequences. *Psychophysiology*, 39(3): 281–91.

Grusec, J. & Redler, E. (1980). Attribution, reinforcement, and altruism: A developmental analysis. *Developmental Psychology*, 16(5): 525–34.

Grusec, J., Kuczynski, L., Rushton, J., & Simutis, Z. (1978). Modeling, direct instruction, and attributions: Effects on altruism. *Developmental Psychology*, 14: 51–7.

Haidt, J. (2001). The emotional dog and its rational tail: A social intuitionist approach to moral judgment. *Psychological Review*, 108: 814–34.

Haidt, J. (2012). *The Righteous Mind: Why Good People are Divided by Politics and Religion*. New York: Pantheon.

Haidt, J. & Joseph, C. (2007). The moral mind: How 5 sets of innate moral intuitions guide the development of many culture-specific virtues, and perhaps even modules. In P. Carruthers, S. Laurence, & S. Stich (eds.), *The Innate Mind*, vol. 3, pp. 367–91. Oxford University Press.

Hall, L., Johansson, P., & Strandberg, T. (2012). Lifting the veil of morality: Choice blindness and attitude reversals on a self–transforming survey. *PLOS ONE*, 7(9): e45457.

Hall, L., Johansson, P., Tärning, B., Sikström, S., & Deutgen, T. (2010). Magic at the marketplace: Choice blindness for the taste of jam and the smell of tea. *Cognition*, 117: 54–61.

Hamilton, L., Carré, J., Mehta, P., Olmstead, N., & Whitaker, J. (2015). Social neuroendocrinology of status: A review and future directions. *Adaptive Human Behavior and Physiology*, 1: 202–30.

Hare, R. (1952). *The Language of Morals*. Oxford University Press.

Harman, G. (1977). *The Nature of Morality*. New York: Oxford University Press.

Harman, G. (1999). Moral philosophy meets social psychology: Virtue ethics and the fundamental attribution error. *Proceedings of the Aristotelian Society*, New Series 199: 316–31.

Harman, G. (2008). Using a linguistic analogy to study morality. In W. Sinnott-Armstrong (ed.), *Moral Psychology: The Evolution of Morality: Adaptations and Innateness*, pp. 345–52. Oxford University Press.

Haybron, D. (2008). *The Pursuit of Unhappiness: The Elusive Psychology of Wellbeing*. Oxford University Press.

Haybron, D. & Tiberius, V. (2012). The normative foundations for well-being policy. Papers on Economics and Evolution. Evolutionary Economics Group. Jena Max Plank Institute.

Heathwood, C. (2006). Desire satisfaction and hedonism. *Philosophical Studies*, 128(3): 539–63.

Hegel, G. (1807/1976). *Phenomenology of Spirit*, trans. A. Miller. Oxford University Press.

Helm, B. (2014). Trust as a reactive attitude. In D. Shoemaker & N. Tognazzini (eds.), *Oxford Studies in Agency and Responsibility: "Freedom and Resentment" at 50*, pp. 187–215. Oxford University Press.

Henrich, J., McElreath, R., Barr, A., Ensminger, J., Barrett, C., Bolyanatz, A., Cardenas, J., Gurven, M., Gwako, E., Henrich, N., Lesorogol, C., Marlowe, F., Tracer, D., & Ziker, J. (2006). Costly punishment across human societies. *Science*, 312(5781): 1767–70.

Herodotus. (2008). *The Histories*, trans. R. Waterfield. Oxford University Press.

Herrmann, B., Thöni, C., & Gächter, S. (2008). Antisocial punishment across societies. *Science*, 319: 1362–7.

Herskovits, M. (1964). *Man and His Works: The Science of Cultural Anthropology*. New York: Knopf.

Herskovits, M. (1972). *Cultural Relativism: Perspectives in Cultural Pluralism*, ed. F. Herskovits. New York: Random House.

Hieronymi, P. (2006). Controlling attitudes. *Pacific Philosophical Quarterly*, 87(1): 45–74.

Hoeffler, S. & Ariely, D. (1999). Constructing stable preferences: A look into dimensions of experience and their impact on preference stability. *Journal of Consumer Psychology*, 8(2): 113–39.

Hoeffler, S., Ariely, D., & West, P. (2006). Path dependent preferences: The role of early experience and biased search in preference development. *Organizational Behavior and Human Decision Processes*, 101: 215–29.

Hofmann, W., Gawronski, B., Gschwendner, T., Le, H., & Schmitt, M. (2005). A meta-analysis on the correlation between the Implicit Association Test and explicit self-report measures. *Personality and Social Psychology Bulletin*, 31: 1369–85.

Hofmann, W., Wisneski, D. Brandt, M., & Skitka, L. (2014). Morality in everyday life. *Science*, 345(6202): 1340–3.

Holroyd, J. (2012). Responsibility for implicit bias. *Journal of Social Philosophy*, 43(3): 274–306.

Holroyd, J. & Kelly, D. (forthcoming). Implicit responsibility, character, and control. In J. Webber & A. Masala (eds.), *From Personality to Virtue*. Oxford University Press.

Homer, P. & Kahle, L. (1988). A structural equation test of the value-attitude-behavior hierarchy. *Journal of Personality and Social Psychology*, 54(4): 638–46.

Horne, Z., & Powell, D. (2013). More than a feeling: When emotional reactions don't predict moral judgments. *Proceedings of the 35th Annual Conference of the Cognitive Science Society*. Berlin, Germany.

Horne, Z. & Powell, D. (forthcoming). Josh Greene is a mendacious idiot.

Huebner, B. (2011). Critiquing empirical moral psychology. *Philosophy of the Social Sciences*, 41(1): 50–83.

Huebner, B. (forthcoming). Do emotions play a constitutive role in moral cognition? *Topoi*.

Iurino, K. & Saucier, G. (forthcoming). Amending the map of the moral domain: Measurement invariance of the moral foundations questionnaire across 27 countries.

Jayawickreme, E., Meindl, P., Helzer, E., Furr, R. M., & Fleeson, W. (2014). Virtuous states and virtuous traits: How the empirical evidence regarding the existence of broad traits saves virtue ethics from the situationist critique. *Theory and Research in Education*: 1–26.

Jensen, A. & Moore, S. (1977). The effect of attribute statements on cooperativeness and competitiveness in school-age boys. *Child Development*, 48: 305–7.

Johansson, P., Hall, L., & Chater, N. (2011). Preference change through choice. In R. Dolan & T. Sharot (eds.), *Neuroscience of Preference and Choice*, pp. 121–41. Oxford: Elsevier Academic Press.

Johansson, P., Hall, L., Sikström, S., & Olsson, A. (2005). Failure to detect mismatches between intention and outcome in a simple decision task. *Science*, 310: 116–19.

Johnson, E. & Schkade, A. (1989). Bias in utility assessments. *Management Science*, 35: 406–24.

Jussim, L. (1991). Social perception and social reality: A reflection-construction model. *Psychological Review*, 98(1): 54–73.

Kahan, D. (1998). The anatomy of disgust in criminal law. *Faculty Scholarship Series*. Paper 112.

Kahan, D., Peters, E., Dawson, E. C., & Slovic, P. (2013). Motivated numeracy and enlightened self-government. *Yale Law School Public Law Working Paper No. 307*.

Kahneman, D. (2013). *Thinking, Fast and Slow*. New York: Farrar, Straus, and Giroux.

Kane, R. (1989). Two kinds of incompatibilism. *Philosophy and Phenomenological Research*, 50(2): 219–54.

Kant, I. (1797/1999). *The Metaphysics of Morals*, ed. M. Gregor. Cambridge University Press.

Katsafanas, P. (2013). *Agency and the Foundations of Ethics: Nietzschean Constitutivism*. Oxford University Press.

Kelly, D. (2011). *Yuck! The Nature and Significance of Disgust*. Cambridge, MA: MIT Press.

Kelly, D. (2014). Selective debunking arguments, folk psychology, and empirical moral psychology. In J. C. Wright & H. Sarkissian (eds.), *Advances in Experimental Moral Psychology: Affect, Character, and Commitments*, pp. 130–47. New York: Continuum.

Kelly, D. & Morar, N. (2014). Against the yuck factor: On the ideal role of disgust in society. *Utilitas*, 26(2): 153–77.

Kelly, D. & Roedder, E. (2008). Racial cognition and the ethics of implicit bias. *Philosophy Compass*, 3(3): 522–40.

Keynes, J. M. (1933). National self-sufficiency. *New Statesman and Nation*, 6(125): 65–7.

Khader, S. (2011). *Adaptive Preferences and Women's Empowerment*. Oxford University Press.

Kim, B. (forthcoming). The locality and globality of instrumental rationality: The normative significance of preference reversals. *Synthese*.

Kim, K. & Johnson, M. K. (2015). Activity in ventromedial prefrontal cortex during self-related processing: Positive subjective value or personal significance? *SCAN*, 10(4): 494–500.

Kittay, E. F. (1999). *Love's Labor: Essays on Women, Equality, and Dependency*. New York: Routledge.

Kluckholn, C. (1959). *Mirror for Man*. New York: McGraw Hill.

Kohlberg, L. (1971). From is to ought: How to commit the naturalistic fallacy and get away with it in the study of moral development. In T. Mischel (ed.), *Cognitive Development and Epistemology*, pp. 151–235. New York: Academic Press.

Korsgaard, C. (2009). *Self-Constitution: Agency, Identity, and Integrity*. Oxford University Press.

Kret, M. (2015). Emotional expressions beyond facial muscle actions. A call for studying autonomic signals and their impact on social perception. *Frontiers in Psychology*, 6(711): 1–10.

Kuhberger, A. (1998). The influence of framing on risky decisions: A meta-analysis. *Organizational Behavior and Human Decision Processes*, 75(1): 23–55.

Ladd, J. (1957). *The Structure of a Moral Code: A Philosophical Analysis of Ethical Discourse Applied to the Ethics of the Navaho Indians*. Harvard University Press.

Landy, J. & Goodwin, G. (forthcoming). Does incidental disgust amplify moral judgment? A meta-analytic review of experimental evidence. *Perspectives on Psychological Science*.

Latané, B. & Nida, S. (1981). Ten years of research on group size and helping. *Psychological Bulletin*, 89: 308–24.

Latané, B., & Rodin, J. (1969). A lady in distress: Inhibitory effects of friends and strangers on bystander intervention. *Journal of Experimental Psychology*, 5: 189–202.

Leiter, B. (2014). Moral skepticism and moral disagreement in Nietzsche. In R. Shafer-Landau (ed.), *Oxford Studies in Metaethics*, vol. 9, pp. 126–151. Oxford University Press.

Levitin, T. (1973). Values. In J. P. Robinson & P. R. Shaver (eds.), *Measures of Social Psychological Attitudes*, pp. 489–585. Ann Arbor: Institute for Social Research.

Lichtenstein, S. & Slovic, P. (1971). Reversals of preference between bids and choices in gambling decisions. *Journal of Experimental Psychology*, 89: 46–55.

Lindquist, K., Wager, T., Kober, H., Bliss-Moreau, E., & Feldman Barrett, L. (2012). The brain basis of emotion: A meta-analytic review. *Behavioral and Brain Sciences*, 35: 121–202.

Loeb, D. (1998). Moral realism and the argument from disagreement. *Philosophical Studies*, 90(3): 281–303.

Luna, D., Ringberg, T., & Peracchio, L. (2008). One individual, two identities: Frame-switching among biculturals. *Journal of Consumer Research*, 35(2): 279–93.

MacIntyre, A. (1998). *A Short History of Ethics: A History of Moral Philosophy from the Homeric Age to the Twentieth Century*. Notre Dame University Press.

Mackie, J. L. (1977). *Ethics: Inventing Right and Wrong*. New York: Penguin.

Macmillan, M. (2002). *An Odd Kind of Fame: Stories of Phineas Gage*. Cambridge, MA: MIT Press.

Manne, K. & Sobel, D. (2014). Disagreeing about how to disagree. *Philosophical Studies*, 168: 823–34.

Masten, C., Eisenberger, N., Pfeifer, J., & Dapretto, M. (2013a). Neural responses to witnessing peer rejection after being socially excluded: fMRI as a window into adolescents' emotional processing. *Developmental Science*, 16: 743–59.

Masten, C., Eisenberger, N., Pfeifer, J., Colich, N., & Dapretto, M. (2013b). Associations among pubertal development, empathic ability, and neural responses while witnessing peer rejection in adolescence. *Child Development*, 84(4): 1338–54.

Mays, V., Cochran, S., & Barnes, N. (2007). Race, race-based discrimination, and health outcomes among African Americans. *Annual Review of Psychology*, 58: 201–25.

McGeer, V. (2015). Building a better theory of responsibility. *Philosophical Studies*.

Mead, M. (1928/1961). *Coming of Age in Samoa*. New York: William Morrow.

Messick, S. (1995). Validity of psychological assessment: Validation of inferences from persons' responses and performances as scientific inquiry into score meaning. *American Psychologist*, 50(9): 741–9.

Messick, S. (1998). The once and future issues of validity: Assessing the meaning and consequences of measurement. In H. Wainer & H. Braun (eds.), *Test Validity*. Hillsdale, NJ: Erlbaum.

Mikhail, J. (2007). Universal moral grammar: Theory, evidence, and the future. *Trends in Cognitive Sciences*, 11: 143–52.

Mikhail, J. (2008). The poverty of the moral stimulus. In W. Sinnott-Armstrong (ed.), *Moral Psychology: The Evolution of Morality: Adaptations and Innateness*, pp. 353–60. Cambridge, MA: MIT Press.

Mikhail, J. (2011). *Elements of Moral Cognition: Rawls's Linguistic Analogy and the Cognitive Science of Moral and Legal Judgment*. Cambridge University Press.

Mill, J. S. (1861/1998). *Utilitarianism*, ed. Roger Crisp. Oxford University Press.

Miller, C. (2013). *Moral Character: An Empirical Theory*. Oxford University Press.

Miller, C. (2014). *Character and Moral Psychology*. Oxford University Press.

Miller, R., Brickman, P., & Bolen, D. (1975). Attribution versus persuasion as a means for modifying behavior. *Journal of Personality and Social Psychology*, 31(3): 430–41.

Mischel, W. (1968). *Personality and Assessment*. New York: Wiley.

Mobbs, D., Yu, R., Rowe, J., Eich, H., Feldman-Hall, O., & Dalgleish, T. (2010). Neural activity associated with monitoring the oscillating threat value of a tarantula. *Proceedings of the National Academies of Science*, 107(47): 20582–6.

Moody-Adams, M. (1997). *Fieldwork in Familiar Places: Morality, Culture, and Philosophy*. Harvard University Press.

Morton, A. (2004). *On Evil: Thinking in Action*. New York: Routledge.

Morton, A. (2013a). *Bounded Thinking: Intellectual Virtues for Limited Agents*. Oxford University Press.

Morton, A. (2013b). *Emotion and Imagination*. Cambridge: Polity.

Neale, S. (2004). This, that, and the other. In M. Reimer & A. Bezuidenhout (eds.), *Descriptions and Beyond*. Oxford University Press.

Neff, L. & Geers, A. (2013). Optimistic expectations in early marriage: A resource or vulnerability for adaptive relationship functioning? *Journal of Personality and Social Psychology*, 105(1): 38–60.

Nesse, R., & Ellsworth, P. (2009). Evolution, emotions, and emotional disorders. *American Psychologist*, 64(2): 129–39.

Nichols, S., Kumar, S., & Lopez, T. (forthcoming). Rational learners and non-utilitarian rules.

Nickerson, R. (1998). Confirmation bias: A ubiquitous phenomenon in many guises. *Review of General Psychology*, 2(2): 175–220.

Nietzsche, F. (1886/1966). *Beyond Good and Evil*, trans. W. Kaufmann. New York: Vintage.

Nisbett, R. & Cohen, D. (1996). *Culture of Honor: The Psychology of Violence in the South*. Boulder, CO: Harper Collins.

Noddings, N. (1984). *Caring: A Feminine Approach to Ethics and Moral Education*. University of California Press.

Noftle, E. & Fleeson, W. (2010). Age differences in big five behavior averages and variabilities across the adult life span: Moving beyond retrospective, global summary accounts of personality. *Psychology and Aging*, 25: 95–107.

Norenzayan, A. & Shariff, A. (2008). The origin and evolution of religious prosociality. *Science*, 322(5898): 58–62.

Norlock, K. (2008). *Forgiveness from a Feminist Point of View*. New York: Lexington Books.

Nussbaum, M. (2000). *Women and Human Development: The Capabilities Approach*. Cambridge University Press.

Nussbaum, M. (2001). *The Fragility of Goodness: Luck and Ethics in Greek Tragedy and Philosophy*. Cambridge University Press.

Nussbaum, M. (forthcoming). *Anger and Forgiveness*. Oxford University Press.

Öhman, A. & Mineka, S. (2003). The malicious serpent: Snakes as a prototypical stimulus for an evolved module of fear. *Current Directions in Psychological Science*, 12(1): 5–9.

Philiastides, M., Biele, G., & Heekeren, H. (2010). A mechanistic account of value computation in the human brain. *Proceedings of the National Academy of Sciences*, 107(20): 9430–5.

Philippot, P., Chapelle, G., & Blairy, S. (2002). Respiratory feedback in the generation of emotion. *Cognition & Emotion*, 16(5): 605–27.

Plotnik, J., de Waal, F., & Reiss, D. (2006). Self-recognition in an Asian elephant. *Proceedings of the National Academy of Sciences*, 103(45): 17053–7.

Poldrack, R. (2006). Can cognitive processes be inferred from neuroimaging data? *Trends in Cognitive Science*, 10(2): 59–63.

Poldrack, R., Wagner, A., Ochsner, K., & Gross, J. (2008). Cognitive emotion regulation: Insights from social cognitive and affective neuroscience. *Current Directions in Psychological Science*, 17(2): 153–8.

Pommerehne, W., Schneider, F., & Zweifel, P. (1982). Economic theory of choice and the preference reversal phenomenon: A re-examination. *American Economic Review*, 72: 569–574.

Pratto, F. & Stewart, A. (2012). Social dominance theory. In D. Christie (ed.), *The Encyclopedia of Peace Psychology*. Oxford: Blackwell.

Prinz, J. (2005). Passionate thoughts: The emotional embodiment of moral concepts. In D. Pecher & R. A. Zwaan (eds.), *Grounding Cognition*, pp. 93–114. Cambridge University Press.

Prinz, J. (2012). *The Conscious Brain*. Oxford University Press.

Prior, H., Schwarz, A., & Güntürkün, O. (2008). Mirror-induced behavior in the magpie (*Pica pica*): Evidence of self–recognition. *PLoS Biology*, 6(8): e202.

Quine, W. V. O. (1960). *Word and Object*. Cambridge, MA: MIT Press.

Quirk, G. & Beer, J. (2006). Prefrontal involvement in the regulation of emotion: convergence of rat and human studies. *Current Opinion in Neurobiology*, 16(6): 723–27.

Railton, P. (1986). Moral realism. *Philosophical Review*, 95: 163–207.

Railton, P. (2008). Practical competence and fluent agency. In D. Sobel & S. Wall (eds.), *Reasons for Action*, pp. 81–115. Cambridge University Press.

Railton, P. (2014). The affective dog and its rational tale: Intuition and attunement. *Ethics*, 124(4): 813–59.

Ranehill, E., Dreber, A., Johannesson, M., Leiberg, S., Sul, S., & Weber, R. (2015). Assessing the robustness of power posing: No effect on hormones and risk tolerance in a large sample of men and women. *Psychological Science*, 26(5): 653–6.

Rasinski, H., Geers, A., & Czopp, A. (2013). "I guess what he said wasn't that bad": Dissonance in nonconfronting targets of prejudice. *Social Psychology Bulletin*, 39(7): 856–69.

Rauthmann, J., Gallardo-Pujol, D., Guillaume, E., Todd, E., Nave, C., Sherman, R., Ziegler, M., Jones, A., & Funder, D. (2014). The situational eight DIAMONDS: A taxonomy of major dimensions of situational characteristics. *Journal of Personality and Social Psychology*, 107(4): 677–718.

Rawls, J. (1971). *A Theory of Justice*. Harvard University Press.

Reilly, R. (1982). Preference reversal: Further evidence and some suggested modifications in experimental design. *American Economic Review*, 72: 576–584.

Reiss, D. & Marino, L. (2001). Mirror self-recognition in the bottlenose dolphin: A case of cognitive convergence. *Proceedings of the National Academy of Sciences*, 98(10): 5937–42.

Richard, F., Bond, C., & Stokes-Zoota, J. (2003). One hundred years of social psychology quantitatively described. *Review of General Psychology*, 7(4): 331–63.

Rist, R. (1973). *The Urban School: A Factory for Failure*. Cambridge, MA: MIT Press.

Roberts, R. (2013). *Emotions in the Moral Life*. Cambridge University Press.

Romdenh-Romluc, K. (2011). Agency and embodied cognition. *Proceedings of the Aristotelian Society*, 111(1): 79–95.

Rosati, C. (1995). Persons, perspectives, and full information accounts of the good. *Ethics*, 105(2): 296–325.

Rosenthal, D. (2009). Philosophy and its teaching. In R. Talisse & M. Eckert (eds.), *A Teacher's Life: Essays for Steven M. Cahn*, pp. 67–84. Lanham, MD: Lexington.

Rosenthal, D. (2005). *Consciousness and Mind*. Oxford University Press.

Rozin, P., Lowery, L., Imada, S., & Haidt, J. (1999). The CAD triad hypothesis: A mapping between three moral emotions (contempt, anger, disgust) and three moral codes (community, autonomy, divinity). *Journal of Personality and Social Psychology*, 76(4): 574–86.

Russell, J., Bachorowski, J.-A., & Fernández-Dols, J.-M. (2003). Facial and vocal expressions of emotion. *Annual Review of Psychology*, 54: 329–49.

Saucier, G. (2009). Recurrent personality dimensions in inclusive lexical studies: Indications for a Big Six structure. *Journal of Personality*, 77(5) 1577–1614.

Saucier, G. (forthcoming). Value hierarchies within and across cultures: A comparative test of 18 value theories.

Saul, J. (2013). Implicit bias, stereotype threat and women in philosophy. In Jenkins, F. & Hutchinson, K. (eds.), *Women in Philosophy: What Needs to Change?* Oxford University Press.

Schneer, J. & Reitman, F. (1994). The importance of gender in mid-career: A longitudinal study of MBAs. *Journal of Organizational Behavior*, 15: 199–207.

Schwartz, S. (1994). Are there universal aspects in the structure and contents of human values? *Journal of Social Issues*, 50(4): 19–45.

Schwartz, S. (2012). An overview of the Schwartz theory of basic values. *Online Readings in Psychology and Culture*, 2: 1. Available at: http://dx.doi.org/10.9707/2307-0919.1116.

Schwitzgebel, E. & Cushman, F. (2012). Expertise in moral reasoning? Order effects on moral judgment in professional philosophers and nonphilosophers. *Mind and Language*, 27(2): 135–53.

Sen, A. (1985). Well-being, agency and freedom. *Journal of Philosophy*, 82(4): 169–221.

Shafer-Landau, R. (1994). Ethical disagreement, ethical objectivism and moral indeterminacy. *Philosophy and Phenomenological Research*, 54: 331–44.

Shafer-Landau, R. (2003). *Moral Realism: A Defense*. Oxford: Clarendon.

Shariff, A. (2011). Big gods are made for big groups: Commentary on Murray & Schloss. *Religion, Brain & Behavior*, 1: 89–93.

Shariff, A. & Norenzayan, A. (2011). Mean gods make good people. *International Journal for the Psychology of Religion*, 21: 85–96.

Shariff, A. & Norenzayan, A. (2007). God is watching you: Supernatural agent concepts increase prosocial behavior in an anonymous economic game. *Psychological Science*, 18: 803–9.

Shaw, A. & Olson, K. (2012). Children discard a resource to avoid inequality. *Journal of Experimental Psychology*, 141(2): 382–95.

Shweder, R. (2012). Relativism and universalism. In D. Fassin (ed.), *A Companion to Moral Anthropology*, pp. 85–102. Oxford: Wiley.

Shweder, R. A., Much, N. C., Mahapatra, M., & Park, L. (1997). The "big three" of morality (autonomy, community, divinity), and the "big three" explanations of suffering. In A. M. Brandt & P. Rozin (eds.), *Morality and Health*, pp. 119–69. New York: Routledge.

Sidanius, J. & Pratto, F. (1999). *Social Dominance: An Intergroup Theory of Social Hierarchy and Oppression*. Cambridge University Press.

Sidgwick, H. (1874/1981). *The Methods of Ethics*, 7th edn. Indianapolis: Hackett.

Simms, L. (2007). The Big Seven model of personality and its relevance to personality pathology. *Journal of Personality*, 57: 65–94.

Singer, P. (1993). *Practical Ethics*, 2nd edn. Cambridge University Press.

Sinnott-Armstrong, W. & Wheatley, T. (2014). Are moral judgments unified? *Philosophical Psychology*, 27(4): 451–74.

Slote, M. (2007). *The Ethics of Care and Empathy*. New York: Routledge.

Slovic, P. (1995). The construction of preference. *American Psychologist*, 50(5): 364–71.

Slovic, P. & Lichtenstein, S. (1968). The relative importance of probabilities and payoffs in risk-taking. *Journal of Experimental Psychology*, 2(78): 1–18.

Slovic, P. & Lichtenstein, S. (1983). Preference reversals: A broader perspective. *American Economic Review*, 73(4): 596–605.

Slovic, P., Finucane, M., Peters, E., & MacGregor, D. (2002). The affect heuristic. In T. Gilovich, D. Griffin, & D. Kahneman (eds.), *Heuristics and Biases: The Psychology of Intuitive Judgment*, pp. 397–420. Cambridge University Press.

Smart, J. J. C. (1956). Extreme and restricted utilitarianism. *Philosophical Quarterly*, 6(25): 344–54.

Snow, N. (2009). *Virtue as Social Intelligence: An Empirically Grounded Theory*. New York: Routledge.

Spitz, H. (1999). Beleaguered *Pygmalion*: A history of the controversy over claims that teacher expectancy raises intelligence. *Intelligence*, 27(3): 199–234.

Sripada, C. (2005). Punishment and the strategic structure of moral systems. *Biology and Philosophy*, 20: 767–89.

Srivastava, S., Richards, J., McGonigal, K., Butler, E., & Gross, J. (2006). Optimism in close relationships: How seeing things in a positive light makes them so. *Journal of Personality and Social Psychology*, 91(1): 143–53.

Stepper, S. & Strack, F. (1993). Proprioceptive determinants of affective and nonaffective feelings. *Journal of Personality and Social Psychology*, 64(2): 211–20.

Stich, S. (2006). Is morality an elegant machine or a kludge? *Journal of Cognition and Culture* 6(1–2): 181–9.

Strawson, P. (1960). Freedom and resentment. *Proceedings of the British Academy*, 48: 1–25.

Strohminger, N. (2014). Disgust talked about. *Philosophy Compass*, 9(7): 478–93.

Sturgeon, N. (1988). Moral explanations. In G. Sayre-McCord (ed.), *Essays on Moral Realism*, pp. 229–255. Cornell University Press.

Suárez, S. & Gallup, G. (1981). Self-recognition in chimpanzees and orangutans, but not gorillas. *Journal of Human Evolution*, 10(2): 175–88.

Sumner, W. G. (1907). *Folkways: A Study of the Sociological Importance of Usages, Manners, Customs, Mores, and Morals*. Boston: Ginn and Company.

Suprenant, C. (2010). Kant's contribution to moral education: The relevance of catechistics. *Journal of Moral Education*, 39(2): 165–74.

Susskind, J., Lee, D., Cusi, A., Feiman, R., Grabski, W., & Anderson, A. (2008). Expressing fear enhances sensory acquisition. *Nature Neuroscience*, 11: 843–50.

Sverdlik, N., Roccas, S., & Sagiv, L. (2012). Morality across cultures: A values perspective. In M. Mikulincer & P. Shaver (eds.), *The Social Psychology of Morality: Exploring the Causes of Good and Evil*. Washington, DC: American Psychological Association.

Swann, W. B., Jr, Rentfrow, P. J., & Guinn, J. S. (2003). Self-verification: The search for coherence. In M. R. Leary & J. P. Tangney, *Handbook of Self and Identity*, pp. 367–83. New York: Guilford Press.

Taylor, C. (1992). *Multiculturalism and the Politics of Recognition*. Princeton University Press.

Tessman, L. (2005). *Burdened Virtues: Virtue Ethics for Liberatory Struggles.* Oxford University Press.

Thaler, R. & Sunstein, C. (2008). *Nudge: Improving Decisions about Health, Wealth, and Happiness.* New York: Penguin Books.

Tiberius, V. (2008). *The Reflective Life.* Oxford University Press.

Tirrell, L. (2012). Genocidal language games. In I. Maitra & M. McGowan (eds.), *Speech and Harm: Controversies over Free Speech*, pp. 174–221. Oxford University Press.

Tom, S., Fox, C., Trepel, C., & Poldrack, R. (2007). The neural basis of loss aversion in decision-making under risk. *Science*, 315(5811): 515–18.

Trawalter, S., Hoffman, K., & Waytz, A. (2012). Racial bias in perceptions of others' pain. *PLOS ONE*, 7(11).

Trivigno, F. (2013). The virtue ethical case for pacifism. In M. Austin (ed.), *Virtues in Action.* New York: Palgrave.

Tversky, A. & Kahneman, D. (1981). The framing of decisions and the psychology of choice. *Science*, 211(4481): 453–8.

Tversky, A., Slovic, P., & Kahneman, D. (1990). The causes of preference reversal. *American Economic Review*, 80(1): 204–17.

Tybur, J., Kurzban, R., Lieberman, D., & DeScioli, P. (2013). Disgust: Evolved function and structure. *Psychological Review*, 120(1): 65–84.

Van Ryn, M. & Fu, S. (2003). Paved with good intentions: Do public health and human service providers contribute to racial/ethnic disparities in health? *American Journal of Public Health*, 93(2): 248–55.

Wager, T., Davidson, M., Hughes, B., Lindquist, M., & Ochsner, K. (2008). Prefrontal-subcortical pathways mediating successful emotion regulation. *Neuron*, 59(6): 1037–50.

Washington, N. & Kelly, D. (forthcoming). Who's responsible for this? Moral responsibility, externalism, and knowledge about implicit bias.

Webber, J. (forthcoming). Instilling virtue. In A. Masala & J. Webber (eds.), *From Personality to Virtue.* Oxford University Press.

Wegner, D. (1994). Ironic processes of mental control. *Psychological Review*, 101(1): 34–52.

Weld, C. (1848). *A History of the Royal Society: With Memoirs of the Presidents*, vol. 1. Cambridge University Press.

Westergaard, G. & Hyatt, C. (1994). The responses of bonobos (*Pan paniscus*) to their mirror images: Evidence of self-recognition. *Human Evolution*, 9(4): 273–9.

Westermarck, E. (1906/1932). *The Origin and Development of the Moral Ideas.* London: Macmillan.

Westermarck, E. (1932). *Ethical Relativity.* London: Kegan Paul, Trench, Trubner.

Wicker, B., Keysers, C., Plailly, J., Royet, J. P., Gallese, V., & Rizzolatti, G. (2003). Both of us disgusted in my insula: The common neural basis of seeing and feeling disgust. *Neuron*, 40: 655–64.

Wiggins, D. (2005). Objectivity in ethics: Two difficulties, two responses. *Ratio*, 18: 1–26.

Williams, B. (1985). *Ethics and the Limits of Philosophy*. Harvard University Press.

Wong, D. (2014). Integrating philosophy with anthropology in an approach to morality. *Anthropological Theory*, 14(3): 336–55.

Wong, D. (2006). *Natural Moralities: A Defense of Pluralistic Relativism*. Oxford University Press.

World Values Survey (2009). 1981–2008 Official Aggregate v. 20090901. Available at: http://www.worldvaluessurvey.org/WVSDocumentation WV1.jsp.

Wright, P., He, G., Shapira, N., Goodman, W., & Liu, Y. (2004). Disgust and the insula: fMRI responses to pictures of mutilation and contamination. *Neuroport*, 15: 2347–51.

Zack, N. (2002). *Philosophy of Science and Race*. New York: Routledge.

Zajonc, R. (1984). On primacy of affect. *American Psychologist*, 39(2): 117–23.

Zajonc, R. & Markus, H. (1982). Affective and cognitive factors in preferences. *Journal of Consumer Research*, 9: 123–31.

Zaki, J., López, G., & Mitchell, J. (2014). Activity in ventromedial prefrontal cortex co-varies with revealed social preferences: Evidence for person-invariant value. *SCAN*, 9(4): 464–9.

Index